India is the Soviet Union's most important trading partner among the less developed countries (LDCs) and the largest recipient of Soviet aid to non-socialist LDCs. Similarly the Soviet Union is one of India's largest trade partners. In this book, Santosh Mehrotra presents for the first time a comprehensive study of this trading relationship and the transfer of technology from the Soviet Union.

The author begins by outlining Indian economic strategy since the 1950s and the role of Soviet and east European technical assistance. He considers Soviet economic interests in LDCs in general and India in particular and discusses the special geo-political relationship between India and the Soviet Union. In part II, Santosh Mehrotra examines Soviet technological transfer to India since 1955. He analyses legal contracts, markets, labour and managerial skills, technical adaptation and the provision of 'follow-up' facilities; and he provides illuminating and detailed case studies of particular industries. In the final chapters, the author analyses Indo-Soviet trade in the 1970s and 1980s covering the payment arrangements and bilateral trading and he compares the terms of the relationship with India's trade relations with the rest of the world.

India and the Soviet Union: trade and technology transfer is an exhaustive analysis of economic relations between an industrialised planned economy and a developing market economy. It will therefore become essential reading for students and specialists of development economics and international relations as well as for governments and institutional economists in international trade and finance.

INDIA AND THE SOVIET UNION: TRADE AND TECHNOLOGY TRANSFER

Soviet and East European Studies

Series list continues on p. 243

INDIA AND THE SOVIET UNION: TRADE AND TECHNOLOGY TRANSFER

SANTOSH MEHROTRA

Jawaharlal Nehru University, New Delhi

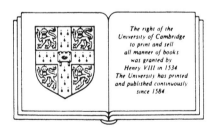

The right of the
University of Cambridge
to print and sell
all manner of books
was granted by
Henry VIII in 1534
The University has printed
and published continuously
since 1584

CAMBRIDGE UNIVERSITY PRESS

Cambridge
New York   Port Chester
Melbourne   Sydney

CAMBRIDGE UNIVERSITY PRESS
Cambridge, New York, Melbourne, Madrid, Cape Town,
Singapore, São Paulo, Delhi, Mexico City

Cambridge University Press
The Edinburgh Building, Cambridge CB2 8RU, UK

Published in the United States of America by Cambridge University Press, New York

www.cambridge.org
Information on this title: www.cambridge.org/9780521362023

First published 1990

A catalogue record for this publication is available from the British Library

Library of Congress Cataloguing in Publication Data
Mehrotra, Santosh K.
India and the Soviet Union: trade and technology transfer /
Santosh K. Mehrotra.
        p.   cm.—(Soviet and East European studies : 73)
Includes bibliographical references.
ISBN 0 521 36202 4
1. India – Foreign economic relations – Soviet Union.   2. Soviet
Union   Foreign economic relations – India.   3. Technology transfer –
Economic aspects – India.   4. Technology transfer – Economic aspects –
Soviet Union.   I. Title.   II. Series.
HF1590.15.S65M44   1990
337.47054–dc20   89–36866   CIP

ISBN 978-0-521-36202-3 Hardback

To my parents,
Sushma and Pia

Contents

Tables

Preface

This study is based on my doctoral dissertation approved in 1985 by the Faculty of Economics, University of Cambridge. The study, especially the part on technology transfer, was made possible by the help of numerous Indian government officials who gave me access to many restricted and unpublished documents and also granted me long interviews. I received considerable assistance from officials, too numerous to name, in the Ministries of Industry, Petroleum, Coal, Steel, Commerce and External Affairs, and a large number of public sector corporations: Steel Authority of India Limited, Metallurgical and Engineering Consultants, Heavy Engineering Corporation, Mining and Allied Machinery Corporation, Bharat Heavy Electricals Limited, Oil and Natural Gas Commission, Indian Oil Corporation, Instrumentation Limited, Bharat Aluminium Corporation and Indian Drugs and Pharmaceuticals Limited (both in their corporate office and their plants). I was particularly fortunate to have secured access to the actual contracts between Indian and Soviet firms, so far not available to any researcher. In addition, many technocrats in public enterprises and officials in government departments provided valuable information during discussions on the subject of Soviet technology transfer to India and Indo-Soviet trade.

I acknowledge with gratitude the comments of Peter Nolan who painstakingly supervised my research. Michael Kaser, W. B. Macpherson and Sumitra Chisti read the entire draft; John Sender and Gabriel Palma read parts of it and offered valuable suggestions. I learnt a great deal from discussions within an East–South study group which met at the Royal Institute of International Affairs, London, during 1983 and 1984; the discussions with Robert Cassen and Alan Smith proved particularly useful.

I owe a deep gratitude to my wife, Sushma, who helped me input the trade data on to the computer; moreover, her perfectionism proved invaluable in terms of the presentation of the manuscript.

Abbreviations

BALCO	Bharat Aluminium Corporation
BHEL	Bharat Heavy Electricals Ltd
BIS	Bank for International Settlements
BPE	Bureau of Public Enterprises
CEDB	Central Engineering and Design Bureau
CIA	Central Intelligence Agency
CMEA	Council for Mutual Economic Assistance
CPE	Centrally Planned Economy
CPSU	Communist Party of the Soviet Union
CPU	Committee for Public Undertakings
DGCIS	Directorate General of Commercial Intelligence and Statistics
DME	Developed Market Economy
DPR	Detailed Project Report
ECE	Economic Commission for Europe
FICCI	Federation of Indian Chambers of Commerce and Industry
FTO	Foreign Trade Organisation
HAL	Hindustan Antibiotics Ltd
HEC	Heavy Engineering Corporation
HSL	Hindustan Steel Ltd
IBEC	International Bank for Economic Cooperation
IBRD	International Bank for Reconstruction and Development
IDA	International Development Agency
IDPL	Indian Drugs and Pharmaceuticals Ltd
ILO	International Labour Organisation
IMF	International Monetary Fund
IOC	Indian Oil Corporation
IP	Indian Pharmacopoeia

LDC	Less Developed Country
MAMC	Mining and Allied Machinery Corporation
MECON	Metallurgical and Engineering Consultants Ltd
OECD	Organisation for Economic Cooperation and Development
ONGC	Oil and Natural Gas Commission
OPEC	Organisation of Petroleum Exporting Countries
PL	Public Law
R&D	research and development
RBI	Reserve Bank of India
RITC	Revised Indian Trade Classification
SAIL	Steel Authority of India Ltd
SDP	Synthetic Drugs Plant (Hyderabad)
SDR	Special Drawing Rights
SEZ	Special Export Processing Zone
SIPRI	Stockholm International Peace Research Institute
SITC	Standard International Trade Classification
UNCTAD	United Nations Conference on Trade and Development
UNDP	United Nations Development Programme
UNECE	United Nations Economic Commission for Europe
USJEC	United States Congress Joint Economic Committee
WEFA	Wharton Econometric Forecasting Association

Note: The word 'billions' refers to US billions – a thousand millions.

Introduction

This study has three major objectives. First, it attempts to analyse Soviet economic interests in LDCs in general and India in particular. Earlier attempts to study India's economic relations with the USSR and eastern Europe had focused on the costs and benefits of the relationship *to India*. The present work started out with the objective of correcting this imbalance. However, this is not intended to be a comprehensive study of Soviet-LDC economic relations; our interest in the latter is limited to the extent that Soviet-LDC economic relations highlight the nature of Indo-Soviet economic relations.

Earlier studies on the subject also ignored or disregarded the importance of geo-political factors in the Indo-Soviet relationship. In the past relations between India and the USSR have been examined either by political scientists or by economists, and both have tended to keep very much within the confines of their disciplines. In the present study we attempt the more hazardous task of examining the interrelationship of the economic and political elements of the relationship. Hence, in part I (which is largely interpretative) we first examine the Soviet contribution to the conception and implementation of India's development strategy; then investigate Soviet economic interests in India; and, finally, examine the mutuality of the geo-political interests of India and the USSR, thereby bringing the 'economic' and 'political' discussion together at the end of part I.

The second objective of this study has been to go beyond the emphasis in the existing literature on Soviet (and east European) *aid* to India. The earlier studies had made an in-depth examination of the financial flows from the CPEs, but technology transfer was not explored in any detail. This, however, is understandable, considering that the study of transfer of technology by developed to developing countries was not such a well-developed field of inquiry in the late sixties and early seventies. Since then the mechanism and effectiveness of technology

1

transfer have become a major subject of research in applied international economics. Nevertheless, as far as is known to this author, there are still no full-length studies of transfer of technology by an industrialised CPE to a developing market economy. Part II of this dissertation, on Soviet transfer of technology to India, is an attempt to fill this gap. (It covers the entire period since 1955, when the first project aid agreement was signed.) However, it should be added that there is no explicit attempt in this study to draw general conclusions in the nature of 'lessons' for other LDCs based on Indo-Soviet economic relations, largely because, as we show, the Indo-Soviet relationship is quite different in many respects from Soviet-LDC economic relations in general.

The third objective, addressed in part III, has been to fill a gap in the existing literature by examining Indo-Soviet trade between 1970 and 1985. Earlier studies of Indo-east European economic relations have covered the period up to the early seventies. Our interest in India's trade with the smaller east European economies is limited to the extent that it throws light on Indo-Soviet trade. There are two reasons for this narrower focus. First, since our concern in the study of technology transfer is with Soviet, rather than east European, economic and technical assistance to India, it seems logical to confine one's attention to Indo-Soviet trade. Secondly, and more importantly, the share of the USSR in Indo-east European trade as a whole has risen sharply to nearly 75 per cent over the seventies, while in the sixties it was around 50–60 per cent. Moreover, India's trade with the smaller east European economies reached a plateau in the early seventies; and there seems little prospect of any rapid increase in that trade even in the eighties and nineties. On the other hand, Indo-Soviet trade has continued to increase rapidly in the seventies and eighties and may well continue to rise through the 1990s. In fact, at the beginning of the seventies, the USSR became India's single largest trade partner, and has regularly shared that position with the USA since then.

In chapter 1 we examine first the intellectual influence of Soviet planning on Indian planners in the fifties, and second, the role of Soviet economic and technical assistance in the implementation of India's development strategy during the Second and Third Five-Year Plans. We also discuss the changes in the macro-economic significance of Soviet assistance since 1969.

The special geo-political relationship between India and the USSR is the subject of chapter 2. Economic relationships between centrally planned and market economies require the mediation of the state as a matter of course; this is much more so than in the case of economic relationships between two market economies. We attempt to establish the interrelationship between the economic and geo-political interests of the two countries and then examine the military dimension of those interests. The military dimension is included because India's defence imports from the USSR have an economic as well as political significance; they acquire economic significance from the fact that they constitute one of the most important categories of Indian imports from the USSR.

In chapter 3 we turn to a consideration of Soviet economic interests in LDCs in general and India in particular. We attempt to explain these interests in terms of the development of the Soviet economy since its First Five-Year Plan, particularly its inability to generate rapid technical progress and the problems with its agricultural sector. The economic relationship with India is something of a special case from the USSR's viewpoint; what makes it special is also analysed.

In part II we turn to an examination of Soviet technology transfer to India. Chapter 4 is devoted to a discussion of aid flows. A comparative evaluation of aid from the USSR and that from other major donors over the 1970s is attempted. In this connection, the authorisation and utilisation of aid as well as terms of aid and its sectoral composition are examined. The overall objective in part II is to assess the role of Soviet technology transfer in developing an independent technological capacity in the sectors to which technology was transferred.

Chapter 5 begins by outlining the methodology for evaluating the effectiveness of technology transfer. In chapter 5 the analysis of technology transfer is based on Indo-Soviet firm level contracts, and in chapter 6 on micro-level industry studies. Chapter 6 contains the analytical results of case studies of projects in the capital, intermediate and consumer goods sectors. Chapter 6 deals with: 1. heavy industries: heavy electricals (Bharat Heavy Electricals Ltd), coal mining machinery (Mining and Allied Machinery Corporation) and steel plant making machinery (Heavy Engineering Corporation); 2. steel industry: a metallurgical design organisation (Metallurgical and Engineering Consultants Ltd), first generation steel plants built with Soviet, British and West German assistance (Bhilai, Durgapur and Rourkela), and second and third generation steel plants built with Soviet assistance (Bokaro and Visakhapatnam); 3. energy and minerals: oil exploration (Oil and Natural Gas Commission), oil refineries (Barauni, Koyali and Mathura), coal mining, and aluminium smelting (Bharat Aluminium Corporation); 4. pharmaceuticals: antibiotics (Rishikesh), synthetic drugs

(Hyderabad) and surgical instruments (Madras) – all part of Indian Drugs and Pharmaceuticals Ltd. These case studies constitute an exhaustive list of Soviet-built projects in India.

As a cautionary note, it is necessary to point out what is *not* attempted in the examination of Soviet technology transfer. First, no use is made of the Little-Mirlees method of project evaluation. Project analysis is a method of making a choice between alternative uses of resources in a clear fashion. Since the technology for these industries was not available domestically, it would have had to be imported. However, in most cases the choice of foreign investors did not exist, e.g. in bulk drugs and pharmaceuticals, oil exploration and oil refining, since transnational corporations were not prepared to transfer technology in these industries except on terms unacceptable to India. But, as we shall see, a choice of investors did exist in the case of other industries, i.e. heavy electricals, heavy engineering and steel. The fundamental reason, though, for not using the L-M method of project analysis is that while the L-M technique is used to answer the question whether or not a project should be (or have been) set up, our interest is rather in the question: how effective was the transfer of technology from the Soviet Union to India? At times the two questions may not be entirely separable; a project which should not have been set up in the first place is unlikely to be a successful example of technology transfer. Indeed, we do not shy away from that conclusion in the case of certain projects where, in fact, an alternative use should have been made of the resources.

Second, no broad comparisons of Soviet and Western technology transfer to India are attempted here. Where possible comparisons are made on the basis of existing secondary literature on technology transfer to India by DMEs. Steel plants and oil refineries are two industries where such comparisons are possible and are attempted. However, a detailed and rigorous comparison of technology transfer occurring in the same sector from two different sources (Eastern and Western) would have to be the subject of another study. None the less, the data base for any future comparison with Soviet technology transfer to India has, it is hoped, been created in part II of this book.

In part III we examine Indo-Soviet trade in the seventies and early eighties. Chapter 7 analyses the payments aspects of the relationship, while chapter 8 deals at length with the real side. In chapter 7 the fundamental analytical question that concerns us is: why has bilateralism (i.e. payments for all commercial and non-commercial transactions in rupees) prevailed in Indo-Soviet trade relations throughout the seventies and eighties, although CPEs including the USSR have been multilateralising trade arrangements with most LDCs. This is also significant considering that in recent years India has multilateralised her trade with three former bilateral trade partners in east Europe: Yugoslavia (1973), Hungary (1978) and Bulgaria (1980). In addition, in chapter 7 we attempt to reconstruct the balance of payments between India and the USSR, since official publications do not give any indication of the overall balance of payments between the two countries. This enables us to estimate defence-related payments (though not the value of total defence imports from the USSR) made by India to the USSR from 1966/7 to 1985/6. Finally, we examine the question of the basis of the determination of the rupee–rouble exchange rate and its impact on India's repayments of Soviet development and defence credits, a question which has been ignored in earlier studies of Indo-CMEA trade. Although the rupee–rouble exchange rate does not directly affect trade (since all aid and trade transactions are conducted in rupees) it lies at the heart of the problem of calculating India's credit repayment obligations.

The final substantive chapter – chapter 8 – deals with Indo-Soviet trade in the seventies and eighties. It is concerned with four questions. The first one arises primarily in the context of bilateral trade and payments arrangements: has bilateral trade with the USSR in the seventies led to trade creation for India or has the trade merely been diverted from hard currency markets? This includes a section on the tricky question of switch trading by Soviet FTOs. An example of switch trading in the eighties is examined in Appendix 5. The remaining three questions examined in this chapter are fairly standard ones: how does the stability of India's export earnings from the USSR, the commodity composition of trade with the USSR, and the terms of trade obtained from the USSR compare with the rest of the world? The examination of the trade relationship gives one certain insights into Soviet economic problems as well as the Indian development experience.

However, no attempt is made in part III to evaluate the effects of trade with the USSR on the domestic economy of India from the point of view of production pattern, internal prices and employment. The ratio of India's total exports and imports to her GDP never rose above 8 per cent between 1960 and 1979; in this respect it is roughly comparable to that of other large economies like the USA, the USSR and Brazil. The impact of Indo-Soviet trade on such variables as production structure, domestic prices and the employment level in India can reasonably be expected to be marginal.

The book ends with a concluding chapter. For India, in the seventies and eighties the macro-economic significance of the Indo-Soviet economic relationship has consisted in mitigating India's balance of payments problems. Petroleum and petroleum products have a dominant share in Soviet exports to India, products which India also buys from hard currency markets. That the USSR has been prepared to sell oil/oil products to India which could have been exported for hard currency suggests that, in Soviet calculations, strategic-political considerations are more important than economic ones.

As regards Soviet aid, it had been an engine of growth of Indo-Soviet trade in the fifties and sixties, and as the share of aid utilised in Indian imports and loans repaid in Indian exports rise, it will resume that role in the eighties and nineties. Soviet transfer of know-how has been very effective, but the transfer of know-why leaves much to be desired. However, the collaborations were only know-how agreements, not know-why agreements.

As regards payments arrangements, it is not in either the Indian or Soviet interests to alter the nearly three-decade-old bilateral payment arrangements. For India the possibility of paying for defence equipment without the expenditure of scarce foreign exchange has precluded multilateralisation. It would be against Soviet interests as well, since India has consistently generated trade surpluses with her since the early seventies. Large trade deficits in convertible currency would be unacceptable to the Soviet Union. As regards trade, the greatest worry to trade planners in both countries has been and will be the declining complementarity between the two economies. Without constant governmental monitoring and attempts to give it a fillip, the trade may stagnate. In the seventies and eighties defence and oil sales by the USSR have enabled it to generate rupee resources which have given bilateral trade a certain dynamism. Whether such dynamism can be maintained into the nineties with lower oil prices and stabilised Soviet oil supplies to India remains to be seen.

Part I

1 The Indian development strategy and the USSR

This chapter is concerned with two questions: first, what influence the Soviet experiment with central planning had on Indian planners in the 1950s; and second, what role Soviet and east European aid played in the implementation of the Indian development strategy as identified in the Second Plan, with its marked shift in favour of capital goods industries.

The influence exercised by the Soviet planning experience was evident both in relation to the use of planning as a strategy and to the particular strategy of planning adopted in India. In 1950 history provided two examples of less developed economies, that of Japan and the Soviet Union, which had achieved considerable growth within the short span of a few decades using two quite different strategies of development. It is a matter of speculation why the Soviet strategy was preferred to the Japanese one by Indian planners. Already in the 1940s, a need for structural reform had been strongly articulated in India, both by industrialists and by the leaders of the national movement. The need for planning as a strategy had been recognised. A commitment to a major role for the public sector in infrastructure and heavy industry development had already been made in a Plan (called the Bombay Plan) produced by the National Planning Committee of the Indian National Congress in 1944. The significance of the Bombay Plan lies not in that any planning model underlay it, but in the composition of the committee that prepared it, which included both industrialists and major Congress leaders. The members included Tata and Birla on the one hand, and Bose and Nehru on the other. Before becoming Prime Minister Nehru often referred in his speeches and writings to the Soviet experience as a model for India (Clarkson 1979, p. 266). The acceleration of industrial development through state investment and planning was thus conventional wisdom for the political and economic leaders of post-colonial India.

The Soviet experience was not the only influence which determined the use of planning as a strategy. Planning as a strategy was also implicit in other influences at work on the Indian intelligentsia at the time. Thus the intelligentsia had produced its own brand of List-type arguments in favour of protection and opposing free trade in India's national interest. The intellectual influences on the intelligentsia included not only Friedrich List but also the Fabian Socialists.[1] A combination of protectionist arguments and socialist influences on this elite resulted in an ideological position against markets, and a belief in industrialisation based on public investment. The essence of 'socialistic' planning, according to the Second Plan, lay in tilting investment in favour of public investment. Unlike its role in Meiji Japan, the public sector in India was not conceived as a transitional phenomenon.[2] It was conceived rather as part of planning as a strategy for creating a 'socialist pattern of society' and as substituting for possible failures of the market mechanism.

Thus it was the pervasive influence of the market failure paradigm and the widely felt need for structural reform that resulted in the adoption of planning as a strategy in the context of post-colonial India. However, this does not fully capture the intellectual influence exercised by the Soviet model. To appreciate the extent of this influence one must briefly review the particular strategy of planning adopted in India's Second Plan.

Once again, the Soviet planning strategy appears to have influenced both senior politicians and the intelligentsia. After about eight years in power – during which the basic structure of the Indian economic strategy had been assembled – Nehru admitted, 'the influence of the Soviet revolution ... [gave] a powerful economic turn to our thoughts'.[3] It must be emphasised that Nehru, apart from being Prime Minister for seventeen years, was also the Chairman of the Planning Commission over that period. He presided over the formulation and implementation of India's first three Five-Year Plans, the second and third of which determined India's development strategy.[4]

What was, then, the precise nature and mechanism of this powerful intellectual influence? It is well known that the Second Plan pattern of industrial investment, with its marked shift in favour of capital goods industries, was deeply influenced by the two-sector growth model developed by P. C. Mahalanobis (Mahalanobis 1953). This model was independently developed by Feldman in the Soviet Union in the 1920s (and later revived by Domar in 1957 in a considerably improved form).[5] Indian planners were unaware of Feldman's model. However, as

Chakravarty notes: 'Indeed, it is quite plausible to argue that Mahalanobis (who had just then visited the socialist countries and with whose economists he had close contact) was impressed with Soviet thinking on industrialization, with its emphasis on the building of the capital goods base' (Chakravarty and Bhagwati 1969, p. 7).

Feldman was the first economist to focus attention on the relationship between the consumer goods and investment goods industries in a plan for rapid economic growth. The main assumptions of his two-sector model were: a long time horizon, a closed economy, the independence of investment allocation from the supply of investment resources and identical capital-output ratios in the two sectors. He came to two important results: first, to that a high growth rate required a high proportion of the capital stock to be in the investment goods sector; and second, that along a steady growth path, investment should be allocated between the sectors in the same proportion as the capital stock. Feldman argued on the basis of his model that given the capital-output ratio, the greater the proportion of the capital stock in the investment goods sector, and the greater the proportion of new investment in the investment goods sector, the higher the growth rate.

Soviet experts participated in the background thinking for Indian planning. In addition to the Polish economist Oskar Lange, one Soviet economist, M. I. Rubinstein, was invited by Mahalanobis to the Indian Statistical Institute, the intellectual centre for the formulation of the Second Plan.[6] Mahalanobis himself went to Moscow (in 1952) to consult Soviet planning experts. Asked whether the Second Plan would have been different without this Soviet participation, Mahalanobis replied that it was helpful to have their sympathy at a top level, which was 'like [having] airforce cover for the army'. Clarkson summarised the Soviet influence thus: Soviet influence on the Indian planning system was first to popularise the general idea of planning among Nehru's colleagues, second to restrain Indian policy-planners from over-enthusiasm, and third to provide both internal political support through their private conversations with Indian leaders and external ideological assistance through their public writings in the Soviet press (Clarkson 1979, p. 267). This view, while being generally correct, ignores the essential point about indirect Soviet influence on the basic strategy of the Second Plan, i.e. the shift in investment allocation to heavy industry.

In principle, within an overall import-substituting strategy, a number of options are open to an industrialising economy, provided the government plans the industrialisation process. Following Raj and

Sen (1961) (or Mahalanobis 1953), the LDC can use its foreign exchange:

1. To import investment goods (e.g. looms), raw materials, fuels, etc., to manufacture consumer goods (cloth).
2. To import capital goods (machine tools) to make investment goods (looms) which in turn produce consumer goods (cloth) and to make intermediate goods (steel) and develop domestic raw material supplies.
3. To import capital goods (machine tools) to make capital goods which in turn are used to make other capital goods, investment goods and so on.

While the first option was followed by most LDCs after gaining independence, India adopted the third option which is similar to the Soviet strategy.

The main lesson of the Feldman model is that the capacity of the capital goods sector is one of the constraints limiting the rate of growth of an economy. There may well be other constraints, such as foreign exchange, urban real wages or marketed output of agriculture. Indeed it is possible that one or more of these is the binding constraint and that the limited capacity of the investment goods sector is not the binding constraint. However, in the early stages of economic growth, a prominent role is often played by the rapid development of this sector. In a closed economy, where the capability of producer goods industries is an operative constraint, a major task of planning for raising the growth rate must be direct investment to expand the capacity of this sector. This was recognised by Mahalanobis at the start of planning in India.

It is unlikely, however, that the Soviet influence extended very much beyond that. Other LDCs, unlike India, approached the USSR from the mid-fifties onwards, for assistance in preparing their national plans. The influence on Indian planning on the other hand was not direct or detailed in the form of actual plan preparation, but rather of an indirect (though no less important) nature in the form of planning strategy.

It is interesting that the Second Plan did not explicitly state the rationale of the shift to heavy industries in terms of foreign trade constraints. Later justification of this strategy by reference to stagnant world demand for Indian exports appears to have been an ex post facto rationalisation (Chakravarty and Bhagwati 1969). At the same time, Mahalanobis did not perceive any difficulties in transforming savings into desired forms of investment. Savings were not considered an independent variable; he showed that a higher allocation of current investment going to investment goods would mean a higher savings rate on the margin and hence a greater rate of growth of output. Such a proposition not only assumed away the role of foreign trade, but also assumed that the government could completely control the consumption-savings balance. As we shall see, while the assumption that there may be no difficulties in transforming savings into investment was a reasonable one for a centrally planned economy, it was not true in the case of a developing market economy like India.

In addition to the considerable intellectual influence of Soviet planning on Indian planners in the mid-fifties, Soviet and east European aid proved extremely useful to the implementation of the Indian development strategy as identified in the Second Plan's pattern of industrial investment. Considering the Soviet sympathy for the Indian strategy, it is hardly surprising that the USSR was among the first few countries to offer economic and technical assistance for the planned development of India. The first loan, for the Bhilai steel plant, was extended in early 1955, during the period of the First Five-Year Plan. At the time the only other donors were the USA and the World Bank.

Not only did Soviet aid commence early on in the planned development of India, the USSR was the first country to commit aid for the duration of a whole Plan in advance, rather than on a year-to-year basis.[7] Almost every Five-Year Plan was preceded by or coincided with the extension of a new loan by the USSR. This is true of the Second, Third (1961–6), Fourth (1969–74), and even the Seventh Plan (1985–90). The peak for loans extended in the 1950s and 1960s came during the Second Plan period.[8] The example set by the USSR, of extending loans for plan periods, was later followed by other donors.

The significance of Soviet aid has been qualitative rather than quantitative.[9] This qualitative significance of Soviet and east European aid lies in: the sectoral composition of aid favouring industry in general and heavy industry in the public sector in particular; strengthening India's bargaining position in relation to Western donors and DME firms;[10] and the mechanism of repaying aid, which linked aid and trade in the Indo-east European economic relationship.

The main usefulness of Soviet and east European aid lay 'in their willingness to give aid for particular projects that are regarded as high-priority investment and to give such aid for public sector development, at times when other major donors, such as the US have shown an extreme reluctance to do so' (Chaudhuri 1977, p. 160). The sectoral composition of Soviet aid over 1956–70 was as follows: steel 49.8 per cent, oil 17.8 per cent, power 15.5 per cent, heavy machinery 9.0 per cent, mining 5.0 per cent. The differences in the sectoral composition of project aid utilised from the USSR and all donors are threefold. First, the USSR gave a much larger share of its aid for steel. Second, a substantial proportion of Soviet assistance went to the oil sector, which was totally ignored by the other donors. Third, other donors (especially the IBRD) gave a fifth of their aid to developing an infrastructure in transport (Chaudhuri 1977, p. 148).

Secondly, the existence of the USSR and east Europe as an alternative source of imports and aid proved beneficial to India in two ways. It encouraged donors from the advanced capitalist world to extend more aid than they had done hitherto, and at more generous terms.[11] Moreover, it strengthened the bargaining position of the Indian government in relation to large firms from the advanced capitalist countries. The indifference of the major international oil companies operating in India to explore for oil in India is too well documented to need repetition here. The American administration's disinclination to extend aid to the Bokaro steel plant primarily because it was to be set up in the public sector is also very well known. When the Soviets offered to set up plants to manufacture bulk drugs, the transnational pharmaceutical companies, which exercised a monopoly over the Indian market for bulk drugs (the basic ingredient from which formulations are prepared), suddenly came forward to set up similar plants in India. Similarly, the Soviet offer to set up oil refineries in India to process crude from Indian wells (explored and developed with Soviet assistance) strengthened the Indian bargaining position with the smaller international oil companies who were prepared to participate in setting up refineries (see chapter 6 for details).

Thirdly, repayment of Soviet and east European developmental and defence credits in the form of Indian exports reduced the burden of repayment. For India, faced with foreign exchange constraints, the advantage of tying aid with trade was obvious. The automatic conversion of aid repayment into trade flows reduced the burden of debt servicing, as long as India's export prices to east Europe remained comparable to prices obtained from the rest of the world. Most studies for the fifties and sixties found that India's export prices to east Europe and the rest of the world were in fact comparable.[12]

From the Soviet point of view, the tying of aid and trade was not a special concession to India alone, but one which became a general practice in Soviet economic relations with LDCs. Soviet and east European development assistance is almost entirely bilateral, the only exception being Soviet and east European contributions to the United Nations Development Programme (UNDP); at the same time, the

USSR and eastern Europe used bilateral trade and payments agree-
ments with LDCs to expand trade with them.[13] The supply effect of
Soviet bilateral aid to India over the fifties and sixties is unmistakable.
Soviet development credits utilised by India over the Second and Third
Plans constituted 82.4 and 66.1 per cent of Indian imports from the
USSR respectively. These shares are much higher than the average
share of aid utilised as a percentage of India's total imports from the
DMEs over the same plan periods (23.9 and 40.7 per cent respectively).
Quite clearly, bilateral aid was used by the USSR from the mid-fifties as
a means of expanding two-way trade which stood at very low levels
prior to the signing of aid and trade agreements. As a result, the total
value of trade between India and the CPEs rose four times between
1960/1 and 1970/1 and the share of east Europe in India's total trade rose
from 0.5 per cent in 1952/3 to 18 per cent in 1972/3.

Soviet (and east European) aid to India, but also Indo-east European
trade, played a critical role in the implementation of India's chosen
development strategy. We have mentioned earlier that India's Second
Plan ignored the role of foreign trade. In fact, Bhagwati and Desai
(1970) have argued that it is unlikely that the assumption in the Second
Plan of 'stagnant world demand for Indian exports', by virtue of which
the shift to capital goods industries, and their domestic production
thereof, was later sought to be justified, was seriously made. This
crucial assumption was not empirically verified. (Perhaps the comfort-
able balance of payments position in the First Plan had lulled Indian
planners into complacency.) The result was that a policy structure
emerged which was strongly biased against exports. In the first three
plan periods export growth was very low. To a certain extent this can
be explained by the lack of domestic policies because even in
traditional exports India's share in world exports fell. However, the
period up to 1969 was not one of rapid export growth for LDCs, and if
we exclude the petroleum exporters, India's export growth up to the
mid-sixties was only somewhat lower than that of other LDCs. The real
difference between India and other LDCs is evident after 1965 when,
right up to the middle of the Fourth Plan, India could not profit from
the boom in world trade (Planning Commission 1981, p. 15). In fact,
but for the very rapid growth of exports to the USSR and east Europe
from the mid-fifties through the sixties, India's export growth would
have been even lower.

The other striking, and from our viewpoint more important, fact
about India's exports in the sixties is the shift in their market distribution. The UK lost her traditional position as the largest market of

Indian exports, an increasing proportion of which went to the USSR, eastern Europe and Japan. Eastern Europe, which took only 8.6 per cent of Indian exports in 1960/1, was taking 21.1 per cent by 1970/1.[14] The fact that one region (i.e. east Europe), which by 1970/1 still took only just over a fifth of India's exports, had accounted for nearly half of the increase in India's exports during the sixties shows that Indian exports to the rest of the world had truly stagnated. It could be argued that the availability of an easier outlet in east Europe through bilateral trade agreements may have reduced the pressure on Indian exporters to sell in hard currency markets.

The slow growth in India's exports to non-east European markets may have been due partly to domestic and partly to external factors. We do not take up in detail the question in India's development about the relative importance of domestic policy and external demand factors in explaining this slow growth. Nayyar (1976), for instance, emphasises the latter: 'Given the trends in *world demand* and *increasing competition* in most of India's major exports, it is most unlikely that, in the absence of bilateral trade agreements with the socialist countries of eastern Europe, India could have increased her total exports as much as she did in the 1960s' (p. 338; emphasis added). Martin Wolf (1982), on the other hand, considers domestic policy factors more important: 'The motivation for this trade [with east Europe] was the problems faced in expanding its exports to countries conducting their trade on a multilateral basis (which, in turn, were largely the *result of India's trade regime*) (p. 39; emphasis added).

Nevertheless, the increase in exports to the USSR and east Europe created the capacity to import goods (in addition to that created by east European credits) essential for the implementation of India's import substitution strategy in particular sectors. The commodity composition of India's imports from the USSR and east Europe shows that machinery (electrical and non-electrical) and transport equipment alone accounted for over 50 per cent of the imports through the sixties (Chisti 1973, p. 81).

It should be pointed out that it is not suggested here that but for east European bilateral aid and bilateral trade/payments agreements, India's import-substitution strategy and marked shift to the capital goods sector would not have occurred. Rather, the argument is that public sector investment in the Second, Third and Annual Plans in the heavy industries, as well as the steel, energy and pharmaceuticals sectors would have been well below the level achieved in the absence of east European assistance. Utilisation of east European aid was only

1.6 and 3.0 per cent of plan expenditure in the Second and Third Plans. However, this proportion would be much higher if only public sector investment were taken into account; naturally, it would be higher still for public investment in sectors which were the recipients of east European assistance.

In the seventies and early eighties, however, the macro-economic role of Indo-Soviet trade and Soviet aid in India's economy changed. First, the share of the USSR (and east Europe) in the expansion of India's exports in this period (26.3 per cent) has been much smaller than in the sixties (43 per cent). Similarly, the Soviet share in the increment in India's total imports in the seventies and early eighties was only 8.6 per cent, while the OECD and OPEC countries accounted for 44.6 and 30.4 per cent of the increase respectively. Secondly, the USSR authorised very little new aid in the seventies. Considering the absence of new aid in the seventies, and the slow growth in trade (relative to the earlier period), the continuing macro-economic significance of the Indo-Soviet economic relationship for the Indian economy lies not so much in providing assistance to India's chosen development strategy as in serving a more limited function, a balance of payments one. Oil and oil products and arms have an overwhelming share in Soviet exports to India, both of which categories of goods India also buys from hard currency markets. The special advantage for India of buying these goods from the USSR probably lies in being able to pay for them in inconvertible rupees, particularly oil/oil products after the oil price increases of 1973 and 1979. Well over half of India's defence imports in the seventies (according to SIPRI) and 60 per cent of India's imports of middle distillates (towards which India's consumption of oil products is biased) and a substantial proportion of crude oil (since 1977) have come from the USSR – all of which are, obviously, paid for through Indian exports. It is in this sense that one may argue that the key investment role played by Soviet aid to, and trade with, India in the sixties has now been replaced by its balance of payments function.

2 Indo-Soviet economic relations: geo-political and ideological factors

One of the main objectives of the present study is to disentangle the political and economic interests underlying the relationship between the two Asian powers, India and the Soviet Union. As regards the economic relationship, it was suggested in chapter 1 that India's interest in the USSR has shifted ground. In this chapter we attempt to establish the interrelationship between the economic and strategic-political elements of the Indo-Soviet relationship. This is necessary because economic relationships between centrally planned and market economies require the mediation of the state much more than in the case of economic relationships between two market economies.

In section 1 we investigate the basis of the strong mutuality of interests, which has a military dimension to it as well. The military dimension of the relationship not only has an economic significance (i.e. defence imports from the USSR constitute one of the most important categories of Indian imports from the USSR, and defence loans are repaid through exports of Indian goods), it also demonstrates the compatibility of strategic-political interests between the two countries. In section 2 we examine the Soviet view of the Indian state with the objective of understanding the ideological factors underlying the close economic and political relations between India and the USSR. Having thus disentangled the political, economic and ideological factors in the relationship, we attempt to draw together the various strands of the argument in the conclusions.

2.1 Geo-politics

When Mrs Gandhi told Leonid Brezhnev (at a civic reception in New Delhi in 1980) that 'Indo-Soviet friendship . . . is of equal importance to both India and the Soviet Union', she was probably referring to the coincidence of interests of the two states on major issues of international and regional politics (*Soviet Review*, December 1980). There has long been a consensus that the Soviets have needed India as a counterweight to China, and that India has used its 'special relationship' with the Soviets to her best advantage regionally, in her relations with Pakistan (over Kashmir (1965) and in the 1971 war) and China on the one hand, and globally, with the USA, on the other. Although there is an imbalance of power, India does retain sufficient flexibility to take a stand on international issues (e.g. the Indian Ocean, the Asian Collective Security system, the Non-Proliferation Treaty) in pursuance of its own national interests to the point of exclusion of those of the USSR.

2.1.1 The mutuality of interests

In the 1950s the primary aim of Soviet foreign policy in South Asia was to counter Western influence. In the 1960s and 1970s, with increasing US involvement in South-east Asia, and later in protecting its oil interests in the Middle East, US interests in South Asia diminished. Soviet policy thereafter became obsessed not so much with the USA as with the containment of China. The decline of US interest in South Asia is reflected in Richard Nixon's foreign policy report to Congress in February 1972, which ruled out competition with the USSR for influence in South Asia. Moreover, since the mid-sixties the USSR has seen itself as an Asian power. The Soviet goal of being perceived as an Asian power was in evidence in Kosygin's mediating role in Tashkent between the Indian and Pakistani heads of government at the end of the Indo-Pakistan war of 1965. A final Soviet objective in South Asia has been to use India as an intermediary in such political forums as the non-aligned movement and economic ones like the Group of 77.

The stability of the Indian state, a crucial prerequisite for the successful execution of these Soviet objectives, is as important to the USSR as to the Indian elite. It is this stability which perhaps distinguishes, in Soviet eyes, India from other friends/allies in the Middle East (e.g. Egypt) and South-east Asia (e.g. Indonesia). Soviet economic and military assistance has served to strengthen the Indian state both domestically as well as in the international arena, and the 1970s have seen the consolidation of India's dominant position in the region. Domestically, the close political and economic relationship with the USSR has enabled the essentially populist party in power to maintain a 'socialist' image. Of the three world powers – the USSR, the USA and

China – the Indian elite sees only the USSR as truly interested in the emergence of India as a major regional power.

The 1970s opened with two historical developments, both of which served to consolidate the growing 'special relationship' between India and the USSR. One of these developments altered the balance of forces within the global triangle (China–USSR–USA), while the other did the same for the regional triangle (USSR–India–Pakistan). The first was the Sino-American détente which was heralded by Kissinger's secret mission (from Islamabad) to Peking (arranged through the good offices of Pakistan) in mid-1971. The second was the Indo-Pakistan war of December 1971 which ended with the dismemberment of Pakistan. The Sino-American détente was perceived identically by India and the USSR as being directed against the USSR. The new power alignment played a major role in India's decision to sign a twenty-year friendship treaty with the USSR in August 1971.[1]

Thus there existed a strong coincidence of Indian and Soviet interests at the beginning of the 1970s which resulted in the Indo-Soviet treaty. However, the hopes that the USSR might have had of the treaty as a step towards an Asian Collective Security system (first proposed by Brezhnev in 1969) were not to be realised, since India did not quite subscribe to that view of the treaty. India's non-aligned conscience probably constrained her from declaring full support for the Soviet Collective Security plan. But since the proposal has not received much support from any non-socialist Asian country, Soviet authors have seized upon any sympathetic statement by Indian leaders and made rather a lot of it. Even Gorbachev's recent concern for Asian security has met with only a cautious response from New Delhi.

The Indian leaders demonstrated that on the question of the Collective Security plan, they were prepared to cooperate up to a point and no further. On the question of naval power in the Indian Ocean, while the Indians appreciate the importance of the presence of Soviet ships as a counterweight to the American presence, they do not wish the Soviets to become the dominant power in the Indian Ocean. A simultaneous reduction in the naval presence of both the USSR and the USA is consistent with India's long-term interest in establishing its own dominance in the region. Thus, again, while Soviet and Indian objectives are similar, they are certainly not the same.

It is this relative similarity of geo-political interests that has prevented any public dispute arising over India's nuclear programme. Like the West, the Soviet Union has publicly opposed the expansion of the nuclear club and exhorted nations to sign the Non-Proliferation

Treaty (which India has consistently refused to sign since 1968). But when India exploded her nuclear device in May 1974, the USSR, unlike the West, merely reported India's action, repeating India's claim that it was for peaceful purposes.

Even the presence of Soviet troops in Afghanistan for nearly a decade was not allowed by the two governments – Indian and Soviet – to drive a wedge between the two countries. The Indian government's stand throughout the conflict in Afghanistan was that the Soviet troops must leave Afghanistan as early as possible, but the American and Chinese governments must also end their military support, through Pakistan, to the Afghan rebels. The Geneva accord on Afghanistan between the Reagan administration and the Soviet government must be respected by both parties. The Indian government has maintained that a stable Afghan government would enable the Soviets to complete withdrawal of troops. The Indian interest is in domestic stability in the South Asian region, which would minimise superpower interference.

2.1.2 The military dimension

The USSR has been India's single most important supplier of defence equipment since the mid-sixties. More importantly, that it has been prepared to transfer defence technology is largely a reflection of the overridingly strong mutuality of geo-political interests between the two. On the other hand, the difference between American and Indian perceptions of global issues have correspondingly been reflected in the very unstable – and from India's point of view unreliable – military relationship with the USA.

Up to 1959, India's armed forces depended exclusively on Western equipment, especially British. Considering that Soviet defence exports to India began only in the early 1960s, it is remarkable how quickly such exports gathered momentum. According to SIPRI, between 1965 and 1969, 80 per cent of all Indian defence equipment imports came from the USSR (*SIPRI Yearbook 1971*). The high Soviet share in India's defence imports, in the latter half of the sixties, can be explained by the fact that after the 1965 Indo-Pakistan war, the USA and Western countries imposed an embargo on arms exports to India. In the early 1970s, the Soviet share remained high for two complementary reasons: the USSR was replenishing Indian stocks during and after the 1971 war; at the same time, the USA stopped all military assistance along with economic assistance.

Having established itself as India's single most important supplier, in 1970–4 the USSR's share fell to 70 per cent of India's arms imports and in 1975–9 to 57 per cent (*SIPRI Yearbook 1982*). In order to place this declining trend in perspective, it is important to point out first that the USSR obviously still remains the most important supplier by far, and secondly, that in recent years India has been fairly successful in diversifying its sources of weapon systems. This second development speaks volumes for the bargaining capacity India has come to enjoy in its dealings with the Soviets.

Perhaps an even more important point which places this trend decline in perspective is the fact that India is one of the few countries outside the Warsaw Pact allowed to purchase Soviet military know-how, as opposed to weapons. As the *SIPRI Yearbook 1983* points out, Western arms manufacturers are increasingly licensing their production to Third World countries, but the Soviet Union is not: 'It had been expected, when the Indian MiG-21 programme began, that this would start a new trend. This has not been the case: the Indian example remains one of a handful of exceptions to the rule' (*SIPRI Yearbook 1983*, p. 368).

The MiG-21 was chosen in 1961 in preference to Western alternatives because the Soviets were willing to make it available for licensed manufacture and also to extend credit for the manufacturing programme. While Lockheed was interested in selling the aircraft to India, the US government, sensitive to Pakistan's worries, refused to allow the firm to transfer technology to India. The significance of the MiG deal lies in the fact that the Soviets had refused the MiG-21 to the Chinese but were willing to license production in India (whose relations with China were fast deteriorating) (K. Subramanyam 1981).

After the Sino-Indian war (1962), India accepted military aid from any country that was prepared to offer it. The USA promised $50m of emergency assistance in 1962/3 and $60m in 1963/4. In May 1964, as much as $500m of military aid, half of it a grant and the rest a loan, was promised for the period 1964–9. But the Indo-Pakistan war (1965) resulted in the cancellation of military aid to both India and Pakistan, with the result that between October 1962 and September 1965 India was supplied with only about $80m as against a promised commitment of $610m.

On the other hand, the USSR, in addition to licensing production of defence equipment in India, has been prepared to set up facilities in India to meet the overhaul and servicing needs of the Soviet air and naval equipment purchased by India. Thus repair and overhaul facilities have been set up in Chandigarh for the Soviet AN-32 medium transport aircraft. Naval vessels purchased from the USSR can be serviced at what is the biggest naval dockyard in the country in Visakhapatnam, constructed with Soviet assistance.

Apart from the mutuality of geo-political interests, there are several reasons why the USSR has emerged as India's most important defence supplier. We have already hinted at the unreliability of American supplies. Moreover, in the USA all military sales over $25m (lethal equipment ceilings are lower at $10m) must be presented to the US Congress for clearance, which means not only delay, but subjection of the recipient's defence policy to scrutiny. Again (only partly on account of the sophistication of American equipment) the USA is normally keen to establish an infrastructure – for instance, military supply missions, training teams and maintenance teams – in the recipient LDC. Unlike Pakistan, India has not been keen on such a broad-based military relationship.

An alternative to Soviet supplies lies in west Europe. However, while west European countries are willing to transfer technology to India, such technology may prove to be rather expensive since the volume of production is lower than those of the two superpowers, and economies of scale are not operative to the same degree. Moreover, the European countries are not in a position to extend long-term credits to India. Finally, in some cases, European defence equipment includes American technology, and the USA could prohibit the sale of such technology.

In these circumstances, it is not surprising that the USSR has emerged as India's most important supplier of defence equipment. Not only was it prepared to extend long-term credits – earlier for ten to twelve years, later for as long as seventeen years (1980 agreement) – but also give low rates of interest (2 to 2.5 per cent); at the same time, repayments are to be made, not in free foreign exchange, but by export of goods, i.e. in the same way as developmental loans are repaid.

In addition, the USSR has been prepared to grant licences for the manufacture of weapon systems. One such agreement (1980) was on the basis of a loan of Rs13bn at 2.5 per cent annual interest, to be repaid over fifteen years after a two-year grace period. India bought seventy T-72 tanks outright; but 600 more were to be manufactured under licence by the Avadi works in Madras. MiG-21 was the first Mach-2 aircraft to be licensed for production in an LDC and a non-socialist country, and now MiG-23 will be the first variable geometry aircraft to be manufactured in an LDC. There is some possibility that even MiG-29s may be manufactured in India.

Consequently, there is a strong new trend in evidence in defence planning: production of major weapons and equipment under licence as a step towards defence industrialisation. Subramanyam, a leading defence analyst, writes: 'Only the USSR has adequate mutuality of interest in India's development of defence technology and necessary resources to support the effort with necessary credit. So India must approach the USSR for transfer of technology rather than weapon systems' (K. Subramanyam 1981).

2.2 Ideology

After the death of Stalin in 1953, the Soviet leadership announced at the 20th Congress of the CPSU (1956) that the foreign policy of the USSR will be founded on the principle of 'peaceful coexistence' of the capitalist and socialist world. As a corollary to the principle of peaceful coexistence, the USSR developed the notion of the peaceful road to socialism in developing countries.

In this context, Khrushchev's report to the 20th Congress of the CPSU, which announced the principle of peaceful coexistence to the world, de-emphasised the potential for revolution in countries. It rather emphasised the international orientation of the potential friends of the USSR; the foreign policies of post-colonial regimes in the new states were given far greater importance than the needs and programmes of communist parties. Not surprisingly, Nehru, once the 'running dog of imperialism', was by 1955 considered an 'outstanding statesman'; Gandhi, for years criticised by Soviet spokesmen, was described by Bulganin (in November 1955) as 'the distinguished leader of the Indian national movement'.[2] This was because the Soviets saw the anti-imperialist potential of the non-aligned movement, of which India was a founder-member.

2.2.1 Soviet view of the Indian state

Bibliographical studies show that India has a central place in any discussion of Soviet development theory. India happens to be the Soviet Union's most analysed LDC. The India Department of the Institute of the Peoples of Asia has a long history going back to Tsarist times. By comparison, the writings on Africa and Latin America were superficial and dogmatic until the late 1950s (Clarkson 1979, pp. 9–11). India was one of the first post-colonial countries with which the USSR established diplomatic relations and, besides, diplomatic relations have remained consistently friendly since Stalin's death. This makes for a stable, though not static, ideological line on India in Soviet orientology.

Although the USSR has neither claimed that India was 'socialist' nor that it was of 'socialist orientation', the question is how was India 'progressive' in Soviet eyes. Here, it is not enough to say that the emphasis was placed upon the state-to-state nature of Soviet aid to large-scale capital projects, modelled on the Soviet experience. According to R. A. Ulianovsky, India has attained a 'middle level of capitalist development'. In this context, the Soviet leadership, like the pro-Moscow, Communist Party of India (CPI), believes that the ruling Congress Party plays a progressive role in Indian economic/political development in three particular respects: it is anti-monopoly, anti-feudal and anti-imperialist.[3]

By giving the label of 'national bourgeois regime' to the Indian state, they endorsed the Congress as 'progressive'. Like the CPI, the Soviets believe that the objective of the national bourgeoisie is to develop an independent economy on a capitalist basis. The Soviets view industrial development by Indian capitalists as being contrary to the interests of imperialism as also to the interests of landlords/princes. Hence, the national bourgeoisie and its political representative, the Congress Party, are thought by the USSR to be both anti-imperialist and anti-feudal. The state is seen to serve a progressive role by building public enterprises and thus loosening the hold of monopolies, both foreign and Indian. By endorsing the Indian Congress as progressive, the Soviets advocated a non-revolutionary perspective for the country's future. The USSR was seeking détente with the USA and in the process assigned a new role for the national bourgeoisie in countries of the peace zone. In the process it revised the fundamentals of Marxism-Leninism and innovated the thesis of peaceful coexistence of the capitalist and socialist world systems. As suggested earlier, it simultaneously developed the theory of peaceful transition to socialism in the new nations. Socialism was to be achieved through a transitional phase described as a 'national democracy' under the leadership of the national bourgeoisie; these countries deserved diplomatic and economic support from the socialist countries. This national bourgeoisie would execute the historic transformation from feudalism and colonialism to pre-socialist capitalism.

This optimistic view of the post-colonial state had not been shared by the Communist Party of China since the late 1950s (although in the seventies Chinese foreign policy has gone through similar manoeuvres). Thus Sino-Soviet differences over the peaceful coexistence thesis, the theory of peaceful transition to socialism, and the nature of the national bourgeoisie in the new nations were reflected in their opposing viewpoints of India. Although in the mid-fifties China exhibited some recognition of the anti-imperialist potential of the national bourgeoisie in these countries, after the Lama revolt in Tibet in 1959 (to which the Indian bourgeoisie's attitude was, at the very least, bellicose) the Chinese were convinced that since capitalism was weak in these new countries, their national bourgeoisie was coming to terms with imperialism in their anxiety to get aid from both power blocs. The Soviet leadership had made India the model of a peace zone country capable of peaceful transition to socialism. India started receiving massive economic aid from 1955 onwards, while aid to China began to decline. The ideological debate between the Chinese and Soviets could not but have had its effects on Sino-Indian relations, and served to strengthen Indo-Soviet relations.

The emergence of concepts such as 'peaceful coexistence' and the 'peaceful road to socialism', therefore, suggests that ideology has become an instrument of Soviet foreign policy towards LDCs. Such an interpretation is confirmed by the Soviet analysis of post-colonial India, which has changed dramatically in tone from the early 1950s to the 1970s, in response to evolving Soviet geo-political interests. Although India is neither socialist nor of socialist orientation, her government is seen as progressive – largely for reasons of foreign policy.[4] As long as the Indian elite is determined to strive for medium, if not great, power status, the Soviet treatment of India as progressive (and its diplomatic, military and economic assistance) entirely suits the interests of the Indian elite.

2.3 Conclusions

What are the future prospects of the Indo-Soviet relationship? The long-term resolution of the Sino-Soviet dispute, it has been suggested, is likely to affect adversely the 'special relationship' known to exist between India and the USSR. That the effect of such a development will be adverse is indubitable; the more important question is, how adverse? It seems unlikely that the political effect would be very damaging. A Sino-Soviet rapprochement will simultaneously create the space for an improvement of the Sino-Indian relationship. More importantly, those who doubt the durability of the Indo-Soviet relationship underestimate the influence of the other Soviet political objectives mentioned at the beginning of this chapter. For example, even if the Sino-Soviet relationship improves, the superpower competition for influence in the Third World in general, and the Indian Ocean in particular, is unlikely to wane. And considering the geographical importance of India's position dominating the Indian Ocean, the Soviet Union will at least need friends, if not allies, in the region. Equally important is the role of India in the non-aligned world. The Soviet self-image of being an Asian power, and not just a European one, would hardly be credible if relations with one of the two foremost countries of Asia were allowed to deteriorate beyond a certain point. Besides, there is a growing Soviet economic interest in India (see chapter 3). This tends to suggest that while the political aspects of the relationship are still dominant for the USSR, its economic interest in India is now much greater than it was ever before. However, it must be added that Sino-Soviet economic ties are expanding very rapidly indeed. Trade turnover has grown very sharply: from $0.6bn in 1982 to $2.6bn in 1986. More importantly, the commodity composition of Chinese exports to the USSR is similar to that of India's exports to the Soviet Union. That is where the Chinese challenge lies.

For India the importance of the political/diplomatic aspect of the Indo-Soviet relationship has changed emphasis: for nearly two decades (the longest period in her post-independence history) she has not fought a war; on the contrary, since 1971 there has been a slow but steady improvement in Sino-Indian and Indo-Pakistani relations. The sense of insecurity of the fifties and sixties, and the consequent need for Soviet diplomatic assistance in international forums has disappeared. But at the same time the striving for medium-power status ensures a steady supply of Soviet and, for that matter, Western arms. As regards the economic relationship India's interest in the USSR has certainly shifted ground in the seventies. In the earlier period Soviet transfer of technology to key sectors of the Indian economy was of paramount importance. As regards trade, it is possible that the availability of an easy outlet in east Europe through bilateral trade took the pressure off Indian exporters to sell to convertible currency areas, but it created the purchasing power to import capital goods. Today, India's economic interest lies in: 1. acquisition of arms without the expenditure of hard currency; 2. acquisition of intermediate products like oil, fertilisers, newsprint and non-ferrous metals, against payment in inconvertible rupees; and 3. the Soviet market, which absorbed almost one-fifth of India's exports through much of the eighties. With such a convergence of interests of Indian capitalists and the Indian state, the likelihood of a dramatic deterioration in the Indo-Soviet relationship seems highly improbable in the foreseeable future.

3 Soviet economic interests in non-socialist LDCs

In order to develop a political economy of Soviet foreign economic relations, especially its relations with LDCs, it is necessary to examine how the domestic needs of the Soviet economy are reflected in its foreign economic relations. This chapter attempts to explain the expansion of Soviet economic relations with LDCs in the 1970s in terms of the compulsions that derive from the specific manner in which the Soviet economy has evolved over the past half-century.

Although the share of Soviet foreign trade as a percentage of its GDP is relatively small (not surprising for such a large economy with major resource endowments), Soviet participation in the international division of labour has expanded rapidly since the late sixties. Thus, while in 1960, three-quarters of all Soviet trade was conducted with other CPEs, within twenty years the share of DMEs and LDCs together in Soviet trade had grown to nearly 50 per cent. At the same time, Soviet economists keep emphasising that although the Soviet (and CMEA) share in world production has expanded enormously, its share in world trade is still very small – hence even now there is enormous scope for expansion. The compulsion to expand is not 'capitalist' (as argued by certain Marxists) but arises from other sources.[1] In section 1 we discuss the domestic economic factors underlying this expansion of Soviet-DME and Soviet-LDC relations in the 1970s and 1980s. In section 2 the implications of these domestic compulsions for Soviet external payments and in section 3 for Soviet foreign trade, in both cases with non-socialist LDCs, are examined. In section 4 the preceding discussion is used to shed light on Soviet economic interests in India.

3.1 Factors underlying expansion of Soviet-LDC economic relations

Over the last twenty years, the (absolute) level of Soviet foreign trade has grown considerably; at the same time, the share of the
market economies, both developed and developing, in Soviet foreign
trade has tended to rise (see table 3.1). This increasing participation in
the world economy has proceeded alongside a decline in the rate of
growth of net material product since the mid-1950s and an increasing
investment cost per unit of output. Since the mid-sixties economic
reforms in the CPEs have been implemented to encourage a transition
from a maximal rate of mobilisation of labour and capital towards
primarily intensive growth (derived from productivity improvements,
i.e. increasing labour and capital efficiency). Policy measures were
taken which were intended to make the Soviet economy generate its
own technological progress at a rate faster than had been achieved in
the past. With the same objective in view, foreign trade and the role of
imported technology expanded in the 1970s.[2]

However, the problem of the failure of the Soviet economy to generate technological progress at a rate comparable to that in the advanced
capitalist countries lay deeply-rooted in the manner in which cen-
tralised planning had developed since the beginning of the First Five-
Year Plan. The problem was perhaps well summarised in Bulganin's
report to the Central Committee of the CPSU in July 1955. Bulganin
enumerated: 1. the autocratic tendencies of the sectoral ministerial
system, trying to secure supplies by a costly vertical integration, instead of relying on the uncertainties of sub-contracting; 2. failure to
secure regular supplies, producing structural under-utilisation of capacity; 3. the neglect of the quality of products, and of the introduction
of new products, due to the purely quantitative methods of planning
and of assessment of performance; 4. the systematic mismatching of
production assortment and the structure of demand – especially in
consumption goods – because of selective over- and under-fulfilment
by enterprises; 5. the cyclical nature of production, with the concen-
tration of output towards the end of the plan period (*shturmovchina*).[3]
These are general problems of the system as it has evolved over the last
sixty years.

Such an environment was not particularly conducive to the generation of technological progress. There was gross distortion in the use of
inputs or in the quality of output because of the physical indicators
used, and almost a cult of gross output ('kult vala') existed. Where the

Table 3.1. *Foreign trade of the USSR: exports and imports by region (percentage share)*

| | Exports | | | Imports | | |
	East	West	South	East	West	South
1960	75.7	18.2	6.1	70.7	19.8	9.5
1970	65.4	18.7	15.9	65.1	24.1	10.9
1975	60.7	25.5	13.8	52.4	36.4	11.2
1976	58.7	28.0	13.3	52.6	37.7	9.8
1977	57.4	26.5	16.0	57.1	33.0	10.0
1978	59.6	24.4	16.0	60.0	31.8	8.2
1979	55.7	29.5	14.8	56.6	35.0	8.4
1980	45.3	36.2	18.5	53.2	35.4	11.5
1981	45.8	34.1	20.1	50.8	34.4	14.8
1985	52.0	25.7	22.3	50.2	27.9	21.9
1986	58.7	19.2	22.1	56.5	25.3	18.2
1987	59.6	20.8	22.7	59.6	22.8	17.6
1988	55.7	21.9	22.4	57.5	25.1	17.4

Notes: East = CMEA countries, People's Republic of China, Yugoslavia, Vietnam; West = OECD countries; South = all other countries.
Sources: Comecon Foreign Trade, 1982; UN, *Monthly Bulletin of Statistics*, July 1985.

supply problem was already acute, the decision to innovate was likely to intensify the supply problem.

A second problem of an organisational nature which militated against innovation was the separation of R&D institutes from the producing enterprises (Berliner 1979; Berliner 1976). Thirdly, both the price and incentive structures seem to militate against innovation. Until recently, the same cost-plus-standard profit principle was applied to the pricing of new products as it was for existing products. The innovator enjoyed no higher price or profit rate for his efforts and hence no special advantage from a technical innovation. Besides, during the period of the growth strategy involving maximum labour and capital mobilisation into industrial production, no special bonus was introduced for innovation. Only in the mid-fifties was a special bonus introduced and since then a number of other bonuses for the same purpose have been added on. However, the major source of managerial bonus still remains the basic bonus dependent on fulfilling the basic enterprise plan targets. Since innovation leads to decline in the current rate of output, the overall effect is that the innovation bonuses merely serve to compensate for some percentage of the basic

bonus. Hence, in spite of these reforms, the prospects for rapid technological progress in the USSR seem to be bleak.[4]

Apart from the need to import technology, another structural compulsion forcing a greater dependence of the Soviet economy (and east
European ones) on capitalist countries – both developed and developing – is the increased need in the seventies for grain imports. It would
be too simplistic to suggest that the contemporary problems of Soviet
agriculture derive from the traditional neglect of investment in agriculture in the Stalin era, 'following not in principle but in practice from the
logic of accumulation and priority to industry and heavy industry in
the original Soviet conditions' (Nuti 1979, p. 265).

Agriculture's continued problems are due, first, to problems with
industrial supplies, and secondly, to institutional shortcomings *within*
agriculture. While the post-Stalin decades were marked by the growing share of agriculture in investment to correct the earlier imbalance,
the output increases, though impressive, have not kept pace with
consumer demand. More importantly, the investment costs of achiev-
ing such output increases have been so high that it would be more
rational for the USSR to depend to a greater extent on imported food.
For the problem with Soviet agriculture is not simply that it suffered
from neglect during the Stalin era and that it is organised and managed
inefficiently. The problem goes deeper and is more complicated than
that. It has been strongly argued, in fact, that a fundamental reform of
the whole economic system is an essential prerequisite. While institutional changes can make a difference to agricultural performance,
the problems of agriculture cannot be dealt with in isolation.

> Soviet industry is incapable of supplying the inputs required. In other
> words, the problems of agriculture are essentially the same as those of
> any other sector of the Soviet economy, and reflect the political and
> economic irrationalities of the system. However, in the case of agri-
> culture, these problems are exacerbated by the soil and climate of the
> USSR. (G. A. E. Smith 1981, p. 5)

At the same time, from the point of view of Soviet ability to pay for its
technology and grain imports, it should be pointed out that in spite of
the CIA's pessimistic forecasts made in the late 1970s for crude oil
output in the 1980s, production has not dipped substantially. Thus the
medium-term prospects of Soviet hard currency earnings should not
entail excessive sacrifice in terms of grain or technology imports.
However, the strain on the balance of payments on account of the
competing demands, on the one hand for agricultural goods from

Soviet consumers, and on the other, for technology imports to increase industrial productivity, will continue to be felt in the medium term. They will also be felt by eastern Europe, as the USSR diverts oil supplies to the DMEs.[5] The problems of Soviet agriculture and the failure of the Soviet economic structure to generate technological progress will force the Soviet authorities into greater reliance on the DMEs and LDCs. In the Soviet literature this phenomenon has been increasingly described as 'interdependence' or even more vaguely as 'greater participation in the international division of labour'.

3.2 The LDC role in relieving Soviet hard currency trade deficits

3.2.1 Soviet trade deficits and resulting debt

The accepted view is that in the late 1960s there took place a policy change by the Soviet leadership resulting in a sudden increase in commercial imports of Western machinery and know-how. By the mid-1950s the sources of extensive growth had been considerably reduced in the USSR and domestic growth had slowed down. However, the existence of the Cold War prevented any increase in East–West trade until the 1970s. Domestic Soviet economic compulsions (following the fall of Khrushchev) as well as an improvement in the international environment through détente resulted in a dramatic increase in East–West trade in the 1970s. The Brezhnev programme to give more attention to the consumer also meant large Soviet imports of Western agricultural goods.

By 1981, the share of Western industrialised countries in the USSR's total imports had risen to 35 per cent from 20 per cent in 1960. On account of the growing reliance on the DMEs for equipment (30 per cent of total trade) and grain, the USSR incurred large trade deficits through most of the 1970s (see table 3.2).[6] During the two rounds of oil price increases, the Soviet trade balance with the DMEs tended to improve at first while Soviet export revenues from energy rose (SITC 3 constituted 66.6 per cent of Soviet exports to DMEs in 1979). But in both periods, the revenue increase led (within one year) to a very rapid growth of Soviet imports from the DMEs, which, in turn, was responsible for a later deterioration in the Soviet trade balance. In spite of the deterioration of the trade balance, the Soviet economy remains much less vulnerable than eastern Europe's. In contrast to eastern Europe, the Soviet balance on invisibles in the current account has been small.

Table 3.2. *East–West trade: Western exports, imports and balances (million US dollars)*

	1970	1971	1972	1973	1974	1975	1976	1977	1978	1979	1980	1981	1982	1983	1984	1985ª
Western exports to:																
Eastern Europe	4,680	5,353	6,797	9,782	14,074	15,762	16,129	16,403	19,610	22,870	24,884	21,062	17,344	16,556	15,860	16,857
Soviet Union	2,812	2,847	4,133	5,954	7,946	13,173	14,422	14,333	16,642	20,039	22,949	24,943	25,690	24,649	24,089	23,264
Western imports (f.o.b.) from:																
Eastern Europe	4,159	4,725	5,725	7,883	10,284	10,934	12,330	13,303	15,334	19,295	21,740	18,950	17,746	17,839	19,594	18,969
Soviet Union	2,501	2,860	3,163	4,904	8,078	8,999	11,040	12,553	13,949	19,846	25,799	25,171	26,342	25,652	26,392	23,614
Western trade balances with:																
Eastern Europe	520	608	1,071	1,899	3,789	4,828	3,799	3,099	4,275	3,575	3,145	2,113	−402	−1,283	−3,735	−2,111
Soviet Union	311	−12	969	1,050	−131	4,173	3,381	1,779	2,693	193	−2,850	−228	−652	−1,002	−2,303	−350

ª Extrapolations, based on January–October.
Source: UNECE, *Economic Survey of Europe*, 1985–6.

Thus its current account balance with the market economies has followed the large swings which are typical of its trade balances. The Soviet Union has been relatively less affected by external disturbances from world markets (as compared to eastern Europe), on account of the structure of its debt (i.e. heavily weighted towards fixed rate credits) and its ability to export increasing amounts of energy in spite of the sluggish overall Western demand for imports (see UNECE, *Economic Survey of Europe*, 1982, p. 266).

It should be noted that a factor influencing east Europe's trade balances, but which is not related to the oil cycle, is the periodic large import of agricultural products by the CPEs.[7] Harvest failures happened to coincide with recession in the DMEs. Thus on the one hand, the recessions have reduced Eastern export possibilities, while on the other, the purchases of food have increased expenditures on imports. The USSR considerably increased its imports of agricultural products from the DMEs in 1975 and the LDCs during 1979–81, while eastern Europe did the same in 1976 and 1980–1. Not surprisingly, borrowing required to cover Soviet deficits increased the net hard currency debt from $600m at the end of 1971 to $12.5bn at the end of 1981.

Soviet grain imports accounted for 40 per cent of hard currency merchandise imports. Without Western grain, Soviet consumers would not have had the increase in meat consumption they realised in the early 1970s, and there would have been a sharp drop in per capita consumption of meat in the late 1970s instead of a levelling off. Although technology imports put pressure upon the balance of payments, the imports were of crucial importance to the Soviet economy in some critical areas, especially in some manufacturing sectors (see Zoeter 1982, p. 484).

In the eighties the Soviet Union (and east Europe) has dramatically reversed the trade deficit with the West into a trade surplus (see table 3.2). This reflects an exceptionally rapid external adjustment undertaken by these economies in response to the debt overhang of the seventies. For most east European economies this took the form of import reductions, but in 1983 and 1984 it took entirely the form of export expansion, especially in the case of the USSR. The rapid expansion of exports reflects a certain rise in the level of re-export activity, especially in the field of fuels trade. However, how fragile this dramatic reversal of the trade balance in the eighties can be was demonstrated when in 1985 a large surplus (for the Soviet Union and east Europe combined) was reduced to some $1bn. This underlines the fact we have stressed, viz., the trade imbalance between East and West is a structural one, and is unlikely to go away in the near future. As the *Economic Survey of Europe* (UNECE 1985–6) forecast:

> While the impact of the oil price drop on global activity is expected to be positive, the implications for east–west trade are not auspicious. The need for western goods is likely to remain high in the east, but revenues from oil exports would suffer. Resort to credits is an option. The conservative stance against debt generally adopted by eastern countries would weigh against a surge in eastern borrowing. (p. 257)

3.2.2 Financing the deficit

While other CPEs have similarly run trade deficits with DMEs, the USSR has been in a much better position to finance its hard currency deficit. First, as has been mentioned above, the USSR is well endowed with oil and natural gas, the world prices of which rose dramatically in 1973 and again in 1979 as a result of OPEC action (of which the USSR is not a member). The second and third factors have been the Soviet ability to sell arms and gold. Since the mid-seventies significant hard currency earnings from sales of arms (to LDCs) and gold have allowed the USSR to hold down its use of Western credits. At the same time, earnings from interest on Soviet assets in Western banks and from invisibles and transfers have usually offset interest payments on the debt. During the 1970s the USSR, which is the second largest producer and marketer of gold in the world after South Africa, was responsible for one-third of the annual world gold production and about one-quarter of the newly mined gold moving in world trade. The USSR tends to market the gold directly according to the need for financing. Gold is one of the USSR's top hard currency earners, with cumulative receipts in the 1970s totalling $15bn – equivalent to about 10 per cent of Soviet hard currency expenditure.

The USSR is one of the two leading sources of arms supplies in the world.[8] There is considerable variation on the estimates of total value of arms deliveries to LDCs by the USSR; the information on that portion of deliveries for which the USSR has received hard currency is even more limited (see table 3.3 for estimates). However, it is certain that in the wake of the 1973 Arab-Israeli war, the USSR was in a good position to supply arms to radical Arab clients who sought to improve and increase their stocks of military hardware. It is interesting that the USA has about three times as many recipients for its exports in the LDCs as

Table 3.3. *Soviet arms sales to LDCs: three estimates, 1970–1982 (million US dollars)*

	1970	1971	1972	1973	1974	1975	1976	1977	1978	1979	1980	1981
SIPRI A	1,136	1,515	1,225	1,537	1,930	2,160	1,554	2,156	3,526	4,104	4,425	3,172
SIPRI B	1,615	1,249	1,469	1,673	1,681	1,867	2,265	2,700	3,153	3,477	3,523	—
USJEC Total (1979)	995	865	1,215	3,130	2,310	1,845	2,575	3,515	3,825			
Hard currency receipts	100	87	122	1,345	1,000	793	1,108	1,500	1,644			
USJEC Total (1982)	775	680	960	2,100	1,980	1,860	2,270	3,810	4,130	4,270	4,670	4,960
Hard currency receipts	400	400	600	1,600	1,500	1,500	1,850	3,220	3,965	3,855	4,200	4,200

Notes: 1. SIPRI figures are trend indicator values at constant (1975) prices. A = yearly figures, B = five-year moving averages.
2. Ericson and Miller (in USJEC 1979) apply the ratio of hard currency receipts to total arms deliveries recorded in 1977 – 43 per cent (itself an estimate the basis of which is not explained) – to the time series for total arms deliveries to derive hard currency sales estimates for 1973–8. For 1970–2 they believe the USSR received hard currency for roughly 10 per cent of its arms deliveries. They admit that in their calculations of the USSR's hard currency balance of payments 'the probability for errors is particularly great with regard to arms' sales'. 3. The basis for Zoeter's (in USJEC 1982) estimates is not explained.
Sources: SIPRI Yearbook 1983; USJEC 1979; USJEC 1982.

the USSR (and it has granted a far greater number of production licences). In spite of this the USSR is the largest supplier to the LDCs; hence, the conclusion is that the countries that receive weapons from the USSR are getting these weapons in very large numbers (see *SIPRI Yearbook 1983*, p. 268).

There is evidence that a considerable part of the arms supplied to Egypt and Syria since 1973 was paid for in hard cash by other Arab countries (Algeria, Libya, Saudi Arabia, Kuwait and other countries). Besides, arms deals with oil countries, Iraq, Libya and possibly Algeria and Iran are payable either in hard currency or in oil and gas, which are equivalent to it since they are re-exported to the West. The increased proportion of Soviet arms sales to the Middle East (in total arms sales) also explains the shift in recent years in the distribution of Soviet military sales to the region towards a higher proportion of such sales going to oil countries – Libya, Iraq, Iran (until the fall of the Shah).[9]

It is next to impossible to calculate what proportion of the Soviet hard currency trade deficit with the West is financed by the hard currency arms sales, since there is no consensus on the level of Soviet arms deliveries to LDCs. Only two of the three estimates for total military deliveries to LDCs presented in table 3.3 make an estimate of Soviet hard currency receipts.

Overall, the 'export dependence' of the Soviet arms industry is probably between one-quarter and one-third for that part of Soviet military industry which manufactures conventional weapons. It is perhaps not coincidental that as the Soviet hard currency deficit with the West has grown and the resultant indebtedness has increased, so the Soviet arms sales to LDCs have expanded. According to the *SIPRI Yearbook 1983*, estimates of the total number of Soviet military aircraft exported outside the Warsaw Pact countries since the mid-fifties range from 6,000 to almost 10,000. An export of 2,520 combat aircraft in the five years from 1977 to 1981 suggests a rising trend. The SIPRI values of annual deliveries to the Third World (table 3.3) lead to a similar con-clusion. During the period 1978–82, the total value of Soviet arms deliveries to LDCs – expressed in constant prices – was approximately double the value for the preceding five-year period.

3.2.3 The shift from bilateralism to multilateralism in Soviet-LDC trade

Quite apart from the hard currency earned in arms sales to LDCs, there is also a possibility that Soviet trade deficits with the West have also been financed by Soviet hard currency trade surpluses with LDCs (see tables 3.4 and 3.5). It is perhaps not surprising that just as the hard currency debt of the East began expanding rapidly, the number of LDCs with which the East trades in convertible currency, rather than through clearing agreements, began to grow.

At the beginning of the 1970s, the total number of East–South trade and payments agreements was 350; the number had risen to 450 by the mid-seventies, so that by now only a few LDCs have no trade and payments agreements with any of the countries of eastern Europe. During the same period, the number of agreements stipulating payments through the clearing system fell from approximately 150 to below 100. This signifies that about 40 per cent of all trade agreements required bilateral clearing, whereas by the mid-seventies their share had fallen to about 20 per cent. What is interesting is that not only was the great majority of agreements between newcomers to trade concluded immediately with convertible currency payments, but many of the old agreements were transformed into agreements foreseeing payments in convertible currencies.

The share of trade between East and South governed by clearing agreements is certainly falling (see table 3.4). According to UNCTAD Secretariat estimates, the share of trade conducted under clearing agreements has been declining since the mid-1960s: in 1965 it was 77.1 per cent; and by 1975 it had dropped 20 percentage points. The tendency was particularly pronounced after 1970, i.e. when the Eastern trade deficits with the DMEs began to rise rapidly in the wake of technology imports. Thus, in the period 1970–5 the trade between East and South in convertible currencies rose almost five times, while trade under clearing agreements doubled.

It is interesting that the thrust towards convertible payments in trade with LDCs has been most noticeable in the smaller east European countries, whose debt service ratios are higher (relative to the USSR), who are more vulnerable to external pressure both from the real and financial spheres, and who are not cushioned by the availability of oil, gold or arms for export to hard currency markets. In 1975 the USSR was carrying out 61 per cent of its total trade with LDCs under clearing arrangements, while the respective percentage for all the other east

Table 3.4. *Trade turnover of east European countries with LDCs under different systems of payment (million US dollars)*

	Bulgaria	Czechoslovakia	GDR	Hungary	Poland	Rumania	USSR	Total
1965								
1. Total trade turnover	178	659	454	298	509	157	2,954	5,209
2. Trade under clearing agreements	144	446	369	187	402	136	2,322	4,006
3. Convertible currency agreements	34	213	85	111	107	21	632	1,201
4. Share of 2. in 1.	80.9%	67.7%	81.3%	62.8%	79.0%	86.6%	78.6%	76.9%
1970								
1. Total trade turnover	325	888	631	454	586	404	4,959	8,247
2. Trade under clearing agreements	244	613	530	342	447	318	3,621	6,115
3. Convertible currency agreements	81	275	101	112	139	86	1,338	2,132
4. Share of 2. in 1.	75.1%	69.0%	84.0%	75.3%	76.3%	78.7%	73.0%	74.1%
1975								
1. Total trade turnover	1,011	1,828	1,558	1,193	1,885	2,042	13,742	23,259
2. Trade under clearing agreements	454	1,117	876	345	451	799	9,226	13,268
3. Convertible currency agreements	557	711	682	848	1,434	1,243	4,516	9,991
4. Share of 2. in 1.	44.9%	61.1%	56.2%	28.9%	23.9%	39.1%	67.1%	57.0%

Source: UNCTAD Secretariat 1977, TD/B/AC.22/2.

European countries together was 42 per cent. However, it may be mentioned that since 1975 the number of hard currency trade partners of the USSR in the Third World has expanded, not diminished. By early 1982 bilateral clearing agreements remained in force with only six of the USSR's trade partners in the Third World – India, Pakistan, Afghanistan, Syria, Egypt and Iran – which together account for no more than 30 per cent of Soviet-LDC trade. By the mid-1980s the number of bilateral trade partners the USSR had in the Third World had fallen to three.

The statistical material available from the UNCTAD Secretariat (see table 3.5) for 1965–75 shows that the USSR had a trade surplus with LDCs in 1965 of $298m; in 1970, $937m; and in 1975, $40m. The LDCs that had clearing agreements with the USSR showed a more balanced trade during the whole period: in 1965 they recorded an import surplus of $133m, and in 1970 an import surplus of $229m. In 1975 these countries even reversed their position, achieving a trade surplus of $659m with the USSR. This reversal of trade balances was arrived at largely as a result of many LDCs, e.g. India and Egypt, meeting their repayment obligations for debts incurred during the 1950s and 1960s. On the other hand, the LDCs conducting their trade with the USSR in convertible currencies registered in the same period higher trade deficits: in 1965, it was $166m; in 1970, $708m; and in 1975, $699m.[10]

3.2.4 Soviet trade surpluses and long-term credits to LDCs

A legitimate question at this point must be whether this Soviet trade surplus can be explained by utilisation of Soviet long-term credits by LDCs, as is claimed by the Soviets. If the Soviet claim is valid, then it cannot be argued that the Soviet surpluses with the South are used to finance their deficits with the West. Vassilev suggests that the former was used to finance the latter during 1961–6, 1961 being the year since when the USSR has had surpluses in most years (Vassilev 1969). Although over that period more than 75 per cent of the Soviet-LDC trade was under clearing agreements, most agreements provided for periodic settlement of outstanding claims being made in convertible currency. However, Vassilev does not give any evidence that the Soviet Union was in fact the recipient of large sums of convertible currency from its LDC bilateral trade partners. On the contrary, an OECD publication found that the settlements in convertible currency were rarely used, and the trade balance was normally carried over to the following trade agreement (OECD 1973, p. 416).

Table 3.5. Trade balances with LDCs of individual east European countries (million US dollars)

	Bulgaria	Czechoslovakia	GDR	Hungary	Poland	Rumania	USSR	Total
1965								
With all LDCs	10	57.0	-6.0	2.0	-45.0	19	298.0	335.0
Under clearing agreements	-1	2.3	-19.8	4.8	-65.7	13.0	132.5	66.1
In convertible currencies	11	54.7	13.8	-2.8	20.7	6.0	165.5	268.9
1970								
With all LDCs	49.0	132.0	-51.0	-38	66.0	66.0	937.0	1161.0
Under clearing agreements	24.7	51.1	62.0	-24.9	10.5	60.6	228.6	412.6
In convertible currencies	24.3	80.9	-113.0	-13.1	55.5	5.4	708.4	748.4
1975								
With all LDCs	287.0	190.0		-39.0	281.0	296.0	40.0	1,055.0[a]
Under clearing agreements	29.2	32.2		-52.1	24.6	83.0	-659.2	-542.3[a]
In convertible currencies	257.8	157.8		13.1	256.4	213.0	699.2	1597.3[a]

[a] Figures for GDR not available.
Source: UNCTAD Secretariat 1977, TD/B/AC.22/2.

For the period 1967–71, Chandra has suggested the possibility that the USSR utilised its trade surplus with LDCs to finance its deficit with the West (Chandra 1977, p. 350). In other words, it is possible the USSR may have used a switch arrangement for settling balances in clearing units at a discount. For some clearing currencies large discounts prevail in international switch markets like Vienna, Zurich and Amsterdam. For example, in 1974 Indian clearing units belonging to Bulgaria were sold at discount rates of 25 to 30 per cent; clearing units from Egypt belonging to east European countries were even sold at discounts of 35 to 40 per cent. Switch arrangements at such discounts, it is suggested, have frequently caused serious financial difficulties for certain developing countries, especially India (cited in Outters-Jaeger 1979, p. 57).

However, no matter how large these switch transactions, they must be but a relatively small proportion of total East–South trade. A crucial question in this respect is what proportion of total Soviet-LDC trade was being conducted in convertible currency. As table 3.4 demonstrates, in 1965, 78.6 per cent of total Soviet-LDC trade (77 per cent for east Europe including the USSR) was being conducted under clearing arrangements, and even by 1970, the figure had only fallen to 73 per cent (74 per cent for all east Europe). It is only after 1970 that the proportion of Soviet-LDC trade under clearing arrangements dropped sharply to 61 per cent (57 per cent for all east Europe). Hence even if the scale of switch transactions is large, it must pale into insignificance when compared with the large absolute values of hard currency trade surpluses of the East with the South in 1970 and 1975 (see table 3.5), and even later.

In order to determine whether Soviet trade surpluses with the South in the 1970s were the result of Soviet exports under credit schemes, we have set out in table 3.6 figures for net credit utilisation by LDCs during 1970–8.[11] To derive the figures for net aid disbursement (column 4, table 3.6) we followed the OECD's assumption which takes amortisation to be approximately one-third of the gross disbursement (see OECD 1973). It should perhaps be emphasised that the calculations in table 3.6 are not to be treated too seriously for any individual year. They should rather be taken as indicators of rough orders of magnitude. In any case they dispel any doubt that the Soviet trade surplus with LDCs can be explained away by Soviet exports under long-term credit schemes. This table makes abundantly clear that the net credit disbursements are well below Soviet trade surpluses with LDCs.

The Secretariat of the UN Economic Commission for Europe

Table 3.6. *Comparison of Soviet credit disbursed to, and trade balance with LDCs (million US dollars)*

Year	Credits extended	Credits disbursed	Net credits	Trade balance
1970	200	390	260	766
1971	1,126	420	280	617.7
1972	654	430	286.6	793.7
1973	714	500	333.3	1,607.2
1974	816	705	470	1,392.5
1975	1,934	500	333.3	766
1976	979	460	306.6	1,200
1977	402	540	360	3,200
1978	3,707	430	286.6	4,200
1979			400	4,700

Notes: Col. 4 has been calculated on the assumption that net credits were two-thirds of gross credits disbursed. See text/footnotes for details.
Sources: CIA 1978; *Comecon Foreign Trade*, 1980.

(UNECE 1978) has attempted to compare the import surplus of LDCs with CMEA countries with the figures for disbursements of CMEA loans to LDCs (unlike the CIA data we have used in table 3.6, UNECE and UNCTAD data is not disaggregated for the Soviet and east European countries). The UNECE's conclusions are the same as ours. The ECE recognises, as we have done, that a portion of the CMEA export surplus can be explained by CMEA exports on credit. At the same time, the ECE Bulletin states: 'Since the import surplus of developing countries was larger than their net borrowings in a number of recent years, some part of their deficit has apparently been financed by a draw-down of currency reserves' (p. 54).

That a surplus exists is not doubted even by east European scholars.[12] However, we cannot be at all certain what proportion of the Soviet trade deficit with the West was financed by Soviet trade surpluses with LDCs.

One possible caveat to the whole argument above, however, could be that a large part of the excess of trade surpluses over net credit utilised (noted in table 3.6) might be caused by trade surpluses on the clearing account. That possibility can reasonably be ruled out for two reasons. First, the share of Soviet-LDC trade under clearing agreements has fallen dramatically over the seventies, so that by early 1982 only six LDCs had clearing agreements with the USSR, accounting for no more than 30 per cent of Soviet-LDC trade. Secondly, of the six LDCs – India, Egypt, Iran, Pakistan, Syria and Afghanistan – at least two of the largest, India and Egypt, have been running trade surpluses with the USSR, since they have been repaying loans extended in the fifties and sixties.

A far more important caveat is that the excess of trade surplus over net credit utilisation could be explained by Soviet arms exports. If the Soviet trade figures do include Soviet arms exports, then there is the additional problem of estimating what proportion of the arms delivered was credit financed.[13] In particular, in order to determine the hard currency gains to the USSR one will need to establish what proportion of the hard currency arms sales was financed or paid for in cash.

We have WEFA (Wharton Econometric Forecasting Association) estimates of Soviet hard currency balance of payments for the early 1980s (disaggregated by DME, LDC and CPE trade partners) (WEFA 1984, pp. 13–14). (WEFA does not differentiate between civilian and military exports by the USSR.) They show that in the 1980s the USSR has consistently had hard currency trade surpluses with LDCs. In fact, it is the hard currency trade surpluses with LDCs, together with gold sales, which account for Soviet current account surpluses in the eighties. These surpluses have enabled the USSR to reduce its hard currency debt to the DMEs in certain years (1982 and 1983). However, the net debt to the West declined by only $3.4bn, while it could have declined as much as $10.6bn. This implies that over 1982 and 1983, the USSR must have acquired *on net basis* $7.2bn of new hard currency assets other than deposits in BIS-area banks. These assets reflect increases in (1) Soviet short-term lending to Western buyers of Soviet oil and raw materials and (2) medium and long-term lending to LDC buyers of Soviet arms, investment machinery, etc. The bulk of the increase in lending occurred to LDCs, according to WEFA, and it involved largely financing Soviet hard currency arms sales in the Middle East. Civilian aid disbursements outside the CMEA were negligible after 1980 (see Alan Smith 1984, p. 7). According to WEFA estimates, 40 per cent of Soviet arms sales are paid for in hard cash or through deliveries of commodities needed by the Soviets. During 1980–3, net new lending to LDCs (mostly to support arms sales) was about $15bn, and by the end of 1983, Soviet hard currency assets in LDCs are estimated to have reached $23–30bn, or two to three times the size of Soviet deposits in BIS-area banks (WEFA 1984).

Our conclusion, therefore, on the question of the LDC role in relieving the Soviet hard currency trade deficits with the West is as follows. The level of information presently available does not fully enable one to separate the civilian and military exports of the USSR to LDCs. Hence we cannot be certain about the existence of a Soviet trade surplus with the LDCs on the civilian trade account. Also, as Alan Smith (1984) argues, there is actually insufficient evidence to indicate that the USSR actually received payment in hard currency for much of its arms deliveries made in the 1970s. However, there is absolutely no doubt that Soviet arms exports to LDCs are playing a crucial role in Soviet hard currency balance of payments. They have enabled the USSR in the eighties to reduce the level of its debts to the West. They have also enabled the USSR to acquire financial assets in LDCs (in the form of hard currency credits necessitated probably by the fall in international oil prices and revenues of the Middle Eastern economies). These credits may, of course, be a considerable risk for the USSR, in the sense that they may never be repaid.

3.3 The LDC role in supplying primary commodity demand

3.3.1 The growing scarcity of raw materials

In 1977, 20 per cent of total mineral and fuel imports of the European CMEA countries came from LDCs. As two east European scholars noted:

> In the 1980s under the influence of a number of factors (inadequacy of domestic resources, the extremely high cost of domestic resource development, the relatively fast rate of growth of minerals and fuels demand, the increasing difficulties and rising costs of imports from socialist sources and the anticipated slowdown in the rate of growth of socialist imports over the long term) most of the CMEA countries are expected to push more strongly towards increasing the share of the developing countries in their total imports of fuels and minerals. (Dobozi and Inotai 1981, p. 54)

This deficit of several key raw materials is largely a reflection of the growing industrialisation and the changing cost relationships between primary and manufactured products.

The irrationality of the pricing of primary products in the USSR till the 1960s resulted in their rather depressed level relative to industrial prices. Following Marx's labour theory of value, the Soviets believed that land has no value because it is not a product of labour. Hence ground rent was not taken into account in price fixing of primary commodities. Moreover, socialist leaders regarded the low cost of living for urban workers and low-priced raw materials as necessary for the consolidation of state power and industrialisation. These pricing practices proved quite detrimental to efficiency, and resulted in the neglect of agriculture and the treatment of minerals in the ground as free goods. Until recently, there seemed to be abundant supplies of raw materials but not such abundant quantities of labour and capital. Hence, in the words of Academician Khachaturov, the enterprise 'prefers to make more economical use of its capital even if it means neglecting natural resources' (quoted by Goldman (1979), p. 185). If the pricing mechanism fails to reflect the full economic costs at an early stage of production, such distortions will be carried through to the rest of the economy. The relative cheapness of raw materials and food led to their extravagant misuse. Thus in the early 1960s, in spite of critical shortages of grain, bread was often fed to pigs and cattle because it was cheaper than other feedstuffs.

The growing concern with comparative cost considerations (especially in the USSR, the chief supplier of raw materials to other CMEA countries) is now making these countries turn to market economies, both developed and developing, especially for such commodities as copper, cotton, fissionable materials, grains, hides, molybdenum, nickel, titanium, tungsten and wool. The consequent tendency has been for raw materials to become 'hard items', in both intra-CMEA and East–West trade.

The DMEs have also been a very important source of primary commodity imports. What is also interesting is that while for the CMEA, LDCs as sources of imports for food and agricultural raw materials have risen from 10.8 to 36.4 per cent and 17.7 to 24.4 per cent respectively between 1955 and 1976 (see table 3.7), for DMEs the share of LDCs as sources of imports of these commodities has fallen over the same period from 46.3 to 29.9 per cent and 39.2 to 23 per cent respectively.

3.3.2 Commodity structure of Soviet-LDC trade

The Soviet trade structure with the DMEs is reminiscent of the typical colonial pattern: in 1977, 83 per cent of all the USSR's hard currency earnings were derived from the export of raw materials.[14] But the colonial pattern holds true of the commodity composition of trade between the USSR/eastern Europe and LDCs as well. Table 3.8 reveals that almost 90 per cent of Soviet imports from LDCs consist of primary

Table 3.7. *Share of LDCs in CMEA trade by commodity category*

	Exports			Imports		
	1955	1976	1984	1955	1976	1984
Total trade	6.1	12.9	16.6	5.7	10.7	11.6
Food	2.2	14.1	25.9	10.8	36.4	41.1
Agricultural raw materials	3.7	8.7	18.8	17.7	24.4	22.5
Ores and metals	3.1	5.7	28.7	1.0	5.8	9.9
Fuels	4.4	6.3	17.8	0.3	24.3	13.6
Manufactures	6.1	12.4	15.3	0.6	2.2	2.5

Source: UN, *Monthly Bulletin of Statistics*, July 1985.

commodities. Since the mid-1970s, over 60 per cent of Soviet imports from LDCs have consisted of food items. For the east European economies as a whole, fuel has been by far the most important category over the period; food and fuel together accounted for approximately two-thirds of total imports from LDCs. What is striking in all this is that the share of manufactures in CMEA imports from LDCs, far from rising, has tended to decline from its peak between 15 and 20 per cent in the early 1970s to under 10 per cent in the early 1980s, in the case of the USSR as well as eastern Europe. While it is obvious that the colonial pattern of trade could not be changed overnight, it is perhaps instructive that at a time when the share of manufactures in total LDC exports was rising, this share in total LDC exports to the CPEs was declining. As a Hungarian economist noted, 'The export of manufactures from the South to the East increased less than either the total exports of manufactures from the South or the total imports of manufactures by the East' (Nagy 1981, p. 316).

Manufactures, particularly machinery and transport equipment, constituted by far the most important export of the CMEA countries. This was mutually beneficial for the LDCs as well as the CPEs; for LDCs, in many cases (India and Egypt) such equipment would not have been available from advanced capitalist countries. At the same time, 'generally, it could be maintained that, given the existing overall pattern of exports of the CMEA, socialist countries are in a position to satisfy their import requirements by exports of a more advantageous commodity-mix in their relations with LDCs than in their trade with DMECs' (Paszynski 1981, p. 36).

All protestations about building a new socialist international div-

Table 3.8. *Commodity composition of the USSR's exports to and imports from LDCs*

	1960 X	1960 M	1970 X	1970 M	1975 X	1975 M	1978 X	1978 M	1979 X	1979 M	1980 X	1980 M	1981 X	1981 M
Food	11.3	44.1	8.3	49.9	9.8	62.5	4.6	66.2	4.9	61.3	5.9	64.7	6.9	70.3
Agricultural raw materials	4.2	49.0	3.0	23.6	3.7	9.2	2.4	8.9	2.0	0.1	4.9	10.0	4.5	10.5
Crude fertilisers, minerals	0.4	0.4	0.6	7.2	0.6	2.6	0.5	2.8	0.3	2.4	4.5	0.2	2.7	0.5
Fuels	16.0	—	5.6	2.0	13.4	12.3	11.5	12.4	16.9	16.5	20.1	8.8	20.7	4.4
Chemical products	3.8	0.4	1.8	1.3	3.2	2.4	1.9	1.4	1.6	1.0	3.0	2.1	2.8	1.1
Iron and steel	8.0	—	4.5	1.5	2.9	0.5	2.2	0.4	2.0	0.3	3.7	0.2	2.3	1.2
Non-ferrous metals	1.8	2.4	1.0	0.6	0.6	0.8	0.4	0.9	0.4	1.2	—	1.9	—	1.2
Other manufactured goods	8.4	3.3	4.7	13.8	3.5	9.2	2.6	6.8	2.3	6.3	7.7	6.5	5.2	6.9
Machinery and transport equipment	26.7	—	33.7	0.1	24.7	0.4	23.6	0.1	23.8	0.1	24.2	0.5	21.1	0.6
Total manufactures		3.7		16.7		12.5		8.7		7.7		9.3		9.8

Note: No commodity group breakdown is stated for a substantial share of Soviet exports. Hence, percentages may not add up to 100.

Sources: UNCTAD, *Handbook of International Trade Statistics*; UN, *Monthly Bulletin of Statistics*, July 1985.

ision of labour notwithstanding, the share of manufactures in total exports of the LDCs to the CPEs (13 per cent) was much less than the share of manufactures in total exports to the DMEs (33 per cent). In retrospect, however, that hardly seems surprising considering that a forecast to broadly this effect had been made in 1969 by a report for UNCTAD prepared by the Moscow Institute of the Economy of the World Socialist System. According to the study, 'within the next fifteen to twenty years, the best prospects for cooperation between the Socialist and the developing countries is that on an intersectoral ("horizontal") basis through the exchange of machinery for commodities and some manufactures, because this practice is in line with national economic plans of both sides. This may at a later date create the prerequisites for subsequent transition to a large scale "vertical" division of labour' (Moscow Institute 1969, p. 8).

3.3.3 Soviet promotion of export-oriented industries in LDCs

The Moscow Institute's study notes:

> From the mid-1950s to the mid-1960s most projects built with the assistance of the Socialist countries of East Europe were designed to meet domestic needs and to replace imports. However, a new tendency has emerged to set up export-oriented enterprises in the developing countries with raw materials. These exports help the developing countries pay for the credits and technical assistance they receive from the Socialist countries. These undertakings supply raw materials which are presently in short supply, but more particularly those expected to be in short supply in the Socialist countries in the future. (Moscow Institute 1969, p. 3)

Several long-term agreements were already in force as far back as 1969 governing the import by CPEs of fuel from LDCs (Afghanistan, Algeria, Iran, Iraq, Egypt). Long-term agreements also covered the import of iron ore, phosphates, copper, etc. According to the same study, the imports of non-ferrous metals, tropical foodstuffs and some other commodities were expected to grow considerably involving an additional expenditure of $2bn annually. At UN meetings, the USSR has since promoted such long-term industrial cooperation, particularly in the extractive sector, as a remedy for several LDC problems: it provides necessary development funds, promotes the setting up of local processing industries, leads to automatic repayment of debt, and in fact since the exports of the LDCs as a rule exceed the volume of the debt burden concerned, it increases export proceeds. Back in the USSR, however, these agreements are justified more in terms of giving the USSR a steady supply of raw materials which are either scarce or increasingly expensive to produce (see table 3.9 and 3.10).

For LDCs which share a common frontier with the CPEs, these policies have led to the formation of border economic complexes, including usually power stations, industrial areas, irrigation systems, and infrastructural facilities operating in the common interest and leading to additional trade exchanges. Until 1978, the return flow was limited to gas and oil, bauxite and iron ore. By 1978, the USSR was receiving: 1. 13bn cu.m. of natural gas a year from Iran and Afghanistan through Soviet-built pipelines, as repayment for economic and military aid; 2. 6 to 7 million tons of crude oil annually from Iraq and Syria from fields the Russians had helped to develop; and 3. 2.5 million tons of bauxite from Soviet-developed mines in Guinea. In March 1978 the USSR made the largest commitment to a single project in the LDCs – $2bn to Morocco to aid in the exploitation of phosphates (i.e. for the fertiliser industry), to be repaid with a thirty-year supply line of 10 million tons of phosphates a year.

In the search for raw materials between the early 1960s and 1978 Soviet geologists had inventoried the metals and mineral reserves of at least twelve countries in Africa, five in the Middle East, two in South Asia and one in Latin America. Gas and petroleum exploration and exploitation assistance was given to fourteen LDCs. According to east European estimates in 1980, the CPEs' import demand from the developing countries may by 1990 reach 80 to 100 million tons of petroleum, 30,000 to 40,000 million cu.m. of natural gas, 30 to 40 million tons of iron ore, 13 to 15 million tons of rock phosphate, bauxite and alumina equivalent to 1 to 1.5 million tons of primary aluminium, and 100,000 tons of copper (see Dobozi and Inotai 1981, p. 54).

According to a statement made at UNCTAD VII (July 1987) by the Soviet Union:

> By the beginning of 1987 agreements had been signed with 21 developing countries on the provision of assistance specifically for the creation or expansion of production capacity at 84 enterprises, whose products will be exported, in full or part, to the Soviet Union. At present 27 buy-back projects are operating in 14 developing countries. Such projects are also underway or already constructed in a large number of least developed countries (Afghanistan, Democratic Yemen, Ethiopia, Guinea, Laos, Mali, Nepal, the Yemen Arab Republic and others) ... At the present stage, buy-back arrangements

Table 3.9. *Share of Soviet imports from LDCs derived from Soviet-assisted projects*

Year	%
1974	12
1978	20
1983	30
1986	47.5

Sources: UNCTAD 1986, ST/TSC/4; UNCTAD 1987, TD/341.

Table 3.10. *Structure of Soviet imports from Soviet-assisted projects in LDCs, 1979*

Product group	%
Foodstuffs	46
Oil	22.8
Machinery	13.3
Light metals	12.8
Miscellaneous	5.1

Sources: UNCTAD 1986, ST/TSC/4; UNCTAD 1987, TD/341.

mainly relate to deliveries of raw materials (oil, gas, non-ferrous metal concentrates and agricultural raw materials), since for the time being such goods still predominate in exports from developing countries. However, as this form of exchange expands in the future, the Soviet Union will import more manufactured goods from these countries. In recent years it has already been purchasing from Soviet-assisted enterprises such manufactured products as batteries, yarn, rugs, blankets and knitted goods. (Declaration of the Soviet Delegation at UNCTAD VII, 13 July 1987, TD/341)

In the USSR, some major projects have been implemented setting up additional production capacities which are supplied with imported goods on a continuous basis. The implementation of such projects has often required what has come to be described, in UN terminology, as tripartite cooperation, involving East, West and South. One example of this is the development of the USSR aluminium industry. A large alumina plant in the USSR is to be supplied with Guinean bauxite as repayment for Soviet assistance to develop the mines. Equipment for the plant has been supplied by France on a compensation basis. Another example of switch deals (mainly in the oil and gas trade) is the multilateral gas agreement between the USSR, Czechoslovakia, Iran and a western European utilities consortium (from Austria, France, West Germany and Italy). Under a general agreement signed in 1975, Iranian natural gas was to be delivered to the USSR, and the equivalent quantity of gas to be delivered from the USSR to Czechoslovakia and western Europe (the agreement was disrupted on account of the Iran-Iraq war). While Soviet-Iranian trade is conducted under clearing agreements, one presumes that the USSR expected to earn hard currency from its own gas exports to western Europe. The phosphates project at Meskal, Morocco, is yet another example of cooperation in raw material production which will have a Western component, in that some orders will be placed in DMEs, especially the USA.

By the mid- to late 1960s, CMEA countries had established a method of determining the effectiveness of setting up export enterprises whose output in full or in part goes to CMEA markets.

Such terms of credit given to an LDC to expand the production of goods for export to a CMEA country are considered reasonable which meet the following requirement:

$$\sum_{t=0}^{T} E \, ex_t \, (1 + I \, ef)^{T-t} \leqslant \sum_{t=0}^{T} E \, im_t \, (1 + I \, ef)^{T-t}$$

where Eex = expenditure (current and capital, taking into account the time factor) for the production and delivery of goods and credit; t = moment of the delivery of the goods under the credit agreement; T = moment of complete repayment of the credit; Ief = normative coefficient of efficiency of capital investments in the concerned CPE; Eim = expenditure for domestic production of goods analogous to imported ones on a scale equal to imports.[15]

3.3.4 LDCs as a source of food

Apart from meeting CMEA needs of agricultural raw materials, fuels and minerals, LDCs have also become extremely important suppliers of food (especially fodder and tropical products) to CMEA countries recently. In the 1970s the USSR completed its transition from its historical role of being a major exporter of agricultural goods to becoming a large net importer of several agricultural products. More specifically, the 1970s saw the conversion of the USSR to a regular large net importer of grain, especially in 1972–3, 1975–6 and again in 1979–81. East Europe significantly increased its purchases of agricultural products in 1976 and 1980–1. These grain imports took place in spite of large-scale investments in capital and fertilisers, as well as improved economic incentives.

At the moment, over 50 per cent of the grain produced domestically is fed to livestock. Hence grain imports are largely for livestock feed which indicates the strong Soviet commitment to meet consumer demand for meat and animal products in the Soviet diet. But, for this same reason, the strategic economic dependence of the USSR on imported grain remains relatively small despite high import–consumption ratios.

The share of LDCs as a source of food imports for the entire CMEA has increased from 10.8 per cent in 1955 to 36.4 in 1976 and further to 41.1 in 1984, and will probably rise even further. A Polish economist predicts that a 'probable area for a considerable increase in import requirements of the CMEA countries is not so much raw materials but food (especially tropical products and fodder) and possibly other consumer items' (Paszynski 1981, p. 41). Dobozi and Inotai (1981, p. 56) also suggest:

> One viable opportunity would be a wide-ranging multilateral cooperation in the exchange of feed for meat, an undertaking that would fit the existing conditions on both sides: the substantial surplus of animal feed in certain developing countries, the large-scale animal husbandry programmes embarked on by some of the European CMEA countries and the growing demand for animal products in a number of developing countries.

There is some concern in the east European literature as to how 'the mutually advantageous nature of economic relations' – effectively, the complementarity of economic structures – between the CPEs and the LDCs can be preserved after the latter eliminate their backwardness. In other words, what about the possibilities of cooperation in the manufacturing sector? The Moscow Institute's study asks: Will the partners be able to ensure a wide exchange of the products, not only in the next ten or twenty years, when it will still be mainly of an inter-sectoral nature (the exchange of manufactures for agricultural commodities and minerals), but also within sectors, especially products of the manufacturing industry, in the subsequent period? (Moscow Institute 1969, p. 33). This will require, according to CMEA experts, the same kind of long-term agreements that have been the practice as regards raw materials, fuel and grain, involving close coordination with the trends of domestic developments. The attempt would be to engineer a structural adjustment in the CMEA economies, which would result in making the two groups of economies essentially complementary.

As the Moscow Institute's study suggests, the CPEs could meet a large part of their needs in fabrics made of natural fibre by imports from LDCs on the basis of industrial specialisation, while concentrating their own efforts on the production of synthetic materials. Similar opportunities exist, it is suggested, in the leather and footwear industry. However, Hungary is perhaps the only CMEA country which has made some headway in this direction (see Lawson 1983).

3.4 Soviet economic interests in India

If there were an ordering of Soviet economic interests in the non-socialist Third World, India's place would perhaps come after the Middle East, even though India has been the largest recipient of Soviet aid (see table 3.11) and is now the USSR's biggest LDC trade partner.[16] The basis of this ordering of Soviet economic interests lies in the Soviet hard currency debt to the West, which in turn results from large Soviet imports of advanced technology and grain since the beginning of the 1970s. As we argued above, Soviet arms sales to the Middle East are a crucial component of Soviet hard currency balance of payments, and are needed to pay for grain (whether from the USA/Canada or Argentina/Brazil) and technology imports (from the DMEs). On the other hand, Soviet trade (both civilian and military) with India is not conducted in hard currency; hence it cannot play any payments role at all in Soviet hard currency balance of payments, considering that the level of switch trade is not known to be particularly high.[17]

Nor does the commodity composition of Soviet imports from India consist of any 'hard' goods such as grain or oil/gas; the latter could be re-exported either to west Europe for hard currency or to eastern Europe thereby saving on Soviet energy exports to east Europe. In fact, the Soviet Union has shown willingness to export 'hard' goods like oil/oil products to India (and even grain in 1973/4, a year characterised by world-wide grain shortages). This strongly suggests the dominance of political, rather than economic, factors in the USSR's interest in India. The dominance of the political element in the relationship is also suggested by the fact that the USSR does not insist on selling arms to India for hard currency. In fact, for India, the special advantage of

Table 3.11. *Soviet economic aid agreements with major LDC partners (million US dollars)*

	1955–64	1965–74	1975–9	Total
Total	3,810	6,260	8,120	18,190
Middle East	1,450	2,520	3,895	7,865
Egypt	1,000	440	0	1,440
Iran	65	725	375	1,165
Iraq	185	370	150	705
Syria	100	360	310	770
Other	100	625	3,060	3,785
North Africa	250	300	2,365	2,915
Algeria	230	195	290	715
Morocco	0	100	2,000	2,100
Other	20	5	75	100
South Asia	1,440	2,355	1,185	4,980
Afghanistan	530	300	450	1,280
India	810	1,130	340	2,280
Pakistan	40	655	225	920
Other	60	270	170	500
Sub-Saharan Africa	490	380	335	1,205
Latin America	30	595	340	965
East Asia	150	110	neg.	260

Source: Valkenier 1983.

buying arms from the USSR is precisely that the defence credits can be repaid in rupees (which the USSR can then use to buy goods in India).

The significance of Soviet exports of oil to India (since 1977), in addition to oil products (which had been exported through the seventies), must not be underestimated. In order to maintain its level of hard currency income from oil exports, given the fall in world oil prices in recent years, the USSR increased the volume of deliveries to the West by 30 to 35 per cent in 1982 and by a further 10 to 15 per cent in 1983. However, Soviet oil production, as is well known, is now levelling off, and nearly half of the increase in sales to the West in 1983 consisted of Middle Eastern oil, resold directly after being acquired from such countries as Libya, Iran and Iraq in exchange for Soviet goods, mainly arms. Hence the opportunity cost to the USSR of exports of oil to India must be measured in terms of hard currency as also in political terms, given that the USSR intends to raise prices and cut quantities of oil exports to east Europe.

However, the dominance of the political element of the Indo-Soviet relationship should not lead one to conclude that there is no mutuality of economic interests. As we argued above, joint production with LDCs of raw materials on a compensation basis has been pursued for a long time (phosphates with Morocco, gas with Iran and Afghanistan, oil with Iran and Syria, bauxite with Guinea). Similar production cooperation in manufactures is relatively limited and mostly confined to the more developed of the LDCs. An agreement with India in 1980 stipulated the construction of several plants whose output would be exported; 1. an alumina plant in Andhra Pradesh (capacity 600,000–800,000 tonnes of alumina per annum); 2. enterprises for the production of canned fruits and vegetables both in finished and semi-finished form; and 3. a phyto-chemical plant (and other pharmaceutical plants) for the production of medicines.

The joint production of manufactures/finished items, as envisaged in the 1980 agreement, is not a new phenomenon. In April 1971 India and the USSR signed an agreement providing for the supply of 20,000 tonnes of raw cotton annually from the USSR which would be converted into cotton textiles in India and re-exported to the USSR. Similarly, the Indian Council for Promotion of Wool and Wool-Product Exports and a Soviet FTO jointly organised mass production of knitted wool items in Ludhiana with long-term Soviet commitments for the import of about 90 per cent of this production. In a similar move, a Soviet proposal to import 500 million metres of cloth a year resulted in an agreement at the end of 1982. India would create new manufacturing capacity, so that there was no diversion to the USSR of existing exports.

In recent years the Soviets have increased their purchases of manufactured consumer goods from India to save spending hard currency in the West. In particular, several Western multinationals have set up plants in India's free trade zones to export to the USSR. Thus the Russians are getting access to quality drugs, toothpaste, soap, shampoo, cosmetics and so on without spending hard currency.

However, in spite of growing exports of manufactures, agricultural commodities still constitute a substantial proportion of India's exports to the USSR. India's leading farm exports to the USSR are: tea, cashews, tobacco, hides and skins, spices, peanuts, castor oil, wool, shellac, jute and horticultural products. Tea is by far India's largest agricultural export to the USSR. Soviet consumers get about 90 per cent of their imported tea from India (the other suppliers being Sri Lanka, Bangladesh and China), and a substantial proportion of their coffee, cashews and peanuts. When China phased out deliveries of tea, coffee, and nuts to the USSR in the early 1960s, the Soviet trade planners looked to India to fill the gap. Since then the growth of Indian exports of beverage crops, nuts, spices and hides has provided Soviet consumers with more adequate supplies of these products, which in the 1950s were often scarce. Indian tobacco temporarily helped replace imported Chinese tobacco in Soviet cigarette factories following the stoppage of Chinese deliveries in 1961. India's share in total Soviet imports of raw tobacco has been quite high – ranging between 20 and 25 per cent – during the seventies.[18]

New areas of cooperation between India and the USSR may now be emerging. At the institutional level, Indo-Soviet economic relations are fairly advanced, but until the late seventies they were confined to institutions at the governmental level. However, since 1977 annual meetings have been held between the USSR Chamber of Commerce and the Federation of Indian Chambers of Commerce; the Soviets hope not only to sell machinery and equipment to India's private sector, possibly on a compensation basis, but also to set up joint projects in other LDCs with private Indian firms. Specific mention has been made of the possibility of Indian firms building power plants in LDCs sub-contracting some part of the work to the USSR, just as the USSR has sub-contracted work to HEC and MAMC (two Soviet-built plants in India) from third country projects. The Soviet Union and India have also agreed to examine possibilities of cooperation in setting up pharmaceutical plants in South-east Asia, West Asia, Africa and Latin America. They have also agreed to explore possibilities of production of formulations in India from bulk drugs made available by the USSR for supply to LDCs. The USSR would also like to see cooperation with the Indian coal industry in third countries. In 1980 an agreement was signed between the Central Mine Planning and Design Institute (CMPDIL) and specialised Soviet organisations to design coal-mines in third countries. Some progress has already been made in heavy engineering, with BHEL, HEC and MAMC having been sub-contracted by the Soviets to provide equipment to LDCs where the Soviets are building plants. Presumably the Soviets would now like India to reciprocate.

Perestroika is affecting the foreign economic relations of the USSR. A new law permitting joint ventures to be set up in the USSR with non-socialist countries was introduced in 1986. Indian firms are beginning to take advantage of this law in the service sector. In addition Soviet firms are planning to set up joint ventures in India with Indian private sector firms. Loans may be extended to private firms. Perestroika may in fact herald a new era of cooperation with the private sector in developing countries.

Part II

4   Aid flows

Before turning our attention to the flows of technology, we will briefly outline the nature of financial flows to India from the USSR and from other major donors during the 1970s and the 1980s to determine whether any changes have occurred compared to the earlier two decades. Section 1 deals with the authorisation, utilisation and repayment of aid; section 2 with the terms of aid and section 3 with its sectoral composition.

4.1 Authorisation, utilisation and debt service ratio

We had suggested in chapter 1 that Soviet and east European aid in the first three Five-Year Plans had played a significant part in the implementation of India's chosen development strategy. In fact aid (from all donors) became increasingly important as planned development proceeded. Net aid as a percentage of plan expenditure rose from 9.1 per cent in the First Plan (1951/2 to 1955/6) to 33.9 per cent in the Annual Plan period and thereafter declined to 11.2 per cent in the Fourth Plan and around 9 per cent in the Fifth Plan. As the importance of aid in plan expenditure declined, so did the significance of Soviet aid. In fact, after a loan was authorised in 1966, the USSR did not authorise another credit for a decade, until 1977. However, in the eighties again there has been a sudden spate of Soviet loans to India.

In terms of total volume of aid *authorised* (see table 4.1) up to the end of the Annual Plans (1968/9), the USSR was the third largest donor to India after the USA and the IBRD/IDA. Soviet aid constituted 11.4 per cent (14.2 per cent including other CMEA countries) of total non-food aid authorised to India.[1] Since all Soviet (and east European) aid was project aid (normally utilised more slowly than programme aid), the Soviet share in total (non-food) aid *utilised* by India up to 1968/9 was lower: 7.8 per cent of total aid (9.6 per cent for all east Europe) and 8.7

Table 4.1. *Authorisation of external assistance (million rupees)*

	Up to end of Third Plan	Annual Plans 66/7–68/9	Fourth Plan 69/70–73/4	Fifth Plan 74/5–78/9	Sixth Plan 79/80–83/4
Total non-food aid of which:	42,008	23,506	38,670	97,274	135,747
Total loans of which:	38,088	21,857	36,708	79,121	119,170
USA	14,197	7,809	4,172	1,882	4,052
USSR and east Europe of which:	6,103	3,215	800	2,083	6,303
USSR	4,946	2,545	—	2,083	6,303
IBRD/IDA	7,245	3,659	13,672	41,879	73,403
UK	3,580	2,054	5,590	9,940	7,877
West Germany	4,452	1,487	3,212	6,391	8,353
Japan	1,659	1,061	3,236	4,530	4,564

Notes: 1. From 1975/6 the UK has extended only grants, not loans. 2. After the end of the Third Plan, no loan authorised by any CMEA country (other than the USSR), except one by Bulgaria (1967/8 for Rs113m) and one by Czechoslovakia (1973/4 for Rs800m).
Source: Ministry of Finance, *Economic Survey*, various issues.

per cent of total loans (10.7 per cent including east Europe). While the USSR was the third largest donor in terms of loans authorised, it slipped to fifth place after the USA, IBRD/IDA, West Germany and the UK, in terms of loans actually utilised (see table 4.2).

The Soviet loans authorised over the period from 1969/70 to 1983/4 (the Fourth, Fifth and Sixth Plans) were so few that the Soviet Union fell to fourth place in respect of authorisations and sixth place in terms of loans utilised. Possibly one reason for the Soviets' disinclination to extend aid for over a decade was the slow rate of utilisation of their loans in the sixties (see table 4.3). In fact, the rate of utilisation of Soviet loans was the lowest up to the late sixties. In fact, it was only after their loans extended in the fifties and sixties had almost completely (i.e. up to 94 per cent) been utilised that the Soviets decided to extend a new loan in 1977. Since Indian public sector projects have normally taken longer than planned to build, it is not so surprising that the rate of utilisation of Soviet loans was the lowest. Another reason, apart from the slow rate of utilisation, for the absence of new Soviet loan authoris-

Table 4.2. *Utilisation of external assistance (million rupees)*

	Up to end of Third Plan	Annual Plans 66/7–68/9	Fourth Plan 69/70–73/4	Fifth Plan 74/5–78/9	Sixth Plan 79/80–83/4	84/5	85/6
Total non-food aid of which:	31,056	23,707	37,726	70,989	99,021	23,537	31,648
Total loans of which:	27,687	21,477	36,198	59,420	82,078	19,633	27,535
USA	12,030	7,275	7,539	1,319	2,981	418	521
IBRD/IDA	5,806	4,450	7,599	22,062	50,537	13,239	18,789
UK	2,936	2,315	5,089	7,838	8,871	1,875	1,592
West Germany	3,421	1,950	3,716	6,010	6,364	1,256	1,324
Japan	1,134	1,449	2,813	4,868	3,801	524	1,509
USSR and East Europe of which:	3,211	2,040	3,442	3,721	2,043	1,080	1,300
USSR	2,871	1,419	2,744	2,494	2,043	1,080	1,300

Notes: 1. 1985/6 estimated. 2. The utilisation of British loans ceased in 1980/1, after which utilisation refers only to grants.
Source: Ministry of Finance, *Economic Survey,* various issues.

Table 4.3. *Rate of utilisation of non-food loans by major donors*

	Up to end of Third Plan	Annual Plans 66/7–68/9	Fourth Plan 69/70–73/4	Fifth Plan 74/5–78/9	Sixth Plan 80/1–84/5
Total	72.7	98.3	93.6	75.0	68.8
USA	84.7	93.2	180.7	70.1	73.6
USSR	58	55.8	[a]	397.7[a]	32.4
IBRD/IDA	80.1	121.6	55.6	52.7	68.8
UK	82.0	112.7	91.0	78.9	112.6
West Germany	76.8	131.1	115.7	94.0	76.2
Japan	68.4	136.6	86.9	107.5	83.3

Notes: 1. The rate of utilisation is the percentage of aid authorised over a period which was utilised. 2. There was an Annual Plan in the year 1979/80.
[a] The USSR did not authorise any aid over the Fourth Plan. Hence 397.7% is the rate of utilisation over the Fourth and Fifth Plan periods.
Source: Ministry of Finance, *Economic Survey*, various issues.

ations was the fulfilment by the late sixties of the Soviet objective in extending bilateral aid: the expansion of trade. Soviet and east European development assistance is almost entirely bilateral, the only exceptions being their contributions to UNDP; the bilateral trade/payments agreements with LDC's, including India, enabled the latter to repay the bilateral aid. Thus the overall combined effect of bilateral aid and bilateral trade was a rapid expansion of two-way trade in the fifties and sixties, which stood at very low levels prior to the signing of the aid and trade agreements. However, by the early seventies the two-way trade had acquired its own dynamic, and did not necessarily need bilateral aid to sustain it (see chapter 8 for details).

One major consequence of the absence of new Soviet loan authorisations in the seventies is the very high debt service ratio (here defined as the debt repaid as a proportion of aid utilised) of Soviet aid as compared to other donors (see table 4.4). From 1966/7 onwards there was little or no net inflow of funds from the USSR; on the contrary, the net flow was *to* the USSR. The only exception is 1974/5, when 2 million tonnes of wheat were shipped to India on a five-year loan (repaid in 1978/9). Only for the USA and the UK (in the late seventies and early eighties) was India's debt service ratio as adverse as it was with the USSR through the seventies.

However, India's debt service ratio with the USSR has become less adverse in the eighties because a series of new loans have been authorised. While only one new loan was authorised in the seventies (Rbls250m or Rs2,083m: 1977), four have been authorised during the eighties (up to 1985): a 500m Rbl (or Rs4,323m) credit in 1980/1, a

Table 4.4. *Debt service as a percentage of aid utilised*

	1970	1971	1972	1973	1974	1975	1976	1977	1978	1979	1980	1981	1982	1983
Canada	4	1	7	5	5	23	56	47	33	200	53	23	88	48
West Germany	55	55	64	63	43	45	47	106	69	61	72	68	69	35
IBRD					475	1,250	300	114	43	79	37	37	50	69
IDA	23[a]	21[a]	27[a]	11[a]	1	1	1	3	3	3	26	13	6	9
Japan	16	[b]	8	25	4	26	21	75	48	65	102	148	73	30
USSR	143	157	439	102	26	192	327	383	139	90	113	80	44	33
UK	25	22	23	30	21	29	78	514	333	407	1,733	[c]	24	2
USA[d]	15	20	76	139	3,502	61	33	83	[b]	88	135	100	747	130
Total	28	26	50	39	163	26	25	44	41	59	36	46	41	41

[a] For 1970–3, figures for repayments to IBRD and IDA not available separately.
[b] Repayment = SDR70m, utilisation = 0.
[c] Repayment = SDR59m, utilisation = 0.
[d] Includes all loans (incl. PL480 loans in rupees, EXIM Bank loans and other loans for 1970–2.

Source: IMF, *Balance of Payments Statistics*, various issues.

140m Rbl (or Rs1,167m) credit in 1983/4, a massive 1bn Rbl credit to the new government in 1985/6, another 1.5bn Rbl credit during Gorbachev's visit to India (November 1986), and yet another 5bn Rbl credit during his second visit to India (November 1988). While these loans may have been planned in any case, the timing of at least two of these loans appears to have had political overtones. It is true that the 1977 loan was extended after most of the existing loans had already been utilised and hence there was an economic basis for giving it; at the same time, it is noticeable that the loan was given within weeks of a new government, led by the Janta party known to be not very well disposed towards the USSR, coming to power in India. Similarly, one of the largest ever loans extended by the USSR to India, the 1bn Rbl credit in May 1985, was given again to a new government led by a young Prime Minister interested in improving relations with the USA (from which authorisations of aid in the seventies had been relatively small).

For the Soviets the economic rationale behind this spurt of new loan authorisations in the eighties is the obvious need to give a fillip to Indo-Soviet trade. In particular, the USSR would like India to increase machinery and equipment imports from the USSR. As we argue in chapter 8, the share of machinery in Soviet exports to India fell dramatically over the seventies; in fact, machinery exports to India are likely to have fallen even in absolute terms, given that in current prices, their total value has remained roughly the same over the decade. It is planned that the share of such manufactured items as fertilisers, steel, plant and machinery will rise from 16.7 per cent under the trade agreement (1981–5) to 47.5 per cent in the following trade agreement (1986–90) (Haribhushan 1985, p. VII-3). However, the Soviets might have felt that the demand for Soviet machinery was unlikely to materialise without the incentive of new Soviet loans.

On the Indian side, the loans are likely to supplement domestic savings. It must be clarified that the paucity of resources for new public investment does not arise because of a lack of savings. In fact, the Indian savings rate has been very impressive since the mid-seventies. In other words, India's balance of payments difficulties and the consequent need for foreign aid have been due more to the economy's inability to transform domestic savings into investment, either domestically or through foreign trade, than to a shortage of domestic savings as such. In a sense, the main contribution of aid to India has been in supplementing the foreign exchange earnings of the country. In the context of the so-called 'two-gap analysis' of the role of aid in the development process, foreign aid to India is to be regarded as bridging the foreign exchange gap rather than the savings gap. However, one would suggest that because of the pressure of non-development expenditure on domestic savings (as argued in chapter 6), the role of foreign aid in supplementing domestic savings may be increasing. One could find evidence for such a proposition in the increasing Indian emphasis and, in fact, insistence on credit for the bulk of its large-scale projects. Among recent Soviet-aided projects, the Vizag steel plant is an example; in fact, the import content of Vizag is somewhat higher than that of the previous Soviet-aided public sector steel plant, Bokaro. Among other projects, the five 'super' thermal power plants (one of which is Soviet-aided), with a capacity of 1,000mW each, fall in the same category, given that they have a large import content, even at the cost of domestic machinery manufacturing capacity remaining unutilised (Economist Intelligence Unit 1982, 3rd quarter, p. 21).

4.2 Terms of aid

The terms of Soviet loans in the seventies and eighties have been softer than those extended in the earlier two decades. Loans in the fifties and sixties normally carried a 2.5 per cent interest, and were given for twelve years with a one-year grace period. The 1977 credit still carried a 2.5 per cent interest rate, but the repayment period was seventeen years with a three-year grace period, which is easier than standard USSR-LDC aid terms. In the 1980s the interest rate has dropped to 2 per cent, although the repayment and grace period have remained the same. It has been argued that the existence of the USSR and eastern Europe as an alternative source of aid in the fifties and sixties probably helped India to get both more aid and more favourable terms from other donors. In particular, the growing volume of US aid to India and the considerable softening of the terms of aid during the time of the Second Five-Year Plan are cited (Chaudhuri 1978, p. 151; Datar 1972, p. 74). It appears that the softening of Western terms of aid has tended in turn to induce the USSR itself to soften its own credit terms over the seventies and eighties. As far as the terms of Western aid donors over the seventies and eighties are concerned, table 4.5 shows that they have stabilised, and have not altered very much from the Fourth to the Sixth Plans.

Although the terms of Soviet loans may have softened, in another respect their loans have remained the same: all Soviet loans are still project-tied. It is true that until the mid-sixties an overwhelming proportion of aid to India from all sources was project-tied. During the

Table 4.5. *Terms of aid from major donors*

	Interest rates (per cent)			Grace period (years)			Repayment period (years)		
	Fourth Plan	Fifth Plan	Sixth Plan	Fourth Plan	Fifth Plan	Sixth Plan	Fourth Plan	Fifth Plan	Sixth Plan
USA	2–3	2–3	2–3	10	10	10	30	30	30
Britain	0	0	—	7	7	—	18	18	—
IBRD	6.25–7.25	4.5–8.5	8.25–9.25	1–10	1–7	3–5	11–20	13–18	14–15
IDA	0.75	0.75	0.75	10	10	10	40	40	40
West Germany	2–3	0.75–3	0.75	3–10	10	10	7–23	20–40	40
Japan	4–5.25	3–4	2.75	5–7	7–10	10	13–18	18	10
USSR	—	2.5	2	—	3	3	—	17	17

Note: The repayment period excludes the grace period.
Source: Ministry of Finance, *External Assistance,* 1980/1.

Second Plan nearly 80 per cent of the aid loans authorised to India were for projects; this figure was round 60 per cent for the Third Plan. Since then there has been an increase in the amount of non-project aid, with its share in the total disbursement of aid being in excess of 45 per cent (Balasubramanyam 1984, p. 175). For example, for Britain, the second largest donor since 1969/70, the share of non-project aid in total loans was 69.9 per cent over the Fourth and Fifth Plans (1969/70 to 1978/9); for West Germany, the third largest donor, it was 68.6 per cent; and for Japan about 47 per cent. But for the largest donor, the World Bank's IDA, the overwhelming proportion of loans extended in the Fourth and Fifth Plans were project-tied (83.7 per cent and 74 per cent respectively).[2] Apart from allowing monopolistic pricing practices on the part of donors, project-tying of aid may give rise to excess capacity in import-intensive industries. When aid is tied to projects, and recipient countries have limited access to other sources of foreign exchange, they may be unable to finance imports of raw materials and spares. It has been argued that the frequently observed excess amounts of spare capacity in Indian industries are due to a shortage of raw materials. However, in the case of Soviet-aided enterprises in India, the reasons for capacity under-utilisation are different, as is argued in chapter 6. Besides, in the Soviet case, the absence of any general purpose programme loans is considerably modified by the arrangement for deferred payment terms. This arrangement governs Soviet supplies of machinery and equipment, including spare parts, completing items and accessories, and replacement equipment for enterprises built in India with Soviet assistance. (The deferred payment terms are extended, according to the inter-governmental protocol, for a period of ten years at an interest rate of 4 per cent per annum. The interest accrues from the date of delivery of the goods and its payment is made in Indian rupees, according to the terms of the trade and payments agreements between the two countries.)

4.3 Sectoral composition

Finally, another respect in which the nature of Soviet aid has not altered very much is its sectoral composition. Between 1956 and 1970, nearly 50 per cent of Soviet aid utilised went to the steel industry; if aid utilisation up to 1980/1 is taken into account, that share rises somewhat to 54.6 per cent (see table 4.6). The corresponding shares for other industries are: power, 15.5 and 13.3 per cent; oil, 17.8 and 17.3 per cent; industry, 9.0 and 13.1 per cent; and mining, 5.0 and

Table 4.6. *Sectoral composition of total aid utilised (percentages)*

| | USSR | ALL DONORS | | | |
	(up to 80/1)	Up to Third Plan	Annual Plans and Fourth Plan	Fifth Plan	Sixth Plan
Power	13.3	7.0	4.4	5.7	19.0
Transport and communication	—	16.9	9.4	7.6	7.7
Steel	54.6	12.7	4.0	4.3	neg.
Industry	13.1	55.4	64.4	37.9	28.1
Agriculture	—	1.0	4.3	18.2	38.2
Oil	17.3	—	neg.	9.4	0.5
Mining	1.7	0.3	neg.	4.1	—
Debt relief, food aid, misc.	—	6.7	13.5	12.8	6.5
Total	100	100	100	100	100

Source: Ministry of Finance, *External Assistance*, 1980/1, and RBI, *Report on Currency and Finance*, various issues.

1.7 per cent. Changes in the sectoral composition of total aid utilised from all donors are summarised in table 4.6. Two points must be noted about the figures for 'All donors': first, the percentages are based on total aid utilised, i.e. both project and non-project aid are included (while all Soviet aid is for projects), and second, the category 'All donors' includes the USSR. It is clear from the table that an overwhelming proportion of total aid from all donors up to the mid-seventies went to industry. Even if only project aid is taken into account, the overwhelming importance of industry in aid utilised still stands. For example, over the Fourth and Fifth Plans, 77.8 per cent of West German project aid, 55.8 per cent of Japanese aid and 44 per cent of British aid went to industry.[3] However, the share of agriculture has been rising constantly with each Plan; in fact, in the Sixth Plan (1980–5) agriculture took the largest share of total aid utilised. The increased share of agriculture in total aid utilised in recent years reflects a shift in emphasis from industrial development to the promotion of agriculture by multilateral aid agencies, especially the World Bank, and the growth in importance attached to agriculture by Indian planners.

Although available data enables us to estimate the sectoral composition of Soviet aid only up to 1980/1, information on Soviet aid authorised in the eighties suggests that its sectoral composition in the eighties and early nineties is unlikely to be very different from the pattern established in the sixties. The sectors for which aid has been extended in the eighties are: steel, petroleum exploration, power, coal mining and modernisation of industrial units in the steel and machine-building sectors in probably decreasing order of importance. Of the total of Rs10,374m worth of project aid for steel extended by the USSR from 1953 to 1983/4, Rs5,342.86m for the Vizag steel plant is yet to be utilised. Approximately Rs4,060m (of the Rs11,600m credit given in May 1985) has been set aside for oil exploration in the areas of Cambay (on the east coast) and the Cauvery river basin (in south India). In the power sector, apart from a thermal power plant (Kahelgaon, 840mW capacity), the USSR may build a 440mW atomic power plant in India, their first ever in the non-socialist world (*Economic and Political Weekly*, 6 June 1985). In fact the massive loan extended in 1988 is for the power sector, both hydro and thermal, to create an additional 6,000mW capacity within the next fifteen years. In addition, two Soviet-designed 1,000mW nuclear power plants are also to be set up.

However, in one respect there is a possibility of a radical departure from past practice. In the last thirty years all Soviet credits have been utilised by India's public sector. But since the late seventies, the Soviets, concerned about the fall in machinery exports to India, have been pressing the Indian private sector to buy capital goods from the USSR rather than from Western sources. So far Indian private firms have not responded very positively to Soviet suggestions. Presently 80 per cent of India's exports to the USSR is accounted for by the private sector but the latter's share of imports from the USSR is less than a third of the total. In order to encourage machinery exports to the Indian private sector, the USSR has been insisting since the mid-eighties on sectoral level balancing of trade, if not enterprise level balancing. This form of barter has been unacceptable to the Indian private sector. However, the Soviet Union has agreed in 1988 to extend a loan of Rbls200m to the Indian private sector. What is significant is that 50 per cent of this loan will be in hard currency. It was first agreed between the Foreign Economic Bank of the USSR and the Industrial Development Bank of India that a loan of Rbls100m will be channelled to Indian private firms which are setting up joint ventures in India with Soviet agencies. Since these joint ventures would need hard currency, an additional Rbls100m in hard currency were extended by the USSR, in view of India's foreign exchange constraint.

5   The collaboration agreements

Having discussed financial flows to India from the USSR, we can now set out the criteria adopted in the latter half of this chapter and in chapter 6 to evaluate the effectiveness of technology transfer from the Soviet Union to India and the degree to which an independent technological capability has been developed in the sectors recipient of Soviet technology.

5.1 Methodology for evaluating technology transfer

An independent technological capability implies the capability to carry out the following six functions in relation to the setting up and running of a project. The first two categories relate to the setting up and the last four to the running of a plant:

1 Pre-investment studies. The first step is a feasibility study, technical and economic (which initially means the commercial feasibility). This involves expert assessment of the technical requirements of the project (including choice of technique) and careful estimation of the costs and benefits to the national economy, involving, inter alia, a detailed market survey.

2 Project execution. This includes the following sub-categories of technological capabilities: basic engineering; detailed engineering; equipment procurement; erection of equipment; commissioning the plant.

3 Process engineering. Process engineering skills are manifested in: trouble-shooting; substitution of raw materials; capital goods stretching (by extending its life, raising its speed); process innovation.

4 Product engineering. These skills imply the capability to: adapt a product to the consumer's needs; improve the product; develop a new product.

5 Industrial engineering. This involves getting the best out of process and product engineering work (3 and 4 above).
6 Linkage capabilities. This refers to capability to undertake horizontal technology transfer, i.e. the duplication or diffusion of the imported technology.

It is primarily the first two of these six categories – project preparation and project execution capabilities – which are the subject of transfer of technology. Process and product engineering capabilities cannot be bought in and must be developed in-house. While industrial engineering capabilities can be transferred, they were never really included in any Indo-Soviet firm level contract. As far as the ability to duplicate or diffuse the technology is concerned, that depends on the degree to which the recipient of imported technology has assimilated the technology; it depends, in other words, on the level of competence acquired in the skills or capabilities noted in the first five categories above. The total technological capability developed within an enterprise must be the combined product of both the technology transferred to it and that which is developed in-house. In our case studies of Soviet technology transfer to India we will have occasion to discuss both aspects, i.e. the technology transferred as well as the capabilities developed in-house by the Soviet-aided enterprises.

The criteria used in the case studies of technology transfer will be as follows:

1 Is there a substantial training component, both on the job in India, as well as in-plant training in the USSR?
2 Does the agreement provide for a sharing of the design and engineering work between the supplier of technology and the acquirer? For instance, in some of the chosen industries (steel and drugs) India has already acquired a certain level of experience which could be utilised in project development.
3 Is there a significant use of local inputs, in terms of construction equipment, services, plant and machinery, wherever possible?
4 Does it set in motion a local research and development process and design capability aimed at making possible a further stage of the project based on a greater proportion of indigenous technology?
5 Is diffusion to other firms of the technology acquired permitted?

Since many of the industries in which technology was transferred by the USSR were in the capital goods sector, we are particularly concerned as to whether the technological requirements for the manufacture of capital goods are present in Soviet-aided enterprises. These technological inputs are: machine-operating skills, manufacturing technology, product design and research and development capacity.

The firm or the industry without this design capacity will have to rely more or less continuously on the supply of product designs and design methods from external sources. Although technical assistance and product design are important for actually making complex equipment, from the point of view of building up the technological capacity of the recipient party it is crucial for the latter to be given the *methodology* used for obtaining the product design. If this is not the case, the recipient will simply receive a design for making the product in question but will not be able to understand how such a design was obtained.

In order to develop an independent technological capacity in any particular sector, an LDC recipient enterprise will have to invest in both an R&D set-up as well as the creation of a product design capacity. The creation of a capacity to design complex equipment and products is mostly a long-term investment in skill formation; it must be developed independently from licensing or collaborations and use the latter for learning purposes. Such a task could be facilitated by the licensing mechanism only when the licenser is willing to provide adequate information regarding the design methodology and to train the licensee's staff engaged in this critical activity. When the licenser is willing to provide the design methodology and/or tries to restrict the training of design personnel, the licensing mechanism is obviously hindering the creation of a technological capacity. The possibilities of obtaining design methodology and adequate training of design personnel are enhanced in those cases in which a number of alternative suppliers exist or when the technology is rather old. We will be keeping these issues in mind while examining Soviet technology transfer to Indian enterprises.

It is generally assumed that if there are 'unpackaged' transfers, it will lead to more 'learning by doing' by local technicians and managers than if the transfer were packaged. But there may also be a cost involved, which might have been avoided if the technology supplier had set up a wholly-owned subsidiary. For example, because of the use of local design engineers and local plant construction, it might take longer to bring the project to the point of production than if a turnkey project had been established; this could occur on account of inexperience and possibly ignorance of the production technique. Or the plant might simply operate less efficiently and produce an inferior product because of deficiencies in design. Or local managers and technicians, being unused to the production process, might operate it less efficiently. It may be true that the fact of having made mistakes on one plant will help the engineers, managers and technicians do better the next time. Yet the problem remains that there may be a price to be paid – in the form of production forgone through delays and inefficiency – in using local technical inputs. In fact, there is no doubt that almost every Soviet-aided project in India suffered from such delays and the resulting cost escalations.

But, equally, it should be borne in mind that wholly or largely foreign ventures may also encounter problems owing to the foreign investor's lack of knowledge of local conditions. In fact, too often in the case of Soviet project aid to India there were serious errors of judgement by Soviet experts regarding requirements of plant capacity. There were also considerable delays by the Soviets in supplying either drawings or equipment or both for projects under construction. But we will not dwell any further on this issue since these kinds of delays and inefficiencies have characterised all public sector enterprises in India, no matter what the collaborator's country of origin may be. In fact, the three major criticisms of Indian public sector enterprises, on the investment side, are that the actual costs of projects have greatly exceeded the original estimates, that both the construction and gestation periods have been longer than planned, and that they often embodied an inappropriate technology or product-mix.[1] It is important here to dismiss Datar's claim that 'the revised estimates for projects financed with East European credits are much higher than other projects'. Datar's conclusion is based on a table (published in a CPU report) on the revision of project estimates of selected public enterprises; it is invalid since the table, in turn, is based on a very small sample indeed (1972, pp. 242–3). Thus the question of delays and inefficiencies does not receive much attention in the case studies of technology transfer that follow since they are not specific to Soviet project aid to India, but are endemic to Indian public enterprises in general.

5.2 The collaboration agreements

An examination of the Indo-Soviet firm level contracts should enable us, to a limited extent, to answer the questions raised in the previous section. However, to what extent the commitments enshrined in the contracts were actually fulfilled will be examined in the following chapter based on the case studies of individual projects. This section, therefore, confines itself to an examination of the features of Indo-Soviet firm level contracts.

5.2.1 Near-turnkey contracts

The contracts of Soviet FTOs (such as Tiazhpromexport or Promashexport) with Indian public sector firms are, in a sense, sui generis, since they are not mere licence agreements, but nor are they turnkey contracts. Strictly, turnkey contracts are those under which a supplier of equipment undertakes the full range of technical and managerial operations needed to establish an enterprise. He later trains local staff to take over the plant which is in working order. In a turnkey contract the foreign firm provides full training at the operational and maintenance levels, but no training at all during the design, construction and phasing-in stages. Soviet-built plants in India are near-turnkey operations since nearly all stages of a project – preparation of a detailed project report (DPR), supply of equipment, technical assistance in erection and commissioning, training of operatives – are a Soviet responsibility and are covered by a project loan; however, they fall short of being turnkey projects in the strict sense because control over the project rests in Indian hands, even though Soviet specialists may run a parallel management in a plant.

This distinction between turnkey and near-turnkey projects becomes clearer if one examines the American proposal on the Bokaro steel plant which preceded the actual agreement with the USSR. The American proposal was not merely to control the design and construction of the steel mill; US Steel Corporation, in fact, wanted a management contract of five to ten years. Only after the expiry of this period would the plant have been handed over to Indian management. Like the American proposal, the Indo-Soviet agreement on Bokaro ensured that the control of design, erection and commissioning remained almost exclusively in Soviet hands (Dasturco, the Indian consultancy firm originally signed on as Prime Consultants, being relegated to a secondary role); however, management remained in Indian hands from the beginning. The latter fact is made much of in all the Soviet literature on foreign aid to LDCs: that while Western firms have insisted at least on equity participation if not total control of enterprises in LDCs, the USSR has not even been interested in obtaining management contracts in Soviet-aided projects. While the latter Soviet claim is justified, the next question (not often asked) is: has such a policy been effective in assisting recipient LDCs in acquiring an independent technological capacity in sectors to which Soviet technology has been transferred? We shall return to this question in detail in the next chapter in the case studies. For the present, however, while keeping this crucial question in sight, we shall confine the discussion to the contracts between Indian and Soviet firms and the terms and conditions therein.[2]

In the early stages of a country's industrialisation, LDC enterprises often enter into turnkey arrangements. At the same time, it is in the interest of the transferrer to sell technology on a turnkey basis partly because it gives him control over the project over a certain period of time, and partly because it enables him to manipulate the price for various components of the technology.[3] It is suggested that a purchasing enterprise in a developing country should not view a turnkey contract as one lump-sum payment for setting up a project. By and large, most Soviet projects in India resulted in the signing of four or five major contracts each involving a separate payment: one each for the preparation of the DPR by the Soviets, the supply of working drawings for the construction of the units of the plant, the supply of Soviet equipment and technical assistance in erection and commissioning including the training of Indian operatives.

As much as possible, not only should the costs be broken down at each stage (as they were in the Indo-Soviet case), but the purchaser should also participate in decision-making at certain stages. It is advisable that, for example, an examination of the DPR should be an essential feature of such an arrangement (as it was in the Indo-Soviet case). More importantly, at the DPR stage, the purchaser should be able to terminate the negotiations if there is evidence to suggest that the benefits from the project may not exceed its cost. As far as we know, only one such Soviet project in India – a pumps and compressors plant – was terminated. For many others, a joint Indo-Soviet decision was taken to expand them even before the economic viability of the first stage of production had been established (see chapter 6). It is again desirable that on completion of basic engineering work, and at the stage of plant construction and selection and purchase of machinery, the purchaser should ensure that competitive bids are obtained for the major items and that the most suitable offers are accepted. As is well known, Soviet loans to India were double-tied: both to project as well as to source. Hence, there was no question whatsoever of inviting competitive bids.[4] While the turnkey contractor, by virtue of his overall responsibility for a project, must have a say in the selection of parties for the major supply and construction contracts, the purchaser should also participate in the selection as far as possible. Again, in the Indo-Soviet case, the purchaser had no choice in the selection of foreign suppliers, partly because quite often Western governments were not happy to finance capital goods projects in India's public sector (though there were some exceptions), and partly because Soviet loans were source-tied. However, the purchaser was permitted to use Indian consultants, construction agencies and suppliers wherever possible, as we show below.

5.2.2 Use of local inputs and design/engineering expertise

As suggested earlier, while the main production units in Soviet-aided projects are both designed and supplied by the Soviets, the rest of the units are designed by Indians and supplied from indigenous sources. This has been the case from the early 1960s onwards. However, in the fifties almost the entire plant, including some of the utilities (e.g. the power plant), was designed and supplied by the Soviets, for example in the Bhilai steel plant and the Barauni oil refinery.

It must be emphasised that, even for the main production units, while the designing and equipment supply are a Soviet responsibility, 'the Customer shall carry out at his own expense and by his own means all the excavation, construction, erection and adjusting work as well as putting the [Koyali] Oil Refinery and the (captive) Thermal Power Plant into operation with the technical consultations of the Supplier's specialists' (Art. 13). The pattern observed in the early sixties was still in evidence in the late sixties and early seventies. Thus in the aluminium project, while the supplier designed the core units, the buyer designed the remaining units, storages, service facilities, transport and its services, and engineering construction and utility networks. So although Soviet-Indian firm level contracts do involve a considerable degree of 'packaging' of technology, they are not turnkey contracts in the strict sense, since they allow scope for some Indian participation.

It should be mentioned that the choice of the mechanism of transfer of technology has a considerable influence on skill formation in the importing country. For example, in Japan, technology was mostly acquired through licence agreements, and this contributed substantially to skill formation and diffusion. Moreover, the technique of 'reverse engineering' (which is illegal under the patent system but is a way of acquiring technology) was used whereby a purchased machine was taken apart and then rebuilt with alterations. Not only was this done without explicit payment for the embodied technology, but this technique also resulted in much learning by doing (UNCTAD 1978,

TD/B/C.6/26). The case for an 'unpackaged' transfer often turns on the argument that a local enterprise will develop skills that it did not possess before, or that local engineers will be taxed with new problems from which they will learn new skills, or that a local research institute will be required to devise some production system which it has not had to deal with in the past.

It is rather interesting that a Soviet study (for UNCTAD) on the experience of the USSR in building up technological capacity states quite categorically: 'In the 1920s Soviet acquisition of foreign technology *only rarely* took the form of "turn-key" projects, but even in those rare cases Soviet workers and engineers were always actively involved in the building of the new mills and factories' (UNCTAD 1980, TD/B/C.6/52, p. 39; emphasis added). Thus one cannot help noticing that while turnkey projects were almost completely out of favour in the USSR at a comparable stage of development, the USSR has itself insisted on near-turnkey arrangements while transferring technology to LDCs.

However, it must be admitted that the Indo-Soviet contracts by no means discourage the participation of Indian expertise and equipment in Soviet-built plants. Thus even the earliest contract at hand (for the Koyali refinery) states: 'The Supplier shall receive the Customer's specialists to participate in the design work in numbers and periods to be mutually agreed upon' (Art. 5.3, Contract 7321). Besides, 'the Detailed Project Report will also contain recommendations regarding the use of Indian equipment and materials for the construction and erection of the Refinery' (Art. 5.2). The later documents make a more explicit reference to the subject.

To what extent these commitments enshrined in the contracts were actually fulfilled will be examined in the case studies of individual projects (see chapter 6). It must be noted that the Indian requirement that collaborators should agree to maximum possible utilisation of Indian equipment and materials was not a feature confined to Indo-Soviet contracts alone.

5.2.3 Clauses relating to diffusion of transferred technology

Another important consideration in examining transfer of technology agreements is whether they allow for horizontal transfer of technology or not. In this regard the Soviet-aided refinery contract states: 'The Customer is not entitled to transfer his rights and liabilities under the present Contract *as well as technical documentations* except to the lawful successors without the Supplier's consent made in writing' (Art. 25, Contract 7321/1; emphasis added). Similarly, the contract for the preparation of the DPR and working drawings of the refinery states: 'The technical documentation prepared under the present Contract shall be used only by the Customer or by his successor duly authorised by the Government of India for the establishment of the enterprise stipulated in para. 1 of the present Contract [the Koyali oil refinery] and they may not be handed over to any other countries' (Art. 18, Contract 7321). The stipulation that such documentation should not be handed over to any other country is perfectly legitimate and a standard clause in such contracts. However, it is equally clear that the Soviet refinery contracts did not permit horizontal transfer to enterprises within India, either of the public or the private sector.

The Bokaro contract in the mid-sixties, however, did allow for such transfer. Thus, Article 2 of the inter-governmental agreement on Bokaro specified: 'The technical documents handed over by the Soviet organisations to the Indian organisations shall be used by the latter *exclusively at enterprises in India*. Such documents shall not be transferred to any foreign physical or judicial entities without prior consent of the Soviet organisations thereto' (emphasis added). The use of the plural 'enterprises' suggests that the Soviets were willing to allow documents and data supplied for Bokaro to be used for other steel plants as well, if such a need were to arise. Presumably the documents were accessible to MECON, the public sector metallurgical consultants involved in Bokaro and HEC (which was manufacturing equipment for Bokaro).[5]

But in the case of the aluminium project, the contract was abundantly clear and gave no ground for a generous interpretation. Thus it specified: 'The Buyer guarantees that – a. the technical documentation, information and other data and documents to be supplied under the present Contract shall not be disclosed *to any third party* except to the extent it becomes necessary to do so solely for its work and operations' (Art. 13.2, Contract 7820; emphasis added). Such stipulations in contracts signed by Indian public enterprises seem surprising, to say the least, considering that the Government of India's *Guidelines for Entrepreneurs* (i.e. private sector firms) require them to insist with collaborators on granting them the freedom to transfer technology horizontally. Thus the *Guidelines* state: 'The Indian party should be free to sub-license technical know-how/product-design/engineering design under the agreement to another Indian party on terms to be mutually agreed to by all the parties concerned including the foreign collaborator and subject to the approval of the Government' (Ministry of Industry, 1979).

In order to place this preceding discussion in perspective, it should be admitted that in practice the absence of freedom to transfer Soviet technology horizontally has not meant any tangible loss to the Indian economy in the sensè of repetitive import of similar technology. The simple explanation for this is that Soviet projects have been established in sectors in which duplication of enterprises has not occurred, since demand for these capital goods has not grown so rapidly as to require repetitive imports (heavy engineering, mining machinery, heavy electricals, drugs and pharmaceuticals). However, steel and oil refining are industries where more than one project has been established with Soviet assistance: in steel, Bhilai and Bokaro were followed by Visakhapatnam more than a decade later, and in oil refining, Barauni and Koyali in the late fifties and early sixties preceded Mathura which came almost fifteen years later. The second steel plant (Bokaro) and oil refinery (Koyali) followed soon after the first one, so that not enough time had elapsed for firms to absorb the technology sufficiently to be able to reproduce it. And it is only when machine-operating skills and manufacturing technology have been absorbed, and product/equipment design capacity developed that the enterprise will become capable of transferring technology to other domestic or foreign firms. Furthermore, it should be pointed out that the latest generation of Soviet-aided projects – Visakhapatnam in steel (scheduled to be commissioned in 1992) and Mathura in oil refining (commissioned in 1983) – are in any case coming up after such a long interval that the old documents are unlikely to be particularly useful given that the technology might have changed considerably in the intervening period.

5.2.4 Settlement of disputes

Another interesting feature of Indo-Soviet firm level contracts is that in case of disputes arising between the signatories, the contract calls for inter-governmental consultations, rather than arbitration, which is the normal practice.[6] Other contracts just mention the inter-governmental agreement in pursuance of which the contract was signed.

That contract disputes are to be settled in accordance with inter-governmental agreements is quite different from the situation operating in relations with advanced capitalist countries. Above all, this shows that the political element of the Indo-Soviet relationship is never very far away even in firm level contracts. This phenomenon is also an illustration of a more general point that institutionally the Indo-Soviet relationship is quite advanced. It has become highly institutionalised over the years and its constituent elements (state-to-state economic cooperation, cooperation between their Chambers of Commerce, friendship societies) each have had an independent trajectory. Whenever problems arise in any of these relatively autonomous areas, recourse is typically made to political authorities, usually in the form of appeals to higher levels.

5.2.5 The price

The purchase price of Indo-Soviet contracts is always quoted on the basis of the gold content of the rouble.[7] The significance of such a clause in the contract is that in case of the devaluation of the Indian rupee (as in June 1967), India's liability would be correspondingly raised by the percentage change in the rupee–rouble exchange rate. This problem rose again in the mid-seventies, when the USSR altered the rupee–rouble exchange rate since the rupee had been depreciating against the major convertible currencies. It was only in November 1978 after several rounds of protracted negotiations that a decision was arrived at on the scaling up of Indian liabilities (see chapter 7 for details).

Yet another unique feature of Indo-Soviet contracts is that Soviet equipment and spares are priced on the basis of weight, rather than individual items of machinery/components being given a separate price tag. Thus the Soviets quote a price for an entire bundle of equipment, with no differentiation for mechanical or electrical equipment, or even for bulky/heavy or sophisticated equipment.[8] It must be pointed out that the price in almost all turnkey contracts around the world is determined in overall terms and without a full and detailed breakdown of the costs of the various elements of expertise and supplies. In such turnkey contracts, even when each stage of implementation has been broken down, it is difficult to determine the additional mark-up at each stage, as negotiations are usually conducted for the package. What is peculiar about the Soviet pricing method is, of course, that whether the supply of equipment or spares is part of a technological package or not, they are still given a package price on the basis of weight, thus compounding the problems of negotiations. It was pointed out by senior public sector executives that the fact that a lump sum payment is made for equipment by tonnage means that, for an Indian negotiator, no price comparison is possible with similar equipment available on the international market.

5.2.6 Guarantees and liquidated damages

When technology transfer comprises supply of basic engineering services, including plant design, etc., it is desirable to include specific guarantees of the quality and performance to be achieved through such services, together with provisions for rectification of engineering and design defects free of cost. All Indo-Soviet contracts provide for such guarantees. It is suggested that provision for liquidated compensatory damages should also be included in licence/turnkey agreements, in the event such rectification is not effected within a reasonable period. An agreement provides for liquated damages when a licenser or supplier specifically warrants the performance of some factor – as, for example, time in the context of delivery of technical documents, equipment, construction of buildings, installation of machinery.[9] No such clause was included in any Indo-Soviet contract, although there were repeated delays in Soviet deliveries for many projects; and the non-inclusion of such a clause remained an issue between the two parties for a long period. (To put the question of delays in perspective, it must be pointed out at the outset that delays in Soviet deliveries are only partly responsible for delays in completion of Soviet-aided projects; equally, if not more, important are the delays by domestic supplier firms. The discussion here is confined to the terms and conditions of the firm level contracts and the inadequacies therein.) Several examples of Soviet delays and problems resulting from the non-inclusion of a liquidated damages clause can be cited. Thus the mining and allied machinery plant (MAMC, Durgapur) was constructed without any definite schedule of construction. In response to criticism of the MAMC and the ministry concerned, the Indian government stated that as the plant was set up with tied credit, it could not insist on a penal clause 'beyond a certain limit' (CPU, *MAMC*, 1969/70, para. 3.20). In the case of the heavy machine building plant of the Heavy Engineering Corporation (HEC), there was a similar delay in Soviet supplies of working drawings, steel structures, equipment and electrical materials. HEC's management told the CPU that the collaborators had not agreed to the inclusion of a clause in the agreement for recovery of liquidated damages (CPU, *HEC*, 1967/8, para. 4.3).

An examination of public enterprises revealed that most of the projects in which time schedules were not included in the DPR were set up with Russian collaboration, and the time schedules for them were prepared after a study of the DPRs.[10] Uncertain of the supplier firms' ability to meet delivery schedules, the Soviet FTOs were presumably cautious in agreeing to any time schedules. Even more interestingly, the Chairman of Bharat Heavy Electricals (BHEL) stated that a time schedule for the completion of the heavy electricals plant at Hardwar was worked out by the Soviet collaborators in one of the volumes of the DPR which was not made over to the Indian authorities.[11]

The delays in supplying equipment to the heavy electricals plant (of BHEL) brought the issue of the penalty clause into sharp focus. It is clear that the Soviets were determined not to include a penalty clause in the contracts. In fact, the Soviets firmly told the Indian government that they would not be able to enter into any kind of agreement where the Indians insisted on a penalty clause (CPU, *BHEL*, 1971/2, para. 2.14). During the discussions over the insertion of a penalty clause between BHEL and the collaborators the Soviets pointed out that there were delays in opening letters of credit by the Indians which resulted in losses to them on account of storage charges and port charges at the port of dispatch and, therefore, they would like a counter-penalty clause also to be included in the contract. However, later they changed their mind and rejected all suggestions about including a penalty clause in contracts.

Hence a protocol was drawn up between India and the USSR (in March 1971) excluding the penalty clause from all further contracts. The Russians insisted that one of the principles was that solutions to all issues would be made by mutual negotiation. The Indian ministry representative explained: 'The problem was that we had to get into this agreement at a time when we needed this equipment and we had to make arrangements under their soft loan agreement. The point was [*sic*] wherever there was competition from others, it would be possible for us to insist on a penalty clause, but in cases where we were more or less driven to the wall, as it were, we cannot include this clause. We can no doubt try to get this clause entered into but if they do not agree to it, mutual negotiation is the only answer' (CPU, *BHEL*, 1971/2, para. 2.14).

5.2.7 Provisions relating to training

A developing country sees in technology transfer not only the immediate access to advanced techniques of production but also a means of educating and training its personnel in the use of technological information and working techniques. It is well known that LDC governments, such as that of India, often require a division of responsibilities between supplier (of know-how or of engineering services or both) and the client so that only highly specialised work is performed by foreign firms; and that by the time the supplier's contract expires, the recipients are fully trained in machine-operating skills and manufacturing technology. In such a division it is implicitly recognised that project costs may go up (and project time be lengthened) because of the higher possibility of error by nationals in the process of learning.

Indo-Soviet contracts provide for formal training to be imparted to the customers' specialists and skilled workers in the USSR. The technical and industrial training is carried out free of charge in Russian (including the teaching of the language), though the seller's expenses connected with living accommodation and food for the buyer's specialists are reimbursed by the buyer.[12] Training by Soviet specialists is also provided on-the-job in the Indian plant. It is noticeable that the earliest contract available (oil refining, 1961) made no mention of the length of time for which the Soviet specialists would stay in India. However, with experience, the customer felt the need to specify the time period in the contract to prevent Soviet specialists from overstaying their brief (for possible reasons for overstays, see chapter 6). In one ministry after another, the author was told of the tendency of Soviet specialists to stay on well beyond the period for which they were needed. Thus the main contract for the preparation of the DPR for Bokaro failed to mention any time period for Soviet specialists. But later the Managing Director of Bokaro wrote to the Soviet embassy in India: 'With reference to para. 6 of Contract 7622 for the designing work, I wish to confirm that Soviet specialists for designers' supervision will be deputed to India for a period of five years and will not exceed on the average.' A similar condition was laid down in the aluminium project contract.

6   Transfer of technology

In chapter 5 we have outlined the methodology adopted in part III for evaluating the transfer of technology from the USSR to India. For the sake of convenience, we summarise those criteria here. We identified an independent technological capacity with the following capabilities in relation to the preparation and execution of projects in manufacturing industry: pre-investment studies, project execution, process engineering, product engineering, industrial engineering and horizontal technology transfer. It is primarily the first two which are the subject of technology transfer; process and product engineering, on the other hand, cannot be bought in and must be developed in-house. The total technological capability developed within an enterprise must be the result of both the technology transferred to it and that which is developed in-house.

The criteria used in evaluating the effectiveness of technology transfer are as follows: 1. the training component, 2. the sharing of the design and engineering work between the supplier of technology and the acquirer, 3. the use of local inputs (i.e. equipment and services), 4. the setting in motion of a local R&D process and design capability, and 5. the diffusion of the technology acquired. We also stated in chapter 5 that the combination of technology transferred and that developed in-house should show itself in machine-operating skills, a mastery of the manufacturing technology and design and R&D capacity. These skills, or technological requirements, have particular importance in the capital goods sector.

The first section, dealing with the capital goods sector, examines Soviet technology transfer to heavy electricals, coal-mining machinery and heavy engineering plants. The second section, on the intermediate goods sector, examines technology transfer to the steel and oil (exploration and refining) industries. The third section, on the consumer goods sector, deals with three plants, all of which are in the drugs and pharmaceuticals industry. In the final section we draw some general conclusions based upon the preceding analysis about the costs and benefits to India resulting from Soviet technology transfer.

It may be useful first to locate the broad governmental policy framework within which the plants (mentioned above) were initially set up. The Government of India's Industrial Policy Resolution of 1956 (which was attached as an Annexure to the Second Five-Year Plan) divided industries into three categories according to whether their future development was to occur in the public or the private sector. The first category consisted of industries the future development of which was to be the exclusive responsibility of the state; the second category were to be progressively state-owned, with all new enterprises in the public sector, but private enterprise was to supplement the state effort; the third category included all remaining industries, to be left to the private sector. Most industries which were the recipients of Soviet technology fell into the first category: heavy plant and machinery required for iron and steel production, for mining, for machine-tool manufacture; heavy electrical plant including large hydraulic and steam turbines; mineral oils; coal; and iron and steel. Only two of the industries which bought Soviet technology were in the second category: aluminium, and antibiotics and other essential drugs. The fact that all Soviet-aided enterprises were in the public sector has serious implications for their managerial efficiency and hence their performance, technological as well as financial – a fact that must be kept in mind while evaluating these enterprises.

Another relevant fact about the policy environment is that the marked shift in investment allocation to the capital goods sector, which characterised the Second Plan, was determined without any reference to foreign trade. Importing at least some of these capital goods, instead of producing them domestically possibly at very high cost, was not even considered; in fact, in general, cost considerations were almost irrelevant in the investment decision. Thus, a simple rule of project preparation is that as part of pre-investment studies, a feasibility study is conducted. However, although preliminary project studies were carried out, in many public sector projects (including Soviet-aided ones) they were inadequate. Thus, regarding the heavy electricals project, a senior civil servant in the Ministry of Industry admitted:

> At the time of venturing on these projects, the overriding consideration in the context of the envisaged development of the power programme in the country was of self-reliance in building electrical equipment in the country. Costs and profitability were secondary

considerations on which little emphasis was laid. Though these aspects were not thoroughly examined at that time because these were need-based projects, studies regarding cost of production and the rate of return and the period when the returns would start accruing had been worked out at subsequent stages. (CPU, *BHEL*, 1967, para. 23)

A feasibility study, apart from demonstrating technical and economic feasibility, must include, inter alia, a detailed market survey. However, no market survey was conducted for the coal-mining machinery project (MAMC). The result of such 'need-based' investment could well be that very large amounts of capital may get locked up in such projects while the capacity remains severely under-utilised (as in fact happened with MAMC). Instead of generating re-investible surpluses, such enterprises became a drain on public resources.

6.1 The capital goods sector

In the fifties and sixties such heavy industries as heavy electricals, mining machinery and heavy engineering were being set up in India for the first time. Since India had almost no experience at all in these industries, there was no likelihood of the sharing of the design and engineering work between the technology supplier and the acquirer, or even the use of local inputs other than construction services. Moreover, since the market in India for these particular heavy industries has not grown very rapidly over the last three decades of planned development, no occasion has arisen to replicate these heavy machinery plants; this implies that no demand has arisen for the diffusion of the technology acquired over the fifties and sixties. Hence the argument in this section is conducted not in terms of the degree of the sharing of engineering work or use of local inputs or diffusion of the technology acquired; rather the concern here is to establish the extent to which the technological requirements for capital goods production – machine-operating skills, manufacturing technology, design, and research and development capacity – have been developed in the enterprises examined. In the following discussion, transfer of 'know-how' normally refers to machine-operating skills and manufacturing technology, while 'know-why' refers to product/process design and R&D capacity.

However, effective transfer of know-how and know-why alone is not the key to the success of an enterprise in the capital goods sector.

The domestic economic environment in which the enterprise operates is equally important. In fact, what is striking about the three enterprises examined in the capital goods sector is their varying performance: one is very successful both technologically and commercially (BHEL), while the other two are complete failures (HEC and MAMC). In this section we attempt to explain the difference in their performance both in terms of the effectiveness of transfer of technology and in terms of the domestic economic environment.

We will now examine in turn the heavy electricals, coal-mining machinery and heavy engineering projects. (For the sake of convenience, they are referred to by the name of their controlling Indian company – Bharat Heavy Electricals Ltd (BHEL), Mining and Allied Machinery Corporation (MAMC) and Heavy Engineering Corporation (HEC).)

6.1.1 Heavy electricals

Since the international heavy electrical equipment market is a very imperfect one, BHEL's entry into the market in the late sixties, as an Indian state-owned manufacturer, constituted a unique development.[1] Just as OECD countries have a purchasing policy for power equipment biased in favour of domestic producers, BHEL too has been afforded levels of protection that enabled it to acquire a near monopoly status in the domestic market. BHEL's contribution to additional generating capacity in India in the seventies has been around 90 per cent. Along with the fact that plan outlays on power through the seventies have been among the largest for any individual sector, this has ensured that BHEL has not faced any demand constraint, at least in the first decade of its existence (though in the eighties this position changed). This has meant that BHEL has had ample opportunity to master the manufacturing technology, and even go beyond to developing product and process engineering capabilities.

We briefly note here the features of Soviet technology transfer to BHEL as well as the technological capability developed in-house by BHEL. The first interesting observation is that the import content of the total plant and machinery installed at the Soviet-assisted heavy electrical plant at Hardwar and a heavy equipment plant set up earlier with British assistance at Bhopal is roughly similar, as table 6.1 demonstrates.[2] We make this point only because, as we shall see later, it has been argued (by Datar and others) that certain Soviet-aided projects

Table 6.1. *Import content of equipment in Soviet and non-Soviet plants*

Source of equipment	Bhopal plant (British)	Hardwar plant (Soviet)
Imported equipment	Rs200m	Rs211m
Share in total equipment cost	77.4%	71.0%
Indian equipment	Rs58.5m	Rs86m
Share in total equipment cost	22.6%	28.9%

Sources: CPU, *BHEL*, 1971/2; BHEL, *Annual Report*, 1964/5.

(e.g. steel plants and oil refineries) were dearer than similar projects set up with Western assistance.

Secondly, there is plenty of evidence that the transfer of technology to BHEL was effective. A World Bank study on the manufacture of heavy electrical equipment in LDCs notes:

> Under favourable circumstances, the learning period for heavy electrical equipment production with well-established technology in an industrial though still developing environment can probably be reduced to 4 or 5 years. In actual fact, it is perhaps likely to reach 7 years or even more, if the environment is unsuitable or if there are unforeseen difficulties. (Cilingiroglu 1969, p. 85)

In fact BHEL, after starting production in the late sixties, appears to have mastered the manufacturing technology by 1973. Until 1973, the manufacturing function occupied the prime place in BHEL. But already by 1974, according to the company's first corporate plan, BHEL was planning to turn from a 'mere manufacturing organisation' into a 'first-rate engineering organisation'. To this end, twenty engineering development centres were established in 1975 for all the major products of the company, 'one product, one engineering centre' (BHEL, *12th Annual Report*, 1975/6). Design cells had already been set up in each unit of BHEL at the same time that the units themselves were established. By the time most of the Soviet specialists left BHEL, Hardwar, in 1976, the manufacturing technology had been fully absorbed. The explanation for the absorption of technology (I was told during personal interviews) was the constant interaction between specialists on both sides, Soviet and Indian.

It must be emphasised that the organisational changes in the engineering function in BHEL in the mid-seventies had been backed by R&D activities at the corporate level. R&D expenditure, which was at an insignificant Rs0.2m in 1971/2, had risen to Rs125m, nearly 3 per cent of turnover in 1976/7; by 1979/80 this had risen to Rs360m or 4.8 per cent of the turnover that year. These are very impressive figures indeed for an Indian public sector undertaking, considering that the public sector spent on an average 0.78 per cent of their sales turnover on R&D during 1978/9. The Soviets, incidentally, have had little or nothing to do with R&D facilities in BHEL.

Thirdly, BHEL's achievements in in-house product engineering have been remarkable, which is further evidence of its assimilation of the manufacturing technology. Thus, BHEL's engineering development centres have integrated and rationalised the different design philosophies embodied in BHEL products acquired from different collaborators, Eastern and Western. In addition to successfully standardising and rationalising existing designs, BHEL engineers have also improved them.

The Soviet design for the highest-rating thermal set to be manufactured at Hardwar was for 200mW. The generator for this set was giving rise to losses in power generated. BHEL, particularly the engineering development centre at Hardwar, has been successful in modifying it and taking the rating of the set to 210mW. Improvements have also been effected in the control instrumentation package for turbines and generators obtained from the USSR. It is understood that Soviet equipment had not been quite adequate in this area. Hence, the heavy electricals plant at Hardwar had developed a new design, and passed on the drawings to another public sector undertaking, to manufacture the instrumentation package. The equipment had now been installed at several power plants and was operating to the satisfaction of BHEL's requirements. The rationalisation of design technology and alterations in the instrumentation package were interrelated, in that the latter became necessary as a result of the former.

Moreover, the Hardwar plant is capable of manufacturing spares for BHEL's products (i.e. generators, boilers, etc.) and thereby meeting the needs of BHEL customers. Spares for the machine tools have also been developed within the Hardwar plant, without resorting to importation of Soviet design documentation for the manufacture of spares. In some cases the assistance of Soviet specialists was sought for the purpose; thereafter they were manufactured either in the Hardwar plant or in the private sector.

Fourthly, BHEL's in-house product engineering and R&D efforts have been so remarkable that the possibility of reverse transfer of technology to the USSR has arisen in certain areas. For example, BHEL has improved the design for the hydro-turbine provided by the

Soviets. The main art of the hydro-turbine lies in the profile of the blade on which water falls. Apparently BHEL has improved the Soviet design and made it more efficient than the original one. Many improvements, it appears, have also been effected in the governing side of hydro-machines. As a result the Soviets have sought BHEL's assistance in this area.

Fifthly, in the past the Soviets were not particularly commercial in their attitude to technology transfer. BHEL had more than twenty separate collaboration agreements with firms from both East and West, but in the experience of BHEL engineers interviewed, while 'the others charged money for every sentence they spoke, this was not true of the Russians'. It was added, however, that in the recent past the Soviet attitude had changed because in the last twenty years Soviet heavy electricals technology had evolved and improved considerably. As evidence of the Soviets' more commercial attitude, it was stated that they would prefer to discontinue deferred payment items granted to India (and BHEL) for equipment imported from the USSR; documents (i.e. working drawings, etc.) now involve immediate payment, though payments for imported hardware are still deferred.

Sixthly, BHEL, like many other Soviet-aided public sector enterprises in India, has shifted to Western technology for its main product-range since the late seventies. For 200–1,000mW technology, BHEL has sought collaboration with Siemens, one of the industry's leaders. All future sets of 200mW upwards will now be of Siemens' (German) design. The main emphasis in technical progress in the heavy electrical industry in the West has been continuously on the increase in the size of the electrical system. While in the larger units the industry leaders nearly dominate the world market, in smaller sizes and in water turbines technology is more widespread, even accessible to producers in LDCs. With Soviet assistance, BHEL has mastered the technology up to 210mW (for thermal units). But since 1983 very few sets of Russian design are being manufactured in BHEL plants (since domestic demand for units smaller than 200mW has tapered off).

However, it was admitted by BHEL engineers that the Soviet-designed equipment is very hardy, and is capable of withstanding mishandling; it has performed well in Indian conditions. The Siemens sets, on the other hand, are not only technically superior, but at the same time very precise, very fine machines which cannot be mishandled. The average plant load factor in State Electricity Board (SEB) run power stations round the country has been less than 50 per cent for a long time now; a major factor in this low capacity utilisation at power stations has been the inefficiency of SEB management and inadequate training of SEB technical personnel. Hence the switch to the more sophisticated Siemens technology may prove to be an uncertain gain.

6.1.2 Heavy engineering

Having examined Soviet technology transfer to BHEL, let us note the features of technology transfer to the coal-mining machinery (MAMC) and steel-making machinery projects (HEC). First, both MAMC and HEC are evidence of a tendency in Soviet-aided plants towards excess built-in capacity. East European countries tend to favour projects involving heavier initial investment, larger scales and longer gestation periods, as a trade-off against lower long-run average costs for reasonable levels of capacity use. The Soviet report (submitted in 1957) on the project argued that to make the heavy machine-building plant 'economical', it should not have a capacity below 45,000 tonnes per annum and that they would welcome starting up a unit with 80,000 tonnes capacity capable of expansion up to 165,000 tonnes. As the Chairman of HEC said later (in 1970): 'The figure of 80,000 tonnes as the plant capacity was indicated by the collaborators based on their experience of working of similar plants in the USSR producing a certain given product-mix.' The result has been that, as public investment for coal-mining and steel plants was not as large as for the power sector, demand for MAMC's and HEC's products has not been as high as that for BHEL, leading to serious under-utilisation of capacity. However, when the demand did become available MAMC and HEC were still unable to deliver the goods, on account of their technological weaknesses.

The technological weaknesses of both HEC and MAMC are the combined result of ineffective technology transfer and a near absence of a culture of application engineering (or product engineering) within the enterprises. The inability of MAMC to deliver arose in large part from the fact that the specifications of machinery requirements of Indian coal-mining companies, which till the early seventies were in the private sector, differed considerably from those laid down by the Soviet consultants in MAMC's DPR. MAMC had been equipped for bulk manufacture of a small range of products; the demand, on the other hand, was for a large range of products but in small numbers. A detailed market survey by either the Indian or Soviet firm prior to the preparation of the DPR should have prevented such a problem from arising, but no market survey was in fact carried out. This situation, taken together with the fact that the coal-raising targets for the Third, Fourth and Fifth Plans proved totally unrealistic, and hence the demand for coal-mining machinery was lower than that anticipated when the plant capacity was planned, meant there was no occasion for MAMC to develop product engineering capabilities.[3] In fact, MAMC's capacity for coal-mining machinery has remained largely unutilised. MAMC responded to this crisis in the early seventies by diversifying into new products, e.g. tractors, railway wagons, equipment for coal washeries and coal beneficiation plant, and bulk handling machinery. Although the USSR offered its own designs and drawings for diversifying production, no further technology was purchased from the USSR by MAMC; like BHEL, MAMC's new collaborators were all Western ones. However, there is a continued dependence on Soviet designs/designers in regard to its original product-mix (i.e. underground coal-mining equipment); thus, in order to fulfil export orders to the USSR (between 1980 and 1985) MAMC had to have Soviet specialists supervise production for the purpose. The proliferation of Soviet specialists, a common problem in Soviet-aided plants, does nothing to bolster the confidence of Indian personnel.

Like MAMC, HEC's problems derived fundamentally from lack of demand. Considering that HEC (which included a heavy machine building plant, a heavy machine tool plant and a foundry forge plant) was set up to manufacture equipment for a 1m tonnes steel plant every year, the actual demand of only 5.5m tonnes over a period of over fifteen years (1966–82) could hardly have provided a sufficient load for it, even on the presumption that the entire equipment needs of the new steel plants were to be met by HEC, rather than at least in part by aid donors. HEC's demand problems were in fact compounded by Soviet transfer of technology to HEC which proved grossly inadequate.

Before we analyse the technological weaknesses of HEC, it is necessary to describe the stages in the design and establishment of a steel plant:

Stage A: initial techno-economic feasibility study of a project and preparation of DPR on acceptance of initial scheme;

Stage B: technological process design and project engineering (including basic design drawings based on which detailed drawings are prepared for production units – coke ovens, sintering plant, blast furnaces, steel-melting shop, rolling mills, etc.);

Stage C: designing of integrated plant layout, and preparation of detailed construction drawings for foundations, building structures, interconnected facilities and services, and technical specifications;

Stage D: design of equipment, preparation of shop drawings for the manufacture of equipment (including system/application and project engineering);

Stage E: manufacture of equipment;

Stage F: construction of steel plant, erection and commissioning of equipment.

While HEC was equipped to manufacture equipment for steel plants (Stage E), it was inadequately equipped for either technological process-design (Stage B) or design of equipment (Stage D). While the Central Engineering and Design Bureau (later called MECON), a public sector consultancy organisation, was established to perform some of the Stage B functions, the Stage D functions have been all but ignored (on MECON, see following sub-section). The result has been that when orders were placed with HEC for Bokaro, India's first steel plant after HEC was commissioned, it could only manufacture the required equipment on the basis of drawings furnished by the Soviets. Thus, as with MAMC, HEC's dependence on Soviet designs continues. Like MAMC, HEC too diversified its product profile to stave off a crisis caused by severely under-utilised capacity. For HEC, similarly, diversification has meant new collaborations which are mostly with Western firms, not east European (apart from one with Czechoslovakia).

This diversification in Soviet-aided enterprises is of two kinds: one, all three – BHEL, MAMC and HEC – have diversified into new products, for which collaboration (or licence) agreements have been signed with mostly Western firms; two, all three have also signed collaboration agreements with Western firms for some of the products which were part of their original product-mix. As an example of the second type of diversification, BHEL's collaboration for turbines, generators and boilers with a Siemens subsidiary (KWU) has already been mentioned. MAMC has collaborated with a British firm to manufacture equipment for the long-wall system of underground coal mining, a system which was planned to be expanded during the Sixth Plan (1980–5). Thus even in MAMC's area of specialisation – underground mining equipment – new equipment is to be based on Western designs, although it appears that MAMC will continue to manufacture equipment for the room and pillar system of underground mining, which currently contributes around 70 per cent of India's total coal production, on the basis of Soviet designs. As regards HEC, as much as

32,000 tonnes of its 80,000 tonne capacity had been created for the manufacture of steel-rolling mills based on Soviet designs; however, with MECON (see following section) having tied up with US (Wean-United) and West German (Schloemann-Siemag) firms, the heavy machine building plant is now manufacturing rolling mills based on their designs.

One needs to examine this phenomenon of simultaneous diversification of the product-mix as well as sources of technology imports in the capital goods sector in some detail. Several points need to be made about this development. First, the diversification of product-mix and technology imports has not in any way tended to reduce HEC's and MAMC's huge financial losses. HEC and MAMC have remained almost throughout the seventies and early eighties two of the fifteen largest loss-makers among central government public enterprises, with the exception of a few years in the mid-seventies when demand was rising for steel equipment (for Bokaro) and for coal-mining equipment (during the Fifth Plan) after the nationalisation of all private coal companies in 1971/2. Second, like MAMC and HEC, BHEL too has diversified its product-mix (and sources of technology). For instance, it now manufactures not only power station equipment but also electrical traction equipment for electric and diesel locomotives as well as electrical equipment for cement, paper, mining, steel, metallurgical and other industries. However, BHEL's diversification was undertaken only after production of its original (Soviet-designed) product-mix had been stabilised, not as a rearguard action aimed at salvaging an investment that, in retrospect, had proved a misallocation of resources.

Most important, this diversification of product-mix and sources of technology imports was symptomatic of a complete absence of technology planning within manufacturing enterprises in the public sector. This indiscriminate dual diversification would probably not have occurred if plans for standardising capital goods had been formulated and implemented. The power-generating equipment industry is a classic case of lack of standardisation in the capital goods sector. Since the main emphasis in technical progress in the West in the heavy electrical industry has been on the continuous increase in the size of the system, SEBs, wherever technically feasible, were pushing for larger and larger capacity sets. The result has been that taken together with imported thermal generating sets (from no less than eighteen countries) there are now twenty sizes in operation in India.[4]

The economic argument in favour of standardisation, particularly relevant in an LDC, is an obvious one: sticking with one size or model of equipment for a reasonable period enables the manufacturer to exploit economies of scale and to lower unit costs through repetitive manufacture. Standardisation should go hand-in-hand with another policy: a judicious combination of selective imports (to meet individual customer needs) with domestic production of certain standard sizes, instead of a blanket policy of producing every product that is feasible from the technical point of view and for which there is a domestic market. In the absence of proper standardisation, the result of indiscriminate import substitution is simply that the import content of domestically manufactured capital goods shoots up. Domestic manufacture normally begins with assembly of imported components, and only gradually is the production indigenised.[5]

Finally, one should note another feature of Soviet technology transfer to the capital goods sector which (as we shall see) may also have some relevance to the question of diversification. The sale of technology by the CMEA countries, especially the USSR, has been mostly in the nature of a one-off sale of design and documentation. In other words, the technology transferred is for a particular size or type of equipment; if improvements are effected to that equipment in the USSR, or new products added to that range of equipment, there is no Soviet attempt to transfer those improvements. Several such instances can be cited (Haribhushan 1985).

It is not wholly clear what underlies this phenomenon. The reason may lie in that the firm level contracts did not include a provision to the effect that any modifications or improvements in technical know-how effected by the supplier over the currency of the contract will have to be passed on to the technology recipient. Such clauses are often included in contracts with Western firms. Formally it requires a corresponding obligation on the part of the recipient that if the latter makes any improvement in the technology during the currency of the agreement, the licenser will have access to that information. However, since the Indo-Soviet firm level contracts were not time-bound in that they had no expiry date, it is hardly surprising that such a reciprocal commitment was excluded. It is more likely that the improvements and modifications were not passed on simply because, unlike capitalist enterprises, enterprises in these administrative economies have no direct interest in foreign trade, and hence no marketing strategy worth the name. The 1987 reorganisation in foreign trade may ease this problem in the future, since many enterprises will trade directly. However, in the past this has put Indian manufacturers, working in association with Soviet enterprises, at a considerable disadvantage vis-à-vis their Indian customers. The manufacturer and customer, who are constantly being bombarded with sales information from interested Western firms, are familiar with the improved and latest versions of Western equipment. Under such circumstances, when the Indian manufacturer is diversifying into a new product, he is more likely to choose between one of several Western suppliers already available rather than seek out Soviet manufacturers, with whom a new, fresh collaboration agreement would be required in any case. As one technocrat from the Ministry of Heavy Industry (with two-and-a-half decades of negotiating experience with the Soviets) said: 'The Soviets' idea of technology transfer is that they will offer you a particular type of excavator – not a range of allied ones. This implies that you must keep going back to them for each product.'

The bureaucratic delays inevitable in going through the whole procedure of signing new collaboration agreements for new products seem to have been a disincentive for Indian negotiators in approaching the Soviets. Administrative delays on both sides – Soviet and Indian – may occur in tandem or even prove to be additive. Meanwhile, the Indian capital goods manufacturers may lose business in favour of imports from the more business-like Western firms. Imports have become easier with new import liberalisation schemes since the late seventies. Hence, it is not so surprising that one inefficient bureaucracy, the Indian, does not necessarily prefer to deal with another inefficient bureaucracy, the Soviet.

In conclusion, one should note another point about Soviet cooperation with enterprises in the capital goods sector built with their assistance. Since MAMC and HEC had suffered severe losses resulting largely from serious under-utilisation of capacity, the USSR had secured several orders in the late seventies for both enterprises from third countries. Even BHEL has been helped to utilise its spare production capacity.

The broader significance of such supplies by MAMC, HEC and BHEL is that since 1973 (when the fifteen-year Indo-Soviet economic agreement was signed) there has been repeated mention of production cooperation and joint ventures by Indian and Soviet enterprises abroad. Although the supplies by MAMC, HEC and BHEL are not in the same category as the proposals in the later inter-governmental agreement (of 1980) to set up export-oriented enterprises in India on a compensation basis, they do seem to be a step in that direction.

In this context the remarkable success of BHEL in exporting technology, both to LDCs as well as to DMEs, is also of significance. BHEL is the single largest exporter of technology from India.[6] The Soviets would naturally like to take advantage of Indian successes abroad. In chapter 2, mention was made of Soviet interest in cooperating with Indian firms in setting up joint ventures in South-east Asia and the Middle East. In fact, the Soviets have specifically mentioned the possibility of Indian firms building power plants in LDCs sub-contracting some part of the work to the USSR. A joint approach could mean, the Soviets suggested, that the USSR will be prepared to extend credit and furnish drawings while both India and the USSR can supply machinery.

6.1.3 Steel plant design

It has been argued in the previous sub-section that while the USSR has been a willing transferrer of know-how, the transfer of know-why has been rather limited. Indian personnel at Soviet-assisted plants have successfully absorbed machine-operating skills and even manufacturing technology (although the degree of absorption of the latter varies between enterprises), partly on account of training imparted both in India and in the USSR and partly in the process of 'learning by doing'. However, little attempt has been made to transfer design methodology with the objective of developing an independent product design capacity in the plants; dependence on Soviet designs/designers was seen to continue in HEC and MAMC. There has been little or no involvement with BHEL in the latter's R&D activities, which are quite considerable compared to other Indian public enterprises. However, the assistance rendered by the Soviets to MECON (Metallurgical and Engineering Consultants), a public sector consultancy organisation, which began primarily as a steel plant consultant, is something of an exception. In other words, the weaknesses of HEC's design wing have been compensated by the relative strength of MECON as a metallurgical design organisation; though, even in regard to MECON, a qualification must be that, right from its inception, its collaborations have not been with Soviet organisations alone but with several Western ones as well.

Although the USSR may not have been MECON's only source of technology, the Soviet contribution to the development of a design capacity in the steel industry is undeniable. The design capacity (in spite of its limitations discussed below) in the Indian steel industry is probably quite well developed even by the standards of such semi-industrialised economies as Brazil and South Korea. Not surprisingly, Indian consultancy exports to LDCs are concentrated in metallurgy (just as Indian industrial project exports are concentrated in power generation). As a UNIDO publication states: 'It is vital that the development and training of designers be simultaneous with the inauguration of an industry.' From the inception of the Bhilai Design Cell in the late fifties to a contract with Gipromez in 1969 and that with Tiazhpromexport in the early eighties, Soviet assistance in the training of designers has been one of the several key factors in the growth of MECON's capabilities.

However, an interesting question is: what would have happened without the Soviet relationship? It would certainly have come into existence; in fact, the Central Engineering and Design Bureau had already come into existence in the late fifties, independent of the Bhilai Design Cell set up by the Soviets. The CEDB had arisen in association with German experts in Rourkela and British experts in Durgapur. (The Rourkela steel plant was built with German assistance, the Durgapur steel plant with British aid.) In the late sixties, CEDB (with which the Bhilai Design Cell had been merged) not only signed a contract with Gipromez, as mentioned above, but also one with an American firm. The two contracts were in a sense complementary: while Gipromez was to render assistance to CEDB in detailed project engineering of steel plants, the contract with the American firm was for assistance in designing equipment (rolling mills). Apart from these collaborations with foreign consultants, both Soviet and Western, CEDB's strengths (CEDB renamed MECON in 1973) also derive from learning by doing. As table 6.3 demonstrates, MECON has been associated with the growth of the major steel plants in the public sector from its inception and has thereby collected considerable know-how. In addition, most of the construction and equipment manufacturing drawings pertaining to these plants were accessible to MECON. Quite clearly, MECON is not simply a Soviet protégé.

So what are MECON's major strengths and weaknesses? For the first stage of public sector plants (except Vizag) the consultancy services were provided by the foreign suppliers. However, even though the Indian consultants became the Prime Consultants from the second stage onwards (except for Bhilai) Indian design capacity remained limited largely to Stage A (preparation of feasibility study and DPR) and Stage C (designing plant layout and project engineering for foundations, etc.) functions in the setting up of an integrated steel plant. MECON could perform Stage B functions (process design and design drawings for basic production units) provided units identical to the ones installed at the first stage of Bhilai and Bokaro were contemplated. Stage D functions (equipment design) were beyond the capability of either MECON or HEC.

MECON had emerged by the late seventies as an independent metallurgical consultant on the world market in its own right. In the metallurgical (and chemical) sector, an active Indian government policy of encouraging the growth of local consultants from the early days of industrialisation has meant that a number of highly successful firms have emerged from the private (M. N. Dastur in iron and steel) and public sectors, including MECON. We saw earlier that BHEL has emerged as India's single largest exporter of industrial projects, and is only one among many Indian firms which form part of a larger scenario of growing technology exports by newly industrialising countries. In consultancy exports, MECON (along with M. N. Dastur) have been important contributors of foreign earnings. Although one reason for promoting the growth of Indian consultancy exports has been the official belief that it would promote the sales of Indian equipment, given the weaknesses of HEC as a manufacturer that was unlikely to materialise. In fact, the striking difference between the success abroad of BHEL and MECON on the one hand, and HEC's and MAMC's exports on the other, is that the former won their contracts abroad in the face of international competition while the latter's exports were arranged through the good offices of the USSR.

6.2 The intermediate goods sector

6.2.1 Steel plants

Since steel is one of the few industries where technology in the public sector was concurrently imported in the fifties and sixties from both Soviet and Western sources, we shall have occasion to compare the experience of Bhilai, Rourkela and Durgapur as recipients of technology from different sources. Secondly, since steel is one of the two industries in which repetitive import of technology has taken place from the USSR, it enables us to assess how Soviet technology transfer to India has evolved over a period of three decades. We undertake the second exercise first, beginning by noting the features of Soviet technology transfer to the steel industry.

Soviet technical and financial assistance to the Indian steel industry is not confined to a heavy engineering plant and a metallurgical consultancy organisation; the USSR has also assisted in building two of

Table 6.2. *Imported and local supplies for public sector steel plants (percentages)*

Steel plant	Capacity (mt)	Equipment Indian	Imported	Structurals Indian	Imported	Refractories Indian	Imported
Rourkela	1.0	—	100	4	96	22	78
Bhilai	1.0	13	87	22	78	6	94
Durgapur	1.0	13	87	28	72	50	50
Expansion stage							
Rourkela	1.8	25	75	78	22	57	43
Bhilai	2.5	18	82	29	71	44	56
Durgapur	1.6	49	51	74	26	96	4
Bokaro first stage	1.7	60	40	94	6	61	39
Bokaro expansion	4.0	88	12	100	—	100	—

Source: UNCTAD 1978, TD/B/C.6/27.

India's four major public sector steel plants and is in the process of building a third. Bhilai and Bokaro, after expansion, each account for 4 million tonnes (henceforth mt) of the total public sector steel capacity of 11.5mt by the end of the Sixth Polan (1985), while Rourkela and Durgapur, the other two public sector plants, have stabilised at 1.8mt and 1.6mt respectively since the mid-sixties. The fifth major plant in the public sector, Vizag, adding a further 2.25mt in the Seventh Plan period, is also receiving financial and technical assistance from the USSR.

The first noticeable fact about Soviet technology transfer to the steel industry is that the indigenous content of supplies – equipment, structurals and refractories – has increased steadily from the 1mt stage of all three first generation plants through to their expansion stage (as table 6.2 shows). The import content of Bhilai at the expansion stage (2.5mt) is somewhat higher than that of the other plants, Durgapur and Rourkela. But there is quite a remarkable drop in the share of imported supplies for Bokaro's first stage. At the 4mt expansion stage, both Bhilai and Bokaro are almost entirely indigenously supplied.

Secondly, while the USSR has permitted an increasing use of local inputs, in terms of plant, machinery and construction equipment, it has not been equally keen on the sharing of the design and engineering work, at least in the steel industry (see table 6.3). As we argued in the previous chapter, the USSR's preferred mechanism of technology transfer is a near-turnkey arrangement. For example, in the late fifties, while the preparation of the DPR for the expansion of Rourkela and Durgapur (the German- and British-assisted plants) was entrusted

Table 6.3. *Consultants for Indian public sector steel plants*

Steel plant	Period	Capacity (mt)	Consultant
Bhilai	1955–61	1.0	Soviet
	1961–6	2.5	Soviet
	1967–	4.0	Soviet
Rourkela	1955–61	1.0	German
	1961–6	1.8	CEDB
Durgapur	1955–61	1.0	British
	1961–6	1.6	CEDB
Bokaro	1965–74	1.7	Soviet
	1975–	4.0	MECON
Vizag	1971–	1.15	Dasturco

Notes: 1. CEDB became MECON in 1973. 2. Dasturco were the associate consultants in Bokaro at both the first and second stages.
Source: Information drawn from various reports of CPU.

independently to CEDB, the DPR for Bhilai's expansion was prepared by Gipromez, with some assistance from the Bhilai Design Cell. Similarly, Bokaro was conceived in the early sixties by the Indian Planning Commission as an Indian plant, from 'conception to commissioning'. In fact, Dasturco, the Indian private steel consultancy firm, had prepared a DPR and been appointed Prime Consultants for Bokaro's 1.7mt stage, well before the Soviets entered the scene in the mid-sixties. However, when the Soviet offer of technical and financial assistance for Bokaro was made, it was contingent on Dasturco being reduced to a secondary role in the project. Again later, in the mid-seventies, at the 4mt stage of Bokaro, the Soviets prepared the DPR and would have preferred to continue as Prime Consultants (information obtained during personal interviews with SAIL officials). But MECON had to persuade the Ministry of Steel and the Russians to be permitted to take over the Russian role as Prime Consultants. MECON finally did become Bokaro's Prime Consultants, while Dasturco continued as the associate consultants.

Although MECON is the Prime Consultant for both Bhilai's and Bokaro's 4mt expansion stage, the process technology is almost entirely Soviet. Most of the units in the expansion stage are, in any case, identical to the first stage; hence, many of the drawings of the first stage are being utilised in the design of the expansion.

Thirdly, as table 6.4 shows, the setting up of the public sector steel plants involved a large-scale training programme abroad for Indian personnel. The reason why the training programme in the USSR seems larger than the others is that both engineers and workers were trained in the USSR, while only engineers were trained for the other plants. The other point about the training programme is that a much smaller number of Indian personnel were required to be trained in the USSR for the second Soviet plant, Bokaro (370 up to December 1976) than for the first one, Bhilai (1,081). This was because a Training Institute had started functioning in Bokaro itself in 1970 where over 2,500 personnel – graduate engineers, senior and junior operatives and artisan trainees – had been trained by 1976. Training in Soviet steel plants for Bokaro was confined to specific areas where specialised techniques were involved.

As regards foreign technicians for Bokaro, a Note by the Planning Commission had spoken of the need for thirty to forty technicians for a limited period. However, US Steel Corporation, which was earlier vying for the project (with the possible backing of US government bilateral aid to India), had wanted a maximum of 670 foreign technicians for a ten-year period. What is interesting is that a roughly similar number of Soviet specialists were stationed at Bokaro: 757 at the peak period of December 1975 (falling to 566 by March 1977). It is equally interesting that (as a former Chairman of Bokaro said in a personal interview) while US Steel wanted a management contract for ten years, the Soviets did not; however, in spite of the absence of any formal contract, in effect the Soviets were managing the plant, through a system of parallel management.

6.2.2 Comparison of three steel plants: Bhilai, Rourkela, Durgapur

Let us now turn to a comparison of the first three public sector plants set up in the fifties: Bhilai (Soviet), Durgapur (British) and Rourkela (West German). The comparison is interesting because the steel industry is perhaps the only public sector industry which has received technology from both Soviet and non-Soviet sources and at roughly the same period of time. The comparison may enable us to determine whether there were any special advantages for India in receiving technology from the USSR. The comparison is largely con-

Table 6.4. *Personnel trained abroad for public sector steel plants*

	Trained up to 1972				Trained between 1973 and 1975			
	Rourkela	Bhilai	Durgapur	Bokaro	Rourkela	Bhilai	Durgapur	Bokaro
Australia	36				2	1		
USSR	4	1,041		187	2	40	5	119
UK	11	12			3	5	2	
USA	407	6			2	1		
West Germany	288	10			57	1	1	
France	1	12			1	1	1	
Japan	5	4				1		
Others	9	27			3	5	1	
Total	761	1,112	674ᵃ	187	70	55	9	119

ᵃ Country-wise breakdown not available.
Source: Ministry of Steel 1976.

fined to the 1mt stage of the three plants, which was completed between 1955 and 1961.

A. *Capital cost* A committee of experts set up to study steel costs in India by the Government of India reported (in April 1966) that the capital costs of the three first generation steel plants built in the fifties were high (at the 1mt stage) compared to similar plants in other countries. It listed at least three items of capital cost which were not normal features of steel plants in other countries: 1. supplies and engineering work were mostly arranged on the turnkey basis from the countries extending the credit; 2. the plants made a provision for additional built-in capacity to be utilised later for expansion; and 3. since greenfield sites were opened for the new steel plants, the acquisition of greater land and construction of modern townships became essential. The gross block (cost of procuring and erecting the fixed assets) per tonne of ingot capacity fell for each of the three plants when they were expanded beyond 1mt: for Bhilai from Rs2,011 to Rs1,452 (2.5mt), for Rourkela from Rs2,350 to Rs2,278 (1.8mt), and for Durgapur from Rs1,950 to Rs1,656 (1.6mt) (Ministry of Steel 1976).

The capital cost at the 1mt stage was the highest for the Rourkela plant (at Rs2,331m); for Durgapur and Bhilai it was roughly the same (at Rs1,990m and Rs2,023m respectively) (CPU, *SAIL*, 1975/6, pp. 126–7). However, Rourkela, apart from having the most sophisticated equipment, also had the highest density of population of equipment. Rourkela is a producer of flat products, for which a greater amount of equipment is required; hence, the fixed cost in Russian terms would be higher.

In terms of capital cost, Bhilai was certainly more attractive than either Durgapur or Rourkela. While the capital cost and import content of the plant was roughly similar in the case of Bhilai and Durgapur (see table 6.5), a higher proportion of the foreign exchange component of Bhilai's cost was met by the Russians than was Durgapur's by the British. If one were to compare Bhilai with Rourkela, not only was a slightly higher proportion of the foreign exchange component of the cost met by Bhilai's supplier, but the terms of the Russian loans were also more favourable: 2.5 per cent interest and repayable over twelve years, to begin one year after the delivery of the equipment, as compared to 5.75 to 6.3 per cent interest, the repayment of which had to be periodically rescheduled on account of foreign exchange difficulties. The Russian loan, as usual, was repayable in rupees – another point in its favour.

Table 6.5. *Capital cost of three integrated steel plants (million US dollars)*

	Bhilai	Rourkela	Durgapur
Plant	316	464	331
Foreign exchange component	206–12	274	201
	(65–7%)	(59%)	(61%)
Portion covered by foreign loan	136	163	74
Foreign loan as percentage of foreign			
exchange cost	64–6%	60%	37%

Notes: 1. Figures in parentheses show foreign exchange component of total plant cost. 2. The table gives costs for 1mt stage only.
Source: HSL, *Annual Reports,* various issues.

B. Operational performance One crucial indicator of the relatively good performance of Bhilai is its high capacity utilisation. Through the seventies and eighties Bhilai's capacity utilisation has rarely fallen below 80 per cent, while Durgapur's has never exceeded 68 per cent; Rourkela's, though consistently higher than Durgapur's, has normally varied between 60 and 80 per cent. There are several factors which explain these differences.

The first is that tonnage-wise, Bhilai's ingot-producing capacity has been (inexplicably) underquoted by Soviet designers. Thus, though the steel melting shop capacity is stated to be 2.5mt, the equipment is capable of producing 3mt (at least in the USSR, according to a senior SAIL executive). This is not the case with Rourkela and Durgapur equipment, so that neither of these plants have ever operated near the rated capacity. Secondly, Rourkela was manufacturing flat products, a much more complicated product than that of either Bhilai or Durgapur. Thirdly, Rourkela used the LD (Linz-Donowitz) or oxygen-blowing system, which was pioneered in Asia for the first time in Rourkela in the late fifties. Since this particular steel technology (i.e. the LD blast furnace) had been introduced only a few years ago even in Europe, not all the technical problems had been mastered. Bhilai and Durgapur, on the other hand, worked on the age-old open-hearth process. US Steel and Bethlehem Steel of the USA introduced the LD system in their own plants only in the mid-sixties. Finally, Durgapur has been repeatedly beset with problems of industrial relations, making normal operation difficult to achieve.

Bhilai's higher capacity utilisation is reflected in its higher net profits. Rourkela's profits, though not as high as Bhilai's, are in strong contrast to Durgapur, which has suffered losses oftener than it has shown profits.

C. Transfer of technology and manpower development The comparatively better performance of Bhilai is a result of a combination of human and technical factors. In the fifties there was an extreme shortage of both skilled workers and engineers to man the steel plants. From the inception of Hindustan Steel Ltd (HSL) its *Annual Report* complained of the difficulties of recruiting experienced steel men. Even as late as 1960/1, HSL's *Annual Report* stated:

> While a large number of graduate apprentices and other junior engineers have been recruited, it has not been possible to obtain the necessary experienced senior personnel . . . To meet the shortage in the middle management personnel, a number of foreign technicians have been engaged for the three plants.

In such circumstances, with machine-operating skills and knowledge of steel-manufacturing technology running at such low levels, 'the in-built rigidity or tolerance in Russian equipment for misuse and mal-operation by the fifty per cent skill-culture of Indian workers' was a great advantage of Bhilai.[7] On the other hand, the more sophisticated German equipment at Rourkela has taken Indian personnel longer to learn to handle properly. Overall this seems like a good argument for LDCs in the early stages of their industrialisation to buy equipment and machinery from the USSR (or other developed CPEs). It was stated that the Russian equipment was normally over-designed. Thus, from the design angle a crane auxiliary hoist may require a 2.2kW motor to drive it; the Germans would give it a 2.5kW motor, while the Russians will give it a 5kW motor. The compulsions of competition in a capitalist economy ensure that German equipment is economical in space, function and cost; the difficulty for an LDC arises since such relatively sophisticated equipment assumes that the level of operating skills in the recipient of technology is as high as in the donor country.

Yet another problem was that the bulk of the personnel trained abroad for Rourkela went to the USA. Besides, most of these trainees were engineers (not workers) who were not going to actually operate the equipment. For Bhilai, on the other hand, both engineers and workers were trained in the USSR. In fact, as many skilled workers/operatives were trained in the USSR as engineers, naturally raising the total number of personnel trained there (see table 6.4). For Durgapur and Rourkela, only engineers received training abroad, mostly in Germany, the UK, the USA and Australia (partly under multilateral

schemes, e.g. the Colombo Plan). Naturally, Bhilai had the advantage
of a larger trained staff available at its disposal compared with the other
two plants. Rourkela engineers faced yet another problem: language
(though in the British Durgapur plant the problem obviously did not
arise). Although there was a system of seconding Indians to German
supervisors at Rourkela, there remained a language barrier, which
compounded the problem of absorbing a more sophisticated technology. On the other hand, every engineer trainee who went to Russia
had to learn Russian.[8] The cumulative result of all these factors has
been that while manufacturing technology was absorbed quite quickly
in Bhilai, it took much longer at Rourkela, and some problems still
remain.

Durgapur's low capacity utilisation can be largely explained by the
fact that it has been dogged by poor industrial relations since two years
after the British experts left. Unscheduled stoppages of work in a
process industry like steel can cause serious problems, since certain
continuously working units like coke ovens, blast furnaces and steel-
melting shops cannot be switched on and off (though rolling mills can
be). Periodic stoppages meant damage to equipment increasing down-
time for repairs resulting in low capacity utilisation. 'But', as a senior
executive stated, 'there was obviously no language barrier in Durgapur
and the kind of problems encountered in Rourkela with operating the
equipment do not exist. Durgapur's import substitution efforts are
adequate; maintenance/repairs and operation technology are up to the
mark. By default we have absorbed the technology.'

As regards spares for equipment, there exists an interesting contrast. In Bhilai there were no problems for the first ten years, since
spares in sufficient quantities had been provided by the suppliers;
when the need for further imports arose, procurement was also easy.
Since the late sixties, HEC and private sector firms have been supplying spares; a number of ancillary firms which have grown around the
steel plant in Bhilai have also been meeting the plant's needs. The
Soviet experts handed over all the necessary drawings and know-how
for spares. Actually, the British too parted with the design drawings
for equipment spares for Durgapur; however, the Germans did not. As
a result, there was continued dependence on German firms for spare
parts. Thus, while imports of spares were costing Rourkela Rs80m per
annum in foreign exchange, spares imports for Bhilai only amounted
to Rs10m per annum (information supplied during personal
interview).

The German engineers in possession of the drawings and operation manual needed for erection/commissioning were generally reluctant to pass them to their Indian counterparts after the expiry of the contract.[9] No drawings were transferred for fault detection; Rourkela has developed these on its own. If in spite of these difficulties, compounded by the relatively greater sophistication of the process technology, Rourkela is a profit-making plant, it is because of its monopoly status in its particular product. Until the mid-seventies when Bokaro started production, Rourkela was the only major flat steel products manufacturer in India.

One aspect of Soviet technology transfer pointed out by several executives was the excellence of their system of preventive maintenance. It is characterised by heavy staffing (almost amounting to overmanning) and narrow specialisation. While the Americans or Germans would supply a minimum number of personnel to execute a job, the Russians preferred functioning in a group.[10]

A related feature of Soviet technology transfer in steel has been the Soviet parallel management in Indian steel plants, similar in fact to the system of party and technical experts working in tandem within the USSR. Thus in the Indian plants they have a General Manager (Works) who is the counterpart of an Indian executive with the same designation; similarly, the Russians have a Chief Engineer (Mechanical) and Chief Engineer (Electrical) who are both counterparts of Indian officers. They even have a parallel system of reporting. Thus, the Ministry of Steel (which has administrative responsibility for the plant making it accountable to Parliament) would receive reports not just from the plant's General Manager (an Indian), but also from the plant's Soviet chief via the Commercial Counsellor of the Soviet embassy in New Delhi, although the latter reports would be of an unofficial character.

The consensus (among Indian technocrats interviewed) about the parallel management phenomenon was that the Russians' concern is simply that the plants run properly, since that affects their image. In Bhilai they were in competition with the Germans and the British. In Bokaro they had taken up the project after the Americans had refused assistance to it. A former Chairman of Bokaro pointed out the similarity between the American proposal of managing the plant for ten years and the de facto (though unofficial) system of parallel management run by the Soviets. It was suggested that the system was acquiesced in at the plant level because it saved the skins of the Indian managers when problems arose. Hence if the ministry is faced with support for the system from two quarters – the Soviets and the plant – it has little choice but to accept the continued existence of Soviet experts at the plant.

Thus while the relationship with the other collaborators has been of a commercial nature, that is not strictly so with the Soviets. For instance, one major difference between the contract for Bhilai on the one hand and Rourkela and Durgapur on the other was that the former called for Soviet operation of the plant at rated capacity for six months. At Rourkela and Durgapur, on the other hand, the commissioning was carried out by the collaborators, and the plant was taken over by Indians after initial starting up. Performance guarantees are normally applicable only for a 24-hour period or at most for a week; this is the practice the Germans and the British followed. Now the Russians follow the latter practice too (e.g. in Bokaro); but Bhilai was more than a contractual or commercial affair. This was further demonstrated by the fact that they deputed some of their most competent experts to Bhilai, including Venyamin Dymsyts, who was later to become Chairman of Gosplan.

The British experts in Durgapur left in 1964, even before its expansion from 1mt to 1.6mt had been completed. At Rourkela, the German technicians left in 1971, a few years after the expansion from 1mt to 1.8mt had been accomplished. At Bhilai, where neither the technology nor the product was as sophisticated as in Rourkela, Soviet personnel have stayed; and not all of the roughly 300 or so at present in Bhilai are there on account of its ongoing expansion to 4mt. Although Indian engineers consider them unnecessary, the responsible ministry officials would be unwilling to displease their political superiors. Clearly the essentially political nature of the Indo-Soviet relationship occasionally also has its repercussions in directly economic terms.

Before we draw this discussion on Soviet technology transfer to the steel industry to a close, one should note some features of the most recent phase in Soviet assistance, i.e. the building of a third new steel plant (Vizag) and the modernisation of old ones (Bhilai and Burnpur). Of the enormous total cost of the 3.4mt plant (Rs40,000m), the foreign exchange component will be 17 per cent (Rs7,000m), of which about two-thirds is being met by a Soviet credit (of Rs4,500m).

What is interesting about this new steel plant is that of the 30 per cent of the total equipment requirements to be imported, only half will be from the USSR, the rest mostly from the West.[11] How did this unique situation come about? The DPR was prepared by the Soviets incorporating Soviet and other CMEA technologies (GDR and Czechoslovakia). However, when the question of extending credit arose, technology imports from the USSR alone were covered and not those from other CMEA countries. The funds of IBEC, the CMEA's international bank for economic cooperation, were not sought to be utilised. The end result was that certain equipment which could have been imported from the GDR, Czechoslovakia and Poland was acquired after floating global tenders and was purchased from Western countries. Some equipment is even being purchased from Bulgaria against free foreign exchange.

In other words, had the CMEA countries adopted a consortium approach, as many large firms from the DMEs often do, all imported equipment for Vizag would probably have been acquired from the CPEs. The CMEA countries operate a division of labour among themselves as regards machinery, as for many other manufactures. For instance, for an engineering project requiring a wide range of machine-tools the Comecon countries do not offer a single window. The Indian customer is required to deal with two or more countries and therefore needs to carry out the coordination and dove-tailing on his own. This too makes it easier for him to deal with firms from advanced capitalist countries.

A final point of interest about Soviet technology transfer to the steel industry is the modernisation of existing steel plants, Bhilai, Bokaro and Burnpur – a new area of Soviet cooperation in the eighties. We argued in chapter 5 that the diffusion of technology acquired will have considerable externalities in terms of technology transfer. In this context a point of interest about the modernisation scheme is that in response to the desire expressed by the Government of India, the Soviets have agreed that all improvements in technology effected in Bhilai and Bokaro can be utilised in other steel plants and by the Indian steel industry as a whole. This Soviet approval for a scheme for horizontal technology transfer is rather unusual for the USSR in its relationship with India, considering the Indo-Soviet firm level contracts have not explicitly permitted such transfers.

6.2.3 Oil exploration and production

From the fifties until the late sixties, seven vertically integrated multinational firms dominated the world oil industry by controlling all its stages: exploration, production, refining, transportation and marketing. But the period after 1955 saw a rapid increase in Soviet crude oil production and an even more rapid increase in exports, which brought the USSR into open conflict with the major oil firms.

First, this undermined the world-parity pricing system. Several governments – particularly the Indian and Cuban – attempted to induce the oil refineries owned by the major oil firms to process cheaper Soviet crude in place of crude supplied by their parent companies at posted prices. Secondly, the USSR was prepared to build oil refineries in poor oil-consuming countries in the public sector and without any equity participation (see next sub-section). Finally, the USSR also emerged as an alternative supplier of technology for oil exploration (see Dasgupta 1971 and Tanzer 1969).

At the same time, the major oil companies, who already owned vast oil refineries in the Middle East, were not keen to explore for oil in areas (e.g. India) where the probability of finding oil was not high, and where new discoveries would only have the effect of replacing crude oil supplies from the Middle East (see Dasgupta 1971, ch. 9). Against this background, the Indian government came to the conclusion that oil exploration would have to be taken up in the state sector (see earlier discussion on Industrial Policy Resolution, 1956). In 1955, except for indigenous crude production of less than half a million tonnes, India's entire requirements (i.e. over 90 per cent) had to be imported. The investment in oil was therefore justified on grounds of the resulting foreign exchange savings.

Only the USSR was prepared to extend assistance for oil exploration. An Indian government statement later explained:

> When it was decided that local exploration should be undertaken, principally but not exclusively as a government enterprise, an approach was made to a large number of countries for technical and financial assistance. Initially, only the USSR and Rumania offered to help. For this reason, a major part of the exploration and production activity in the country today is carried on with the support of these countries.[12]

To summarise Soviet technology transfer to the oil exploration/production industry, their contribution lay in 1. providing most of the equipment for exploration; 2. carrying out seismic surveys, both on- and offshore; 3. training a very large number of ONGC personnel in India; and 4. assisting in establishing a design institute and an R&D establishment. The Soviet influence is most evident in drilling technology; the design concept in oilfield development in India was derived from the Soviet Union. However, the Soviet technological influence on ONGC is confined to onshore exploration and drilling, which has contributed a relatively small proportion of domestic production since production from the offshore Bombay High structure started in the mid-seventies. Most of ONGC's technological capability in offshore drilling has been derived from Western sources.

The overall economic impact of Soviet assistance was to break the complete monopoly exercised by the international majors in India by enabling the growth of the public sector in all stages of the oil industry – exploration, production, refining and distribution. This led to a foreign exchange saving in several ways: 1. public sector oil exploration and production reduced crude imports to some extent; 2. the Soviet crude offer in 1960 enabled India to take advantage of discounts on the posted prices of the crude oil purchased by foreign companies;[13] and 3. public sector refineries resulted in further foreign exchange savings by reducing remittance of income by wholly foreign-owned refineries.

6.2.4 Oil refining

The foreign-owned refineries in India had refused to refine Soviet-supplied crude, claiming that they had an agreement with their parent firms in the Middle East. Moreover, the minimal exploration efforts undertaken by the oil companies in India had yielded no results. So naturally, when crude was actually discovered with Soviet assistance in India it was logical for the Indian government to seek Soviet assistance to set up oil refineries as well. Thus the Gauhati and Barauni refineries in east India were set up to refine crude from wells discovered in Assam, while Koyali in the west has been refining oil from wells in Gujarat.

Till the early sixties all the four refineries in India were foreign-owned. However, the setting up of public sector refineries from the early sixties onwards strengthened the Indian government's bargaining position in future negotiations in respect of equity ownership (e.g. in the two joint sector refineries at Cochin and Madras). It also enabled independent companies (outside the circle of the seven international majors) to bid in the Indian petroleum industry. For example, in 1965, in its Madras refinery bid, Burmah-Shell was prepared to accept a 51 per cent share for the Indian government and restricted dividend payments for itself.

In 1984/5 India had twelve oil refineries, ten of them in the public sector (all the four foreign-owned ones having been nationalised in the mid-seventies) and two in the joint sector. Three of the ten public sector refineries (Barauni, Koyali and Mathura) were built with Soviet technical and financial assistance and two with Rumanian. Together,

Table 6.6. *Capital costs of public/joint sector oil refineries*

Location	Capacity (mt) 1	Total cost (Rsm) 2	Foreign exchange component (Rsm) 3	% 4	Collaborator 5
Gauhati	0.75	159.9	64.3	40	Rumania
Barauni	3.0	489.8	266.3	54	USSR
Koyali	3.0	286.0	132.9	46	USSR
Cochin	2.5	282.5	181.3	64	Phillips (USA)

Notes: 1. At the 2mt stage, the total cost of Barauni was Rs464m and that of Koyali Rs262m. The third mt in both cases cost merely another Rs25m or so each. 2. All four refineries went on stream between 1961 and 1966. 3. *Public Enterprises Survey* gives a lower figure for foreign exchange component of Barauni and Koyali: Rs177m and Rs96m respectively.
Sources: BPE, *Public Enterprises Survey*, various issues, and CPU, *Indian Oil Corporation*, 1967 and 1973/4, for column 2; Ministry of Finance 1980/1 for column 3; Vedavalli 1976 for figures on Cochin.

the three Soviet-built refineries account for 16.6mt of refining capacity of a total capacity of roughly 34mt.

Marshall Goldman, and later, Asha Datar, have argued on the basis of a comparison of Gauhati (Rumanian) and Barauni (Soviet) on the one hand, with Cochin (private sector) on the other, that the Soviet and Rumanian plants were dearer than the plants built with the collaboration of the private sector (Goldman 1967, pp. 95–100; Datar 1972, pp. 247–51). If the attempt is to establish the profitability to the donor, then surely the foreign exchange component of the total cost, rather than the total cost per se, is the more important criterion; Cochin's foreign exchange component, as a percentage of total cost is far higher than that of any other refinery (see table 6.6). Moreover, since Cochin was to refine imported crude, the collaborators (Phillips) were prepared to accept a lower overall price for Cochin, as long as high profits in crude imports were ensured.

Since Barauni, Gauhati and Cochin were built on a turnkey or near-turnkey arrangement, it is more likely that they were more expensive than if the technology had been obtained in an 'unpackaged' form. However, given the oligopolistic nature of the international oil industry in the late fifties and the lack of Indian experience in refinery technology, the unpackaging of the technology may not have been a realistic alternative.

It is true that the foreign exchange and total cost of the first Soviet-built refinery, Barauni, is much higher than that of the second, Koyali. Datar may be right in suggesting that for Koyali the Soviets may have had to revise their costs downwards 'for political reasons' (Datar 1972, p. 249). But it is equally likely that Barauni's foreign exchange costs are so high primarily because it was undertaken as a near-turnkey operation. For Koyali, on the other hand, a large proportion of the design work was done by Indians, and a substantial share of the equipment was procured indigenously. Since equipment supply and design work account for an overwhelming proportion of foreign exchange costs, Koyali's lower overall and foreign costs are hardly surprising.

The first generation of refineries, like all the first generation steel plants, were designed entirely abroad – both the private as well as the public sector ones. Thus the three foreign-owned refineries set up between 1954 and 1957, as well as the first two public sector ones at Gauhati (Rumanian) and Barauni (Soviet), were designed by the collaborators. But drawing upon the experience of these two public sector refineries, the contract with Tiazhpromexport for the third, Koyali, provided for 40 per cent of the design work (for the 2mt stage) to be the responsibility of Indians. Accordingly, a nucleus of a design cell (later called Design Organisation) was set up in Koyali, with the help of Soviet training, to undertake the designing of the refinery (IOC, *6th Annual Report*, 1964/5). Later, having been so closely associated with the first stage of Koyali, Indian design engineers went on to prepare successfully all the detailed drawings for the 3mt expansion of both Koyali and Barauni, on the basis of drawings available from the previous stage.

As regards the use of Indian equipment, Vedavalli writing about the foreign-owned refineries established in the fifties notes: 'Although the refineries did make some attempt to substitute for imports in the sixties, not much was achieved until the public sector entered the field of petroleum refining' (Vedavalli 1976, p. 178). The Koyali refinery utilised about 60 per cent of equipment and materials from indigenous sources for the 2mt stage and about 75 per cent for expansion to 3mt (CPU, *IOC*, 1973/4, para. 7.16). The import content of equipment for auxiliary services fell with each Soviet-assisted refinery. For example, for Barauni, the tanks needed to store products in a refinery were supplied by the Soviets; for Koyali and, of course, Mathura, the tanks were of completely Indian fabrication, while conforming to Indian design. The cooling unit was provided by the Soviets in Barauni; for Koyali and Mathura it was indigenous. The power plant for Koyali and Barauni was imported; in Mathura it was Indian. The water treatment plant in Barauni was Soviet; for Koyali and Mathura indigenous. The electrical distribution system for Barauni was supplied by the collaborators; in Koyali, it was partly indigenous and partly Soviet, and by the late seventies, for Mathura, it was entirely indigenous. (Information gathered during personal interviews.)

This trend was accelerated during the construction of the joint sector refinery at Madras (in collaboration with the National Iranian Oil Company) in 1967 and 1968. However, the first major breakthrough in Indian design and construction of refinery projects came with the construction of a 2.5mt public sector refinery at Haldia (West Bengal) with Rumanian and French assistance (commissioned 1974). This project was executed by Engineers India Ltd (EIL), a public sector engineering consultancy organisation (set up in 1967/8).[14] While Soviet firms had been Consultants for Barauni and Koyali up to their expansion to 3mt, EIL was the Consultant not just for the Haldia refinery, but also for the expansion of Koyali to 7.3mt (commissioned 1978) and the third Soviet-aided refinery at Mathura (capacity 6mt; commissioned 1983). As a result, the overall foreign exchange content of the capital cost of Haldia was only 19 per cent while that of Mathura was even less at 12 per cent (of which Soviet participation accounted for 8 per cent).

Clearly indigenous technological capability has increased with every succeeding project. Thus the technology for all non-patented units of a refinery has been fully absorbed. This includes many of the basic units making up a refinery – atmospheric distillation unit, vacuum unit, bitumen unit and vis-breakers. However, for the three most recent refinery projects (Haldia, Koyali expansion and Mathura) foreign assistance is still being utilised in the form of know-how/process design for specific units (involving the purchase of licences) and some imported equipment.[15]

As in the case of equipment supply and design work, an increasing proportion of training to Indian personnel has been imparted in India and by Indians. While for Barauni a large number of Indians were trained in the USSR, for Koyali fewer were trained abroad, for a shorter time period and only for special units (e.g. the catalytic reformer). For the Mathura refinery, almost no training was given in the USSR. Similarly, the maximum number of Soviet specialists in Mathura at any time was about twelve to fifteen, compared to approximately a hundred in Koyali and two hundred in Barauni. Further evidence of the Indian command over refinery technology is that Indian specialists dictated the design basis for Mathura, while for Koyali and Barauni it was dictated by the Soviets. For Koyali and Barauni the design basis furnished by Indian specialists hardly made a ten-page document; for Mathura it was a huge volume. It is also useful to note that for equipment in Soviet-built refineries, India has been able to manufacture the spares (or substitute equipment with other indigenously available equipment or components). For Barauni and Koyali, the Soviets provided the design documentation for spares with the equipment. Such drawings of spares that were not given had to be prepared by the Central Design Organisation. For Mathura, most of the spares will be indigenous, because the equipment is indigenous.

However, it must be recognised that this technological capability is not only the product of earlier Soviet assistance. Three new refineries had been set up in the fifties by the international majors (Esso, Caltex and Burmah-Shell). As Vedavalli notes:

> The [private sector] petroleum industry in India has also had an effect on the country's economy in the form of technological linkages, such as training labour and introducing new technologies. The setting up of refineries initially attracted managers, technicians, and skilled labour from abroad to work for the oil companies. But the companies have undertaken training schemes at all levels in order to employ local personnel as rapidly as possible: as a result by 1970 the number of expatriates in the three private foreign companies had been reduced to a maximum of one or two people. (Vedavalli 1976, p. 179)

However, as we said earlier, there was no contribution of the private sector refineries in the field of design. Whatever progress was achieved in this field followed the rise of the public sector in the industry. Secondly, although the foreign-owned refineries made some attempt to substitute for imported equipment, not much was achieved until the public sector entered the field of petroleum refining. Thirdly, the entry of the state, with Soviet and Rumanian assistance, into oil refining improved its bargaining position and enabled it to secure better terms in the setting up of the joint venture refineries in the sixties. Fourthly, state-owned refineries financed with Soviet credits had a more favourable balance of payments impact than did the foreign private refineries (Vedavalli 1976, pp. 167–71). Finally, the major backward linkage of the refining industry is crude oil exploration and production. The terms of the refinery agreements with the three major oil companies stated that they were to obtain crude supplies from the Middle East; there was no incentive to take part in oil exploration. However, the public sector refineries were established specifically to refine crude oil from fields discovered and developed with Soviet assistance.

6.3 The consumer goods sector

6.3.1 Pharmaceuticals

Like the oil-refining industry, the pharmaceuticals industry in India was also dominated in the fifties by large transnational corporations. Although formulations technology is relatively simple, Indian manufacture of formulations did not develop since the transnationals controlled the raw material supply through the international patent system. Pharmaceutical manufacturing technology consists of two components: raw material manufacture (i.e. bulk as it is called) and dosage form fabrication. The technology of formulation fabrication is simpler and more widespread than that of bulk drug production. Pharmaceuticals is now perhaps the only major industry in the world which depends on patent-generated monopoly to protect its innovations. The main role of Soviet assistance lay in breaking the monopoly of drugs transnationals over bulk supplies to Indian firms. Another important contribution of Soviet assistance in the area of drugs was assistance in the production of essential drugs. The adverse balance of payments effects of the presence of foreign subsidiaries in the pharmaceuticals industry may be balanced by such benefits as generation of employment and production of life-saving essential drugs. However, it is well known that the output of the foreign sector in the Indian drugs industry is concentrated in inessential products such as tonics, cough syrups and the like, primarily for the consumption of the higher income groups. It is equally well known that in order to handle the health problems of LDCs what is required is a basic needs approach (as insisted upon by UNCTAD and the World Health Organisation). Among other things, such an approach would involve a national drugs policy; the first step in formulating such a policy is for every country to draw up a list of drugs essential to the well-being of a majority of the population.

Apart from the product-mix of drug transnationals, it is equally important that the foreign subsidiaries in India contributed only 11 per cent of the total tonnage of bulk drug production and about 27 per cent of turnover even as late as 1978/9. They have concentrated on the low capital-intensive and high profit area of formulations, in which foreign subsidiaries have a massive 44 per cent of the domestic market. On the other hand, the public sector, comprising Hindustan Antibiotics Ltd (HAL) and the Soviet-aided Indian Drugs and Pharmaceuticals Ltd (IDPL), supply 28 per cent of the capital and technology-intensive bulk drugs produced in India, while their share of formulations (an area dominated by foreign brand names) is under 6 per cent. Hence, it is in the two key areas of essential drug production and bulk drug production that the contribution of Soviet financial and technical assistance lies.

It was well known in the fifties that Soviet technology in drug production was a poor substitute for the technology available with the west European and US transnationals. In 1956, when the drugs projects in the public sector were being discussed, an Indian delegation, after visiting several countries, including the USSR and east Europe, recommended that the government should adopt a selective approach, buying technology for different groups from different sources. The Kane Committee recommended:

> It must be admitted that in the antibiotics field the techniques employed in western Europe and in the USA are more advanced [than in the USSR] and the yields are higher [per unit of raw material consumed]. A similar position exists with respect to some of the vitamins. Since the cost of production of a drug will depend to a great extent upon the yields obtained in each process, it would appear desirable to explore other sources of collaboration in these fields before taking final decisions. (CPU, *IDPL*, 1968/9, para. 2.1)

The question is why, in spite of the recommendation of a committee of experts against buying Soviet technology in a package, did the Indian government seek Soviet technical assistance in precisely that form? A partial explanation lies in the government's reason for rejecting the option of purchasing technology from the transnationals. The reason was twofold: first, the payment terms with the drug transnationals would have been onerous; and second, even if India accepted the payments (technical fees, royalties, etc.) involved, patent restrictions would have prevented a complete transfer of technology.

It could be argued that if the transnationals were prepared to invest in India, why should transfer of technology have been so important? Literature on the subject of technology transfer has shown that foreign firms prefer to transfer technology through foreign investment, which gives them the power to control the management and policies of local firms in the host country with a view to securing control over the accumulation of surplus and its disposal. In fact, the extent of foreign ownership of capital helps to determine the degree of sophistication of technology that is offered by the latter (Balasubramanyam 1973, p. 51). In India the relative desire and potential for control varies from industry to industry. In general, foreign control is concentrated in technology-intensive and patent-protected industries like machinery and pharmaceuticals (K. K. Subramaniam 1972, p. 281).

The government, therefore, was probably justified in believing that, as in the case of oil exploration, the transnationals would be uninterested in investing in India, particularly since all the bulk drugs (i.e. intermediates for production of formulations) were being imported from them. Even if the transnationals agreed to a joint venture, heavy royalties would have had to be paid in order to acquire the patents (as was, in fact, pointed out by the Kane Committee). The government's view was reinforced by the result of negotiations conducted by them for certain drug intermediate products. In 1955 the Italian firm Montcatini was commissioned to prepare a survey report on the best manner of producing these intermediates. The German transnational Bayer and the UK's ICI volunteered to prepare their own report. The terms quoted by the German firm seemed much tougher than those offered by the Soviets. Bayer offered a supplier's credit at 7.5 per cent interest, continuous payment of royalty and 10 per cent immediate payment of the total sum. The Soviets offered financial assistance on concessional terms (though harsher than usual): 2.5 per cent interest, a grace period equal to the period of delivery of machinery and equipment plus one year, and a period of repayment (excluding grace period) of seven years; as usual, the loan was repayable in rupees rather than hard currency. It must be noted that the Soviet loan for IDPL was the harshest ever extended to India, requiring repayment within seven years rather than the usual twelve years in the fifties and sixties and twenty years in the seventies and eighties. The government concluded that in the circumstances the USSR was the most suitable collaborator even though their technology was 'second best'. However, no comparative assessment was made of the total foreign exchange to be expended by way of technical fees and royalty and likely capital cost (and import content thereof) at which the units of IDPL could be set up with Soviet assistance.

A subsidiary reason for choosing to collaborate with the USSR was that the designs of the plants were readily available from them. In a note to the government Kane stated:

> Experts of the USSR have designed pharmaceuticals and drugs plants for some east European countries [Czechoslovakia and Rumania] and China. Some of these units have capacities similar to those recommended for establishment in India by the USSR team of experts. The drawings and details of equipment are therefore readily available and if it is decided to seek their collaboration, there may be a saving in time. (CPU, *IDPL*, 1968/9, para. 2.2)

The disadvantage, however, was that several items were included in the product-mix which the Kane Committee had advised against either on technological grounds (e.g. vitamins, antibiotics) or because they were already being manufactured in India (e.g. penicillin by Hindustan Antibiotics Ltd). But it must be emphasised that the Indian government was not negotiating a single project. It was rather negotiating a package deal for four projects in the medical industry – an antibiotics plant, a synthetic drugs plant, a surgical instruments plant and phytochemicals plant (the last of which never materialised). Hence its bargaining capacity as regards the inclusion in the product-mix of individual items for particular projects was likely to be relatively limited.

Some of the features of the technology transfer to IDPL may now be noted. First, at the project preparation stage there was no great concern either on the Soviet or Indian side about cost estimates or profitability of the plants. In fact, the Soviet DPR was found to be based on inaccurate or insufficient data. IDPL's Chairman informed the CPU that when the feasibility report (1958) was submitted by the Soviets, their stated objective was to set up the plant; however, they did not say that the plant would make a profit.[16] The Soviets merely stated that in making these recommendations for the development of the Indian medical industry, they had borne in mind the objectives of freeing the country from the import of these drugs, utilisation of indigenous resources and rationally utilising Soviet credit. In their view the benefits were not to accrue to the plant, but to the economy as a whole in the form of foreign exchange savings (CPU, *IDPL*, 1968/9, para. 8.13). It may be argued that the objective of freeing the economy of import dependence is not an obviously desirable goal and could be achieved through protection and private foreign investment. However, as we have argued above, since the transnationals were supplying the basic inputs for drug formulation in India, the foreign exchange cost (in hard currency) of foreign investment in this research-intensive, patent-protected industry would have been considerable.

The second feature of Soviet collaboration in the public sector pharmaceutical industry is that the advantages of foreign exchange savings and transfer of know-how must be balanced against the costs of purchasing technology which, as we have argued above, was inferior to that available on the world market. The Soviet DPR had, for instance, provided for norms to be attained at each stage of production. For many years, the process deficiencies of Soviet drug manufacturing technology led to lower efficiencies, higher time-cycles and higher rejection rates in both the antibiotics and synthetic drugs plants.

Repeated modifications had to be carried out to the manufacturing process because the Soviets had no patents of their own. They had to bypass the existing patents and evolve a new procedure. In fact the Soviets were probably experimenting with the antibiotics project of IDPL to get around the patents.

Yet another factor complicating the transfer of technology was that the USSR State Pharmacopoeia was not accepted in India. Drugs marketed in India have to satisfy the requirements of Indian Pharmacopoeia (IP) which had accepted the British and US pharmacopeia in order to market foreign drugs. The pharmacopoeial standards of the USSR were lower than those of the USA, Britain or even in exceptional cases IP. Hence the market requirements also forced modifications in IDPL's products.

The modifications resulting from the deficiencies in Soviet know-how led to long construction and gestation periods. Consequently, the capital cost estimates of IDPL projects were revised five times between 1961 and 1968. The increase in capital costs of 117 per cent for the antibiotics plant and 90 per cent for the synthetic drugs plant between the first estimate and actual expenditure was the highest percentage increase for any Soviet-aided project, and quite remarkable even by the standards of Indian public sector enterprises.

Thirdly, the technological problems and process deficiencies mentioned earlier were resolved by the joint efforts of Soviet and Indian technologists. The latter were assisted in this task by the Soviet provision for an R&D laboratory, a pilot plant and an Engineering Design Workshop and by Soviet supplies of special laboratory equipment. Training for the antibiotics and synthetic drugs plants was carried out in the USSR for 113 Indian personnel. The research wings of the two drugs plants focused their attention on improving the existing technology of drugs and effecting import substitution in raw materials wherever possible. Although IDPL's R&D effort has not resulted in new products or drugs being discovered, in certain products IDPL was, in the early eighties, in a position to carry out a reverse transfer of technology to the USSR.

Fourthly, IDPL's experience of transfer of technology from the USSR was dominated by the provision for excess built-in capacity, a feature of Soviet technology transfer we have encountered before. For instance, the capacity provided for in the antibiotics plant was well above that initially requested by the Indian government.[17] The synthetic drugs plant was similarly burdened, although to a lesser degree, with excess capacity for certain drugs. The obvious result was a severe under-utilisation of capacity with inevitable effects on financial performance. In addition to excess built-in capacity, the surgical instruments plant of IDPL encountered another problem which has been a feature of Soviet technology transfer – narrow product-range. A catalogue of any standard firm producing surgical instruments would probably contain 2,000 to 3,000 items. Only a few of these items are required in large numbers. Most sophisticated instruments are hand-made and required in small quantities. However, IDPL's surgical instruments plant was conceived and designed as a plant for mass production of only 166 types of instruments. Incredibly enough, no market survey was carried out prior to the decision on the product-mix. Even the instruments produced by the plant were found unacceptable in the domestic market, either because they were too heavy or had different specifications from those Indian doctors were used to. The plant's capacity was partially utilised by exporting almost the entire output to the USSR for nearly a decade after production started; after exports stopped (because Soviet prices, according to IDPL, were too low), its capacity has remained almost entirely unutilised.

Drugs and pharmaceuticals are a research-intensive high technology industry. IDPL spent 1.5 per cent of its net sales in 1981/2 on R&D (1.7 per cent in 1980/1 and 1.6 per cent in 1979/80), which, however, is low by international standards, with the transnationals spending over 10 per cent of sales turnover on R&D. The most senior research scientist of IDPL's Research Centre considers this expenditure on R&D to have been effective:

> The R&D Wing of IDPL Hyderabad, which has now [1981] developed into a full-fledged Research Centre for development of chemical technology and drug research, has not only been instrumental in assimilating and updating the original technology imported from the USSR but also played a role in indigenisation of the technology and further diversification of the product-mix. (Sridhar 1981)

The Soviet collaborators originally designed the Synthetic Drugs Plant (SDP) to produce 851 tonnes of basic drugs. The capacity was doubled to 1,697 tonnes without any foreign collaboration. This was achieved by rationalisation of processes and the introduction of eleven new products to the original product-mix of sixteen. In the second phase of expansion, it is planned to raise the SDP's capacity to 3,179 tonnes of bulk drugs with thirty-six drugs in the product-mix. And as the same Research Centre scientist goes on to claim: 'The entire diversification of the product-mix during the Second Phase Expansion Programme during the Fifth Plan period has been carried out by its own R&D.'

Perhaps equally impressive is the fact that technology for some of the products bought from the USSR has been improved and has now been transferred by IDPL to the USSR, e.g. antibiotics yield, Vitamin B1 (for which Kane had advised against buying Soviet technology).[18]

It should be added that the senior scientist does qualify his claims about IDPL's research efforts:

> However, our R&D effort has been mainly concentrated on the development of technologies more or less on the beaten lines or in assimilating and updating the imported technologies ... Our R&D has done precious little in the field of discovering any new drugs or products. Our dependence on foreign discoveries is complete ... There is a considerable lag in establishing their technologies within the country. (Sridhar 1981)

However, a complete evaluation of IDPL must take into account the externalities and linkage effects of setting it up. First, of IDPL's domestic sales of drugs, around 60 per cent (in value terms) consist of formulations, the remainder being in the form of bulk drugs (ready for preparation of formulations), which are sold to the foreign, organised private, and small-scale sectors of the pharmaceuticals industry in India (IDPL, *Annual Reports*, various issues). Before IDPL came into being, bulk drugs were almost entirely imported from the drug transnationals abroad. However, many transnational subsidiaries also set up plants to produce bulk drugs in India after IDPL entered the market; India's strategy of import substitution provided a seller's market protected by high tariff walls and import restrictions. IDPL was thus responsible not only for breaking the transnationals' monopoly over the supply of bulk drugs, but compelling them to produce bulk drugs domestically. By the mid-seventies nineteen foreign firms were engaged in bulk drug production; foreign units accounted for 34 per cent of the number of bulk drug producers and 38 per cent of the total investment (but they contributed only 11 per cent of the total tonnage of bulk drug production and about 27 per cent of turnover) (Ministry of Petroleum and Chemicals 1975, p. 86). It is interesting that IDPL supplied bulk drugs not only to many small and medium firms, but to foreign firms as well. On the other hand, the nineteen foreign subsidiaries producing bulk drugs in India did not make even a part of their production available to Indian firms (Ministry of Petroleum and Chemicals 1975, pp. 136–40). It has even been suggested that public sector firms (IDPL and HAL) have not been utilising their formulations capacity deliberately, thus subsidising the private and foreign sectors by selling them bulk drugs (CPU, *IDPL*, 1973/4, para. 2.271; CPU, *HAL*, 1975/6).

Secondly, Indian firms, both in the organised and in the small-scale sector, have benefited since IDPL began supplying bulk drugs to them. This relieved them from the uncertainty of direct imports and from the control of transnationals which had been supplying them at high prices or under restrictive conditions.

Thirdly, nearly three-quarters of IDPL's sales of formulations go to government departments and hospitals, rather than to the open market (IDPL, *Annual Report*, 1975/6). However, this also implies that not only does the public sector have an insignificant share of total formulations sales in the country (under 6 per cent), its formulations might have encountered difficulties in penetrating the domestic market which, as we suggested earlier, is dominated by the transnationals (44 per cent) and the organised private sector (32 per cent); this is not so surprising considering formulations production is a low technology, non-capital intensive and high profit area activity.[19] A likely reason for IDPL's inability to penetrate the domestic formulations market appears to be that by 1981, IDPL product prices were still not very competitive. Moreover, IDPL has suffered from the typical bane of the public sector – a weak marketing strategy.[20] Drugs and pharmaceuticals, unlike heavy industries or oil refining, is not a public sector monopoly or even a near monopoly. It is one of the two industries (along with aluminium) in which, according to the Industrial Policy Resolution of 1956, the public and private sectors were permitted to coexist. Hence, in the absence of a strong marketing strategy, IDPL will be unable to penetrate the domestic market in the face of fierce competition from the foreign and the organised private sectors.

6.4 Conclusions

Having highlighted the points of analytical interest from our enterprise-level case studies, we can now summarise the benefits and costs of Soviet technology transfer to India.

6.4.1 The benefits of Soviet technology transfer

1. Servicing Soviet (and east European) project aid imposes quite a different form of burden on the Indian economy compared with Western loans. While payments of interest and repayment of principal on Western loans are in hard currency, Soviet loans are repaid in

rupees; the rupees are utilised by the USSR for the purchase of goods and services in India, according to trade and payments agreements signed between the two countries. This, as we have argued above, was a crucial reason for choosing the USSR as a collaborator in several projects. As long as two conditions are met, i.e. the prices secured by India for her exports to the USSR at the margin are at least as good as those obtained elsewhere, and secondly, exports to the USSR are not diverted from hard currency markets, the burden of servicing Soviet loans should be lower. We show in chapter 8 that these conditions were usually met.

2. Soviet project aid enabled the Indian government in several cases to break the monopoly of transnational companies in the Indian market and improved the bargaining position of the government vis-à-vis the transnationals. Oil exploration in the public sector and the state-owned oil refineries not only broke the transnationals' monopoly, but also resulted in considerable foreign exchange savings for the economy. Foreign exchange savings also resulted from the concessions the Indian government was able to extract from foreign oil companies during future bids for oil refineries (e.g. Madras). In the drug industry, the establishment of public sector bulk drug manufacturing plants with Soviet assistance led to the expansion of bulk drug production in India by the drug transnationals.

3. The planned character of the Soviet and Indian economies made it possible for the USSR to: a. commit project aid for the duration of an entire plan, and b. extend project aid for investments of an interlocking character. Several examples of the latter phenomenon can be cited. The USSR provided assistance not only for a machinery plant for underground coal mining (MAMC), but also helped set up a workshop for repairing underground coal-mining equipment (Korba), apart from building coal washeries and transferring technology to the coal-mining industry. Similarly, apart from providing equipment and technical assistance for three steel plants, a steel plant machinery-making plant (HEC) and a steel plant design organisation (MECON) also received assistance. Again, an instrumentation plant (Kotah) was built to make precision instruments for steel plants, petro-chemical plants, power stations, etc. Finally, capacity was created in HEC (and BHEL) for manufacturing oil-rigs for use by ONGC. Thus, in a sense, Soviet assistance has led to the creation of vertically integrated industrial complexes. These enterprises were meant to be capable of constructing, erecting and commissioning whole steel plants or power stations on a turnkey basis. In other words, these enterprises were created as

part of a whole strategy of import-substituting industrialisation with the objective of giving the Indian economy technological and production capability in basic and capital goods industries.

4. Since the Soviets are committed to handing over charge of the project soon after erection and commissioning is complete, their cooperation in building a project generally included the training of Indian personnel.[21] However, training of Indian personnel was not a special attribute of Soviet technology transfer. It is true that training in the USSR took place on a very large scale in the steel industry which was particularly short of personnel in the fifties. Most enterprises examined demonstrated that machine-operating skills and the manufacturing technology had been well absorbed and assimilated; some had gone beyond the mere assimilation of manufacturing technology, and demonstrated considerable product/process engineering capabilities. Those enterprises which had not developed the latter capability had not had sufficient opportunity to do so, i.e. they were usually faced with a chronic lack of demand for their products.

The Soviets encouraged a significant use of local inputs, in terms of construction equipment and services and plant and machinery, wherever technically feasible. We found strong evidence of progressive indigenisation of equipment in the two sectors – steel and oil refining – which have been recipients of Soviet technology on more than one occasion and over a period of time.

5. Although the USSR has not been as keen on sharing design and engineering work as using local inputs, Indian consultants were usually associated in Soviet-aided projects. Since the first stage of the first steel plant (Bhilai: 1mt) and of the first oil refinery (Barauni: 2mt) was executed on a turnkey basis, there was no question of sharing of design and engineering work. However, over time, more and more of the design work, particularly for off-site facilities, was undertaken by Indian consultants. For the main production units, while the basic design has come from the Soviet Union, the detailed engineering has been done by Indian consultants within the broad parameters laid down by the Soviets. In any case, an increasing proportion of total consultancy services in the steel and oil-refining industries was provided by Indian consultants with successive projects.[22] Again, while the DPR for all Soviet-aided projects was normally prepared by the Soviets, Indian design engineers were usually associated with them.

While the Soviets' preferred mechanism of technology transfer was the near-turnkey arrangement, and the original Soviet contracts only required the transfer of know-how rather than know-why, later on the

Soviets did assist in the setting in motion of a local design capability in certain sectors. In addition, in the coal-mining industry, the Central Mine Planning and Design Institute has been the recipient of Soviet design technology in the seventies (mostly on a contractual/commercial basis). As far as HEC and MAMC are concerned, the weakness of their design capability is undeniable, but admittedly that alone was not responsible for their abysmal overall financial and technological performance; domestic factors were at least equally, if not more, important. Besides, HEC's design weaknesses were, to some extent, compensated by MECON's strengths. While several industries were the beneficiaries of Soviet design methodology (while others were not), Soviet efforts at setting in motion a local R&D capability were confined to certain industries (e.g. drugs and oil drilling).

An R&D laboratory and pilot plant was set up at IDPL's synthetic drugs plant at Hyderabad; pharmaceuticals is a highly research-intensive industry, and in the circumstances (considering the inferiority of Soviet drug-manufacturing technology), an essential prerequisite for assimilation of technology by IDPL. The second R&D lab was for ONGC, the Institute of Drilling Technology at Dehradun, set up in the seventies. A third, a Research, Development and Design Centre for the aluminium industry, was also in the process of being set up in the early eighties with Soviet assistance (extended through multilateral channels, i.e. UNDP).

6. We noted that an aspect of Soviet technology transfer is the excellence of their maintenance system. In general, Soviet industry is characterised by large repair workshops and high maintenance and repair expenditure. In the absence of product/price competition characteristic of market economies, product designs in Soviet-type economies remain stable for fairly long periods and the obsolescence rate is rather low; hence the need felt by Soviet enterprises for capital goods stretching. Not only is there no competitive pressure to change machine tools and equipment, but the problems of administrative planning may mean uncertainty in getting spare parts, thus encouraging enterprises to be 'self-sufficient'. Besides, it must have been advantageous in a capital-scarce economy like the pre-war Soviet economy to have a well-organised maintenance system, particularly in the highly capital-intensive industries. In a similarly capital-scarce economy like India's at the eve of its industrialisation, an excellent system of preventive maintenance aimed at stretching the life of capital goods is equally important. However, in a more developed economy like the USSR today the maintenance facilities often betoken a severe equipment

problem: in addition it may not be sensible to concentrate skilled personnel in these sections. Soviet economists have argued that the life of their capital equipment is too long, no sensible evaluation of the maintenance/replacement trade-off being made.

7. We found that Soviet equipment was observed to be less sophisticated but more hardy than similar Western equipment. Indian engineers had found Soviet equipment to be normally over-designed, and probably for that reason hardier, and hence capable of with-standing mishandling. In this sense, Soviet technology was perhaps more 'appropriate', particularly given the low skill level prevailing in India. In fact, the excellence of the Soviet maintenance system and the hardiness of Soviet equipment constitute two strong arguments for LDCs to buy technology from the USSR.

8. Finally, on the basis of the limited comparison attempted above, one can argue that India's experience as a recipient of Soviet technology compares favourably with her experience as a recipient of Western technology. In some respects we found that the Soviets were more willing transferrers of know-how in the steel industry (e.g. see section 6.2.2 above comparing Bhilai, Durgapur and Rourkela). In the oil-refining industry, we found that significant progress in the sharing of design and engineering work between the supplier of technology and the acquirer as well as the use of local inputs was achieved only with the emergence of the public sector with Soviet/Rumanian assistance. It is rather difficult to pin down the reasons underlying India's more favourable experience as a recipient of Soviet technology. It is true that while the relationship with other collaborators had been of a wholly commercial nature, it was not strictly so with the Soviets. Although this is wholly conjectural, it can be argued that particularly up to the mid-sixties, the Soviets saw themselves in competition with the West in India (and the Third World in general), and were using 'economic relations as a political weapon'.[23] Valkenier argues that from 1953 to 1964, the Soviet Union was using economic relations as a political weapon, but from 1965 onwards, the pursuit of economic advantage became increasingly dominant. (See also the discussion of the politics of foreign aid in India in Eldridge 1969.) Hence, they were keen on demonstrating the advantages to India (and the rest of the world) of collaborating with socialist countries. Whatever the reasons, the advantages to India were obvious. However, Soviet technology transfer to India has not been without its costs, and it is to these costs that we now turn our attention.

6.4.2 The costs of Soviet technology transfer

Before we attempt to analyse the costs of Soviet technology transfer, it is necessary to point out that the performance of India's public sector leaves much to be desired; it is rather difficult to separate out those of its problems that derive from the aid-relationship from those that are the result of managerial deficiencies and the difficulties of pioneering a capital goods sector in an underdeveloped economy. As we pointed out in chapter 4, on the investment side Indian public enterprises have been criticised for the actual costs of projects greatly exceeding the original estimates and the construction and gestation periods having been longer than planned. But these are problems that occur not only in Soviet-aided public enterprises, but also in those which are recipients of Western technology. On the operational side, it was expected that with the passage of time, a growing proportion of the funds required for public sector industry would have been found from the internal resources of the investing enterprises. But this expectation has not been fulfilled and the rate of return in a majority of these enterprises is well below target. The difficulty of one's task becomes clear when one realises the sheer variety of the financial performance of Soviet-aided enterprises. For instance, while HEC, MAMC, IDPL and BALCO have remained through most of the seventies and early eighties among the fifteen largest loss-makers among central government public enterprises, at the same time BHEL, ONGC and IOC have been among the top ten profit-making public enterprises.[24] Since we have not carried out a comprehensive comparative assessment of the Indian public sector's experience as a recipient of Soviet and Western technology, the following discussion of the costs specific to Soviet technology transfer to India must be taken as suggestive or tentative, rather than definitive. In a word, two points must be kept in mind: one, it is possible that the problems discussed below may also have occurred in other public enterprises which were recipients of Western technology; and two, the delays and cost escalations characteristic of Soviet-aided enterprises in India were endemic to Indian public enterprises in general.

1. Some of the problems of Soviet-aided enterprises in India have derived from the interaction of two inefficient bureaucracies. For instance, two of these enterprises, the mining and allied machinery plant and the surgical instruments plant, proved complete disasters. These two cases were quite unprecedented even by the standards of the Indian public sector. Both enterprises were set up to manufacture

products with specifications for which there was absolutely no demand in India. Besides, on account of the narrow product-range these enterprises were equipped to manufacture, they were in a position to meet only a miniscule part of the overall demand for coal-mining machinery and surgical instruments in the economy. A similarly narrow product-range was transferred to the precision instrument plant; the product-mix for process control instrumentation was highly imbalanced from a systems requirement point of view. Accordingly, a large-scale diversification was undertaken with Soviet assistance in the late sixties, and a repetition of the fiasco – resulting from mass production of a narrow product-range – associated with the two earlier enterprises was thereby prevented.

2. In general Soviet-aided enterprises in India exhibited a tendency towards excess built-in capacity. The availability of Soviet credits enabled Indian negotiators and decision-makers to take the line of least resistance against Soviet suggestions about high built-in capacity. 'Gigantomania' had been characteristic of Russian industrial plants even during the Witte period, long before the gigantic projects of the Soviet First Five-Year Plan (1928–33) were even conceived. In an administratively planned economy, which is primarily a supply-constrained, not demand-constrained economy, the government's control over production and investment ensures that a demand constraint for producer goods will normally not arise. But in a developing market economy like India, demand factors must of necessity be carefully weighed before investment decisions are taken. Quite often demand projections by Indian planners were simply over-optimistic.

However, the problem was compounded by a certain rigidity on the part of the Soviets: existing plant sizes were simply transferred to India without any adjustments being made to the capacity of the plant (HEC, MAMC). In fairness to the Soviets, however, it must be pointed out that available evidence indicates that foreign firms from advanced capitalist countries have also done little to adapt and restructure technologies transferred under technical collaboration agreements. It is only when they have had a financial stake in the ventures that they have provided such assistance (Balasubramanyam 1973, ch. 5).

3. We found that a peculiar feature of Soviet technology transfer was that although the plants were Indian controlled, the Soviets ran a parallel management. While the practice may have its advantages to the extent that it indicates the Soviets' commitment to 'their' plant, it also involves costs since it often implies a proliferation of Soviet specialists. The costs may be twofold: one, the extra payment necessi-

tated on the technical assistance account; and two, the dependence on Soviet specialists generated as a consequence.

4. Yet another problem with Soviet technology transfer observed was that the sale of technology had been mostly in the nature of a one-off sale of design, documentation and equipment. Only such technology that had become well-established and proved itself was passed on; in other words, at the time of the transfer the designs were already probably ten years old (the usual figure quoted by Indian engineers during interviews). However, no design improvements or updated models were passed on later; the designs are for a particular size of equipment and the technology and its parameters remained frozen at that point of time. At least in the case of technology licensing agreements with firms from advanced capitalist countries a reciprocal commitment by the contracting parties to pass on any improvements effected during the currency of the contract makes it possible for the recipient to have access to the improvements effected by the licenser.[25] However, no such provisions were included in the Indo-Soviet firm level contracts when the enterprises were set up; the setting up of these plants was obviously conceived as a one-off sale of designs and equipment. A related problem, often caused by the too narrow product-range transferred by the Soviets, was that it compelled the enterprises to keep going back to the Soviets for new products. At other times, though, diversification was undertaken by buying technology from Western sources.

5. Finally, we found strong evidence for the suggestion in the literature on technology transfer that turnkey contracts involve a high price for the recipient. Both in the case of the first generation steel plants as well as the oil refineries, which were executed on a turnkey or near-turnkey basis, it was observed that the capital and foreign exchange cost of these projects was high relative to later plants/refineries. This was found to be the case whether the contractor was a Soviet or a Western firm. We also found that the import content of the heavy electricals plants purchased from the UK and the USSR, and the steel plants purchased from Germany, the UK and the USSR, was roughly the same. However, the import content of Soviet (and Rumanian) refineries was lower than that of the joint sector refineries built in the sixties.

As for the future, in the 1990s Soviet technology transfer to India will remain concentrated in the four core sectors – steel, coal, oil and power – to which Soviet technology was transferred in the four decades since India's planned development commenced. Equipment for manufacturing steel, mining of coal, exploration of oil and generation of power will continue to be imported; to this extent there will be continuity. But it is unlikely that the Soviet assistance will be utilised for investment in plants to produce capital goods or consumer goods. In the Indian perspective plan for the period 1985 to the year 2000 the thrust areas in industry are electronics, biotechnology, telecommunications, plastics and man-made fibres, and computers. These are areas in which there is a relative technological lag in Soviet industry (Amann, Cooper and Davies 1977; Amann and Cooper 1982; Amann and Cooper 1986). Given that India is undergoing a phase of modernisation, the emphasis has shifted to buying the best in the world.

Given also that intermediate industries (e.g. coal, oil, power and steel) have remained an area of economic activity reserved for the public sector, Soviet technology transfer will continue to be largely concentrated in the public sector. Nevertheless, there is a greater interest in the Soviet Union to collaborate with the Indian private sector. The USSR Chamber of Commerce has been emphasising to its Indian counterpart (Federation of Indian Chambers of Commerce) since 1977 that the USSR may be willing to collaborate with the Indian private sector in joint ventures in India, involving the export of Soviet machinery and the import of the resulting product on a compensation basis. More progress has been made in this sphere than in the case of joint plants in third countries. An interesting Soviet suggestion is that India can help construction activity and running of enterprises in the USSR, by not only supplying machinery, but also skilled workers and technologists, especially because the USSR is experiencing shortage of such personnel.

Soviet machinery exports to India can expand if either a. the USSR transfers technology to India's private sector using the licensing mechanism or through joint ventures, or b. the Indian private sector is persuaded to buy equipment and machinery on a semi-commercial basis on deferred payment terms. However, the east European countries are much more active in this field than the USSR. East European countries have been participating in joint ventures with the Indian private sector for a long time.[26]

However, the international economic relations of the USSR are changing under Gorbachev. In the wake of a new Soviet law (1986) joint ventures are planned to be set up in the USSR in collaboration with non-socialist countries. Hotels are being constructed in the USSR by Indian firms. But many more joint ventures are planned in India than in the USSR. In addition the Indian private sector, which has traditionally had dealings largely with the Western world, could be persuaded to buy machinery from the USSR on a semi-commercial basis. Deferred payment terms (for ten years at 4 per cent interest p.a.) on deliveries of machinery and equipment may already be on offer by the USSR. A cooperation agreement in 1977 between the USSR Chamber of Commerce and the Indian counterpart (FICCI) ought to fill the information gap existing in the Indian market about Soviet machinery; regular annual meetings have taken place between the two bodies since 1977. The incentive for increasing imports of machinery from the USSR is that an increase in Indian exports to the USSR may depend on higher machinery imports (although the difficulty here is that the exporters and importers are usually not the same people). An increase in Indian exports could only come about through the USSR generating more rupee funds; given the Soviet difficulty in increasing oil/oil product exports to India, rupee funds could only come from the sale of Soviet arms or machinery.

Part III

7   Bilateral payments

Bilateralism, with its emphasis on planning of imports and exports and bilateral balancing, suited the requirements of the CPEs' foreign trading system. When new trading arrangements with LDCs were established for the first time in the fifties, the CPEs of eastern Europe were already trading with each other on a bilateral basis. The CPEs' trade relations with LDCs were also established on a bilateral basis, and those which were not were gradually bilateralised. Like the LDCs, the CPEs were suffering from an acute shortage of convertible currencies. Hence, it was natural for the USSR's trade with India to have been on a bilateral basis.

This chapter on bilateral payments arrangements between India and the USSR attempts to answer the following questions:

1 Why does bilateralism (i.e. payments in rupees) still prevail in Indo-Soviet trade in the late eighties, although the CPEs have been multilateralising trading arrangements with most LDCs?

2 Since Soviet defence credits to India are repaid through bilateral trade, what has been the magnitude of defence-related payments by India to the USSR (between 1966/7 and 1985/6)? Calculations for the period up to the mid-sixties have already been made by Datar (1972). This whole subject is interesting because defence imports are possibly the single most important category of Indian imports from the USSR. To estimate defence-related payments, we attempt to reconstruct the balance of payments between India and the USSR since official statistics of neither country reveal balance of payments data with individual countries.

3 Why did the rupee–rouble exchange rate become a major issue in Indo-Soviet economic relations during the seventies? The rupee–rouble exchange rate does not affect trade transactions since all trade is denominated in rupees (and all trade is conducted in world market prices). But the exchange rate between these two inconvertible cur-

rencies lies at the heart of the problem of calculating India's credit repayment obligations to the USSR.

7.1 The rationale for continuing bilateralism

The reasons for India (and for that matter, other LDCs) entering into bilateral trade and payments agreements with the CPEs in the mid- to late fifties have been widely discussed and are fairly well understood.[1]

The essential reason lies in the foreign exchange constraints faced by India (and other LDCs) in the initial phase of import-substituting industrialisation. Although Mahalanobis provided no explicit justification for his export pessimism, nevertheless the Second Plan was formulated on an assumption of stagnant world demand for India's exportables.[2] The reality of the foreign exchange constraint facing India was brought home in the late fifties: the sterling balances accumulated during the Second World War were quickly depleted by 1955/6 under pressure from capital goods imports, and India was confronted with a balance of payments crisis.

In the early fifties, India's trade with the CPEs had been conducted on a multilateral basis and carried on in convertible currency. By 1956, although the rupee had become the unit of account, surpluses and deficits were still settled in sterling. At this stage, the agreements were regarded as an instrument of expanding India's trade, rather than a saving of hard currency. The foreign exchange crises of 1955/6 changed that arrangement; by 1959/60 payments arrangements with CPEs had been altered so that all payments were now made in inconvertible rupees. This was the culminating act in the gradual transition from multilateralism to full bilateralism via a partial bilateral payments agreement.

Thus full bilateralism was established between India and the CPEs at the beginning of the sixties. Through the late sixties and early seventies, therefore, there was a spate of studies examining the experience of India's (and other LDCs') bilateral trade/payments agreements with CPEs.[3] Their conclusions were quite similar: that bilateralism had resulted in a net increase in India's exports, that the composition of imports had been quite favourable to India, and that the terms of trade with the CPEs were at least comparable, if not better than, those obtained from the rest of the world. In other words, the overall impact on India's economy of Indo-east European trade was a positive one.

In the fifties, the CPEs were responsible for beginning a new phase of bilateralism in international trade when they first started engaging extensively in international trade outside the CMEA (Outters-Jaeger 1979, pp. 10–14). There were sound economic reasons (given many problems of their economies, hinted at in chapter 3) for CPEs' preference for bilateral trade. Apart from the trade restrictions by Western countries, and inexperience in Western marketing methods, the reasons included the nature and often the low quality of the products which they were offering (mainly primary commodities and basic manufactures), and inconvertible currencies. As most of the CPEs were suffering from severe hard currency shortages, convertible currency was devoted to obtaining high-priority imports for raising the economy's growth rate.

However, by early 1982, the bilateral clearing system remained valid in trade relations of the USSR with only six LDCs – Afghanistan, Egypt, Iran, Pakistan, Syria and India. India too had begun a trend of multilateralising its trade with the CPEs – with Yugoslavia in 1973, Hungary in 1978 and Bulgaria in 1980. That process, however, appears to have been halted, since no alterations to existing trading arrangements have been effected since 1980.

In order to explain the continuation of the bilateral payments agreements between India and the USSR, one has to investigate whether the reasons (just discussed) for the establishment of these agreements in the late 1950s have altogether disappeared in the 1980s. Such an investigation necessarily involves a review of the payment arrangements since 1960.

7.1.1 Balance of trade and net credits utilised in the sixties

The most striking feature of India's balance of trade with the USSR in the 1970s is that every year (except for two years) it has been in surplus; overall, India had accumulated a balance of trade surplus between 1970/1 and 1981/2 of Rs12,354m (not adjusted for incomplete coverage). This is in contrast to the situation in the 1960s when, entirely financed by Soviet credits, India was able to maintain an overall trade deficit amounting to Rs347.3m for the period 1961/2 to 1965/6, and Rs181m for 1966/7 to 1969/70. The net credits utilised over the same periods were Rs1,551.3m and Rs301m respectively.

It is noticeable that in the early sixties the net credits utilised by India (Rs1,551.3m) are much higher (in fact four-and-a-half times higher) than India's trade deficit with the USSR over the same period (1961/2 to

Table 7.1. *Comparison of Indo-Soviet trade balance with net credits utilised by India (million rupees)*

	Indian exports	Indian imports	Balance	Credit repayment	Credit utilisation
1970/1	2,098	1,061	1,037	602	367
1971/2	2,087	873	1,214	306	140
1972/3	3,048	1,144	1,904	488	85
1973/4	2,860	2,547	313	474	137
1974/5	4,213	4,089	124	477	140
1975/6	4,166	3,098	1,068	464	266
1976/7	4,540	3,160	1,380	818	258
1977/8	6,567	4,420	2,147	1,233	241
1978/9	4,106	4,690	−584	1,103	215
1979/80	6,382	8,242	−1,860	447	480
1980/1	12,263	10,137	2,126	334	450
1981/2	16,610	11,564	5,046	204	226
1982/3	16,697	14,132	2,565		400
1983/4	13,058	16,586	−3,528		747
1984/5	18,796	17,881	915		1,080
1985/6	19,374	16,728	2,646		1,300
Total	136,865	120,352	16,512		6,532

Sources: DGCIS, *Monthly Statistics of the Foreign Trade of India*, various issues; Ministry of Finance, *Explanatory Memorandum on the Budget of the Central Government*, various issues.

1965/6). From this fact Datar rightly concluded that to the extent that India has not been able to finance a deficit on its current balance (invisibles are known to be minimal) equal to the amount of net development (and defence) credits utilised, India was giving technical credits to the USSR. (See Appendix 4, pp. 204–5 below, on technical credits.) Under the bilateral payments arrangements prevalent with the USSR (and other CPEs), balances accumulated with the USSR constituted a waste of credit finance, and in that sense, reduced the nominal value of the credit finance. Datar calculated that the technical credits given by India to all east European countries (though mainly to the USSR) during 1956/7 to 1960/1 and 1961/2 to 1965/6 amounted to 16 per cent and 8 per cent of the net development credits utilised (Datar 1972, p. 101).

Given that the technical credits extended by India work out to such a small proportion of credits utilised, perhaps the more interesting conclusion based on Datar's finding relates to the real (as against the payments) side of the economic relationship:

> The need for India to give technical credits has arisen to a large extent from India's difficulty in finding acceptable imports to absorb her export earnings in Eastern Europe and from the slowness with which the East European countries have, on occasions, fulfilled export commitments. The difficulty in finding goods has two possible consequences. First, India may have had to import unnecessary goods. Secondly, India may have pre-paid her debts. (Datar 1972, p. 90)

The commodity-mix of imports from the USSR in the fifties and sixties does not suggest that unnecessary goods were imported, i.e. imports consisted largely of capital goods crucial to the implementation of India's import-substitution strategy. There was, though, some pre-payment of Soviet credits for Bhilai between 1962/3 and 1964/5 (according to an Indian government representative's evidence before the Parliamentary Estimates Committee).

Datar's conclusion that already in the early sixties India was finding it difficult to import suitable goods from the USSR has to be taken seriously because at a later stage of India's development (from the mid-seventies onwards) India did (and continues to) have difficulty in identifying suitable imports which the USSR is, at the same time, prepared to supply. India was not the only LDC in the early sixties with substantial credits from CMEA countries, yet unable to find the appropriate goods to import – Burma and Argentina were faced with similar problems. Some of the problems, of course, derived from the non-transferability of balances with one CMEA country to another within the bloc.

The problem disappeared in the case of India largely as a result of the payments for defence imports. In fact, it is rather significant that the explanation for most of the excess of net Soviet credits utilised over the trade deficit (with the USSR) between 1961/2 and 1965/6 lies in defence imports. (Defence imports began about 1960.) Defence equipment constitutes by far the single most important category of imports from the USSR through the 1970s and 1980s (with the exception of crude petroleum and petroleum products). Quite clearly, the pattern had been set early. Between 1961 and 1965 defence imports were perhaps exceeded only by imports of complete plant and equipment (item 16 in the Soviet trade classification): defence imports, according to Datar's calculation, came to Rs750m while equipment imports amounted to Rs2,000m.

Our own calculations show (table 7.2) that although in the latter half

Table 7.2. India's balance of payments with the USSR, 1966/7–1985/6 (million rupees)

	1966/6–1969/70 Receipts	Payments	1970/1–1981/2 Receipts	Payments	1982/3 R	P	1983/4 R	P	1984/5 R	P	1985/6 R	P	Total (1970/1–1985/6) R	P
Current account														
1. Merchandise imports (c.i.f.)		5,880		55,025	16,697	14,132	13,058	16,586	18,796	17,881	19,374	16,728	135,304	120,352
2. Merchandise exports (f.o.b.)	5,699		68,940											
3. Adjustment for incomplete coverage				500										500
4. Invisibles	n.a.	n.a.	n.a.	n.a.										
5. Total current account	5,699	5,880	67,379	55,525									136,865	120,852
6. Net current balance		181		13,915									16,013	
Capital account														
7. Development credits utilised	1,855		3,005		400		747		1,080		1,300		6,532	
8. Development credits repaid		1,554		6,950										12,810
9. Repayment of defence credits		120		7,909										9,735
10. Total capital account	1,855	1,674	3,005	14,859									6,532	22,545
11. Net capital balance		181		11,854										16,013

Sources: Rows 1, 2: DGCIS, *Monthly Statistics of the Foreign Trade of India*, various issues; row 3: estimated from *Monthly Statistics*; rows 7, 8: Ministry of Finance, *Explanatory Memorandum of the Budget of the Central Government*, various issues; row 9: estimated.

of the sixties the problem of the trade deficit falling short of net development credits utilised did not disappear, it was certainly reduced dramatically. The trade deficit in this latter period stood at Rs181m, while the net credits utilised were Rs301m, a difference of just Rs120m. We take this difference (Rs120m), or at least a very large part of it (in the absence of substantial invisibles transactions between the two countries), to be payment for defence imports over the four-year period 1966/7 to 1969/70. The reason for the substantial reduction in this difference in the latter half of the sixties as compared to the first half (1961/2 to 1965/6) is the threefold increase in repayments of development credits, from Rs521m in the first half to Rs1,554m in the second half.

Another way of conceptualising the problem of this difference is, as suggested above, to regard it as repayment of defence credits. If we take Datar's calculation of payments for defence equipment during 1961/2 to 1965/6 – Rs750m – to be correct, then the payment of Rs120m between 1966/7 and 1969/70 does seem rather small. However, it is possible that the explanation for this reduction in defence-related payments in the late sixties lies in two factors not mentioned so far. First, the first defence imports (agreement signed in 1959/60) were financed by a *commercial* credit for five years (as distinct from long-term credit) (K. Subramanyam 1981). It was only in 1964, once the Sino-Soviet split was well under way and the Soviet need for friends in South Asia became clear, that the USSR modified the five-year credit agreement to a ten-year one, thus easing the burden of repayment.[4] However, by then presumably a substantial proportion of the 1959/60 credit must already have been repaid, leaving little to be repaid during the latter half of the sixties. Secondly, the earlier period (duration five years) witnessed two wars (with China, 1962 and Pakistan, 1965), which might have necessitated emergency imports requiring immediate payment instead of on credit. Equally importantly, it is noticeable that if we include the early seventies as well in our calculations (i.e. a period which witnessed the Indo-Pakistan war of 1971), then the cumulative figure for defence-related payments to the USSR over 1966/7 to 1972/3 rises sharply to Rs2,869m.

In order to maintain a sense of perspective on all these figures on defence-related payments, it must be remembered that actual imports of defence equipment may be much higher in any given year than is suggested by the payments made. The actual value of defence equipment imports in any given year (or period) could only be computed (and even then only roughly) by using indirect methods (like the building-block approach) used by such organisations as the CIA or SIPRI. The absence of accurate volume and price data and the price differentiation practised by defence suppliers in different markets makes any figure for actual value of defence imports (exports) subject to large margins of error. Our aim in the tables and text is only to compute the repayments of defence credits, in circumstances in which the value of defence credits extended is not known. This is a quite different situation from the one concerning development credits: data on utilisation and repayment of individual developmental loans is available from several Indian official publications.

7.1.2 Balance of payments in the seventies and eighties

India had a trade surplus with the USSR from the beginning of the seventies up to 1985/6 except for three years, 1978/9, 1979/80 and 1983/4. During the period 1970/1 to 1985/6 India's aggregate trade surplus with the USSR amounted to Rs16,513m (unadjusted for incomplete coverage). This trade surplus was occasioned by two factors: 1. repayment of development credits, and 2. repayment of defence credits. According to the bilateral trade and payments arrangements between India and the USSR (see Appendix 1 on mode of payment), repayments of both developmental and defence credits have been effected through exports of goods since 1959/60.

Since Indian official publications do not publish balance of payments with individual countries, we have attempted to reconstruct India's balance of payments with the USSR from 1966/7 to 1985/6. It is reasonable to suggest that not all of India's trade surplus with the USSR was used for repaying defence and development credits. For instance, there may have been unrecorded imports or payments for invisibles or errors and omissions.

Datar had, in fact, found that there was incomplete coverage of imports for the Bhilai steel plant in the fifties and sixties and had estimated the unrecorded imports to be valued at Rs360m between 1956/7 and 1965/6. We found that unrecorded imports over 1970/1 to 1981/2 came to Rs500m. For some curious reason, in 1977/8 a certain portion of Indian petroleum product imports from the USSR does not figure in the total for Indian imports from the USSR that year. (For detailed discussion of coverage of Indian import and export statistics with special reference to Indo-Soviet trade, see Appendix 2.)

A second possibility could be that we are not taking adequate account of invisibles in constructing the balance of payments. However, it appears from all accounts that, apart from interest payments and payments for technical assistance, the value of invisible transactions between India and the USSR is minimal.

Interest payments are included in row 8 of table 7.2. The figures for row 8 are taken from the *Explanatory Memorandum of the Budget*, which does not give separate figures for the repayment of principal and payments of interest. However, from *External Assistance* (1980/1) we have calculated the *total* civilian interest payments between 1966/7 and 1981/2 to be Rs1,135m – i.e. less than 2 per cent of total imports over the same period.

Since technical assistance is paid for from development credits, it is also included in row 8. Datar (1972, p. 105) took technical assistance to be 20 per cent and 15 per cent of credits utilised over 1956/7 to 1960/1 and 1961/2 to 1965/6 respectively. In the late sixties and seventies technical assistance could not have constituted more than 10 per cent of credits utilised, given the improvement in technological capabilities and the rise in number of skilled personnel in India, and the falling share of Soviet equipment supplies and design work in Soviet-aided projects in India.

We have assumed that the travel and embassy expenditure by the Soviets in India and Indians in the USSR roughly balance out. As regards shipping, India has had bilateral arrangements with the CMEA countries since 1956. According to these arrangements, trade between the two countries should move mostly in ships owned by the two countries. An UNCTAD document noted (in 1979) that this element of the agreement is observed in practice in the Indo-Soviet Shipping Service. Hence, in the case of shipping as well we have assumed that the credits and debits tend to balance out, particularly over a long period of time (like 1970/1 to 1985/6).

Having thus established that there is an *actual* surplus on India's net current and capital balance with the USSR in the seventies, we have taken this residual to consist of repayment of defence credits. As table 7.2 demonstrates, between 1970/1 and 1985/6 the cumulative Indian trade surplus with the USSR stood at Rs16,013m. The total credit utilised over the same period was Rs6,532m. The aggregate repayment of developmental loans over the same period amounted to Rs9,735m. Thus, while a proportion of the Indian trade surplus can be explained by repayment (amortisation plus interest) of developmental loans, the residual (Rs16,013m + Rs6,532m – Rs9,735m) of Rs12,810m must almost entirely (except for errors and omissions) consist of repayment of defence loans.

It must be re-emphasised that the sum of Rs12,810m does not constitute the value of defence equipment imported from the USSR over the period 1970/1 to 1985/6. The value of defence equipment actually delivered must almost certainly be higher; Rs12,810m is merely the figure for repayment for defence loans extended in the sixties and seventies (on the precise value of which we have no information) which would have come up for repayment. Considering that Datar had come up with a figure of Rs750–1,000m for Indian defence payments to the USSR over a five-year period 1961/2 to 1965/6, i.e. at a time when the USSR was perhaps not the largest donor (of defence credits and equipment) to India, our figure of Rs12,810m over a sixteen-year period does not seem unreasonable.

It should be of interest that repayment of development credits (net of utilisation) accounts for a smaller percentage (20 per cent) of India's cumulative trade surplus over 1970/1 to 1985/6 than does repayment of defence credits. For India, the possibility of paying for defence equipment without expending scarce foreign exchange is too attractive an arrangement to permit an early multilateralisation of Indo-Soviet trade. In our opinion, this is by far the most important reason for the continuation of bilateralism in India's trade/payments arrangements with the USSR a quarter of a century after the introduction of bilateralism between the two countries. It can be reasonably predicted that, unless India's foreign exchange position improves dramatically, we can expect bilateralism to prevail in Indo-Soviet trade well into the next decade.

Although the possibility of continued Soviet interest in bilateralism in trade with India has already been suggested in chapter 2, it is worth repeating that the USSR too has considerable interest in purchasing consumer goods from India to save spending hard currency in the West.

7.1.3 Experience of multilateralisation with other CPEs

Perhaps another reason why India would not like to multilateralise her trade with the USSR was her experience with multilateralisation with Yugoslavia (since 1973), Hungary (since 1978) and Bulgaria (since 1980). While India's trade with her bilateral trade partners has remained relatively balanced between 1973 and 1983, she has consistently had a trade deficit with her multilateral trade partners since the trade was multilateralised. The reason is that while Hungary and Bulgaria have been able to increase their exports to India, the latter's exports to them have remained relatively stable. In fact, the Indian government now believes that trade with these smaller CMEA countries should have been multilateralised only gradually. If trade with certain CPEs was not expanding, the way forward should have been settlement of net balances in free foreign exchange as a first step within the bilateral framework of planning trade exchanges. This was not done in the case of India's trade with Bulgaria and Hungary; instead, a decision was taken to go fully multilateral straightaway. It is interesting that Bulgaria has now agreed to a balanced plan for an exchange of goods with India, within a multilateral relationship. Even Yugoslavia, with whom rupee payments were abandoned in the early seventies, has now entered into planned balanced deals with India.

The reasons why India may not have been able to expand her exports to these multilateral trade partners in east Europe are possibly twofold. First, as far as manufactured consumer goods are concerned, Indian exports suffer from a disadvantage in that transport costs to east Europe are higher than they are for west European exporters. Secondly, these CMEA countries can get suppliers' credits from Western producers, which Indian exporters are in no position to provide (in hard currency). Hence, while India has been unable to expand her exports to these countries, her imports have not fallen. The commodity composition of India's imports from these countries explains why her imports have not declined: 50 per cent still consist of machinery and equipment.

So every indication is that India is unlikely to multilateralise her trade with the other CPEs. The Soviet Union itself is unlikely to be keen to multilateralise her trade with India. In fact, while discussing the five- to ten-year long-term plan for economic cooperation, the opinion of the Soviet government was informally sought in the late seventies on a possible changeover to a multilateral system of payments with them as well as the other CMEA countries. The Soviet response was categorically in the negative (Kumar 1985). They, however, indicated no objection to India changing the payment system with other CMEA countries. This points to 1. the Soviets' own long-term planning, and 2. to their appreciation of the fact that whereas the USSR can maintain growth in trade, the smaller CPEs perhaps cannot. The Soviets presumably recognise that the economic interest of the smaller CPEs may lie in multilateralising their trade with India. The Soviets may be right in the sense that Indo-east European trade has not grown much in the seventies. That may be because of the growing lack of complementarity between India and east Europe. There is evidence of this slow growth in Indo-east European trade in table 8.3 below, which shows that India's imports from the USSR as a percentage of imports from east Europe as a whole have risen considerably over the seventies and early eighties. Whether Indo-east European trade will necessarily increase as a result of multilateralisation is uncertain; what is certain is that India is unlikely to be keen to multilateralise Indo-east European trade in a hurry.

7.2 Credit repayments and rupee–rouble exchange rate

All trade transactions between India and the USSR are invoiced in rupees. The prices charged by India and the USSR are supposed to be based on international prices. Since both Russian and Indian prices are quoted in rupees, the exchange rate between the rupee and rouble is of no importance in trade transactions. The exchange rate is of relevance only in relation to two sets of transactions: 1. invisible payments by India (e.g. Indian tourists travelling to the USSR, Indian embassy expenditure in the USSR, payments for Soviet technical assistance); 2. repayment of principal and interest on development and defence credits utilised. If the exchange rate changes, India's payment obligations would change correspondingly. As we have seen, India's invisible payments are relatively small. Hence we shall be largely concerned with the effect of exchange rate changes on India's credit repayment obligations, which as we know, are effected through export of goods.

In the earlier literature on Indo-east European trade there is almost no discussion at all of exchange rates. That was because the exchange rate between the rupee and east European currencies had remained stable until the devaluation of the Indian rupee in June 1966, and even later, until 1972. According to the long-term trade and payments agreements, the exchange rate between the rupee and the rouble (both inconvertible currencies) is determined by the gold content of the two currencies. In purely legal terms, the gold content of both currencies had remained constant until mid-1966, and since the gold content of currencies was an accounting fiction used for calculating the exchange rate between any two currencies (until the breakdown of the Bretton Woods system in 1971), the rupee–rouble exchange rate had also remained stable.

At the time of India's devaluation (in 1966) the gold content of the rupee and the rouble had some relevance as the world exchange rate system was then based on an arrangement of fixed parities. Since the rupee was devalued by 57.5 per cent in 1966 (i.e. the rupee's gold parity declined while the rouble's remained the same), India's rupee payment obligations should have increased correspondingly, i.e. by 57.5 per cent. However, since neither the rupee nor the rouble are traded on international foreign exchange markets, their gold content was, even before 1971, a fictitious concept. Moreover, because of the close relations between the two countries, the problem was resolved quite quickly through a compromise. The rupee was devalued by 47.5 per cent against the rouble, i.e. by a smaller magnitude than that against the freely traded currencies. Thus when the rupee was devalued, the outstanding repayments due to the USSR were revalued by nearly one-half.

Since 1971 all the currencies of the world have lost their mythical gold content. Instead of being based on fixed gold parities, exchange rates are left to find their own level on a day-to-day basis. Since both the rupee and the rouble are inconvertible, neither being traded on foreign exchange markets, the exchange rate could be arrived at through some hard currency which is traded in the international markets. The problem of arriving at a mutually acceptable rupee–rouble exchange rate arose because the rupee (which was pegged to the pound sterling from August 1971 to September 1975) depreciated against sterling over that period by about 39 per cent. (Since September 1975 the rupee has been pegged to a basket of major currencies.) The USSR, therefore, pressed for a devaluation of the rupee against the rouble as well, implying the need for a revaluation of India's debt repayment obligations to the USSR.

The Indians seemed unprepared to accept the Soviet view that the gold content of the rupee vis-à-vis the rouble had fallen because the rupee, linked as it was to sterling, had depreciated against other prominently traded currencies. First, the exchange rate of the rouble against other traded currencies is determined by the USSR quite arbitrarily to suit the exigencies of its foreign trade. Thus, the cross rates of the rouble against major convertible currencies are rarely in alignment. Secondly, since India's outstanding obligations to the USSR are normally denominated in rupees and the trade transactions are settled in rupees, the simple logic of arriving at the cross exchange rates between the rupee and the rouble via third currencies was also not acceptable to India. India therefore insisted on a mutually agreed solution which should be fair to both sides.

One way of resolving the problem is to denominate repayment obligations in terms of a commonly acceptable currency, e.g. the SDR, which is an internationally accepted basket of currencies. But as long as the USSR asserts its right to fix its exchange rate against all traded currencies as it sees fit, there is no easy solution. In any case, the USSR does not accept the SDR.

An agreement was finally reached in November 1978 (after protracted negotiations between 1974 and 1976) based on a specific basket of currencies.[5] In all probability, this basket is close to that used by India (since September 1975) to fix the exchange rate of the rupee. Quite clearly both development and defence credits repayment obligations will now be increased; however, the 1978 rupee–rouble agreement reflects some compromise on the part of the USSR.

Three features of the rupee–rouble agreement stand out. First, the extent of the depreciation of the rupee against the rouble vis-à-vis its 1966 level was about 20 per cent, whereas on the cross rate basis the devaluation should have been around 40 per cent. Thus the extent of depreciation of the rupee, and therefore the extent of upward adjustment of India's outstanding obligations to the USSR, were less than they would have been if one arrived at the new rate via the major convertible currencies. Secondly, the USSR agreed to the repayment of the enhanced part of the obligation over a period of forty-five years as if it were an interest-free loan; the grant element of the enhanced obligation was as high as 85 per cent. Finally, repayments already effected by India against past credits at the old rate were considered as final and no extra liability is to arise on that account. It is learnt that the outstanding amount to be repaid in 1978 stood at Rs1,000m approximately.

A final noticeable feature of the rupee–rouble agreement is that the rupee–rouble exchange rate would be subject to revision from time to time, and that there would be no gold clause in any future contracts between parties in the two countries. Thus the principle of gold parity, which had remained an irritant through the seventies, was finally buried. It has been agreed that if there is a change of up to 3 per cent (plus or minus) in the exchange rate between the rupee and the basket currencies (which are all convertible currencies), there would be no change in the rupee–rouble rate. The latter will only change if the basket rate changes by more than 3 per cent. If the rupee–rouble exchange rate is altered, then India's repayment obligations will be changed correspondingly through negotiations.

There are now three exchange rates in existence between the rupee and the rouble. One applies to credit agreements and commercial transactions, which is by far the most important, and is known as the

Table 7.3. *Rouble–rupee exchange rate*

From	To	Official rate Rouble 1 = Rs	Basket rate
	Up to 24–11–1978 (inclusive)	8.333	
25–11–1978	15–06–1979	10.0000	
16–06–1979	10–08–1979	9.6938	
11–08–1979	04–04–1980	9.9974	
05–04–1980	09–11–1980	9.6378	
10–11–1980	25–02–1981	9.3407	
26–02–1981	13–03–1981	9.7396	
14–03–1981	21–03–1981	9.4189	
22–03–1981	18–04–1981	9.7074	
19–04–1981	09–09–1981	9.4137	
10–09–1981	23–09–1981	9.7247	
24–09–1981	24–06–1982	10.0259	
25–06–1982	30–12–1982	9.6997	10.2518
31–12–1982	12–02–1984	10.0176	10.5878
13–02–1984	28–07–1984	10.3306	10.9186
29–07–1984	24–10–1984	10.6728	11.2803
25–10–1984	14–02–1985	10.9934	11.6192
15–02–1985	12–07–1985	11.3442	11.9900
13–07–1985	08–09–1985	10.9917	11.6174
09–09–1985	09–11–1985	11.4340	12.0849
10–11–1985	19–01–1986	11.7821	12.4528
20–01–1986	05–02–1986	12.1527	12.8445
06–02–1986	23–04–1986	12.5231	13.2360
24–04–1986	16–07–1986	12.9577	
17–07–1986	20–09–1986	13.3743	
21–09–1986	03–12–1986	13.8669	
04–12–1986	22–01–1987	14.3049	
23–01–1987	mid-1988	14.7923	

Source: Reserve Bank of India, *Report on Currency and Finance*, various issues.

official rate. The second one is for contracts under the Deferred Payment Protocol of 30 April 1981 (renewed 23 December 1985) for deliveries of machinery and equipment from the USSR to India; this is known as the basket rate. Both these rates are determined by the exchange rate between the rupee and the sixteen basket currencies. There is, however, a differential between the 'official' rate and the so-called 'basket rate', as is obvious from table 7.3. The reason, it is understood, is that the deferred payment terms (4 per cent interest, ten-year repayment period) are softer than ordinary suppliers' credit terms. It appears that the Soviets believe that the machinery and equipment on deferred payment terms are internationally competitive and hence a basket rate higher than the official rate is justified. The third rupee–rouble exchange rate, which applies to non-commercial transactions, i.e. embassy expenditure, tourists, etc., is determined via the US dollar. In other words, it is simply a cross rate between the two inconvertible currencies.

Appendix 1 Mode of payment

We quote below extracts from Article 7 of the five-year Trade Agreement, signed 10 December 1980, between India and the USSR, to give an idea of the mechanism of payments for trade and credit transactions.

'1. All payments of commercial and non-commercial nature between India and the USSR will be effected in Indian rupees. 2. For the purpose of paragraph 1 of this Article: a. the Bank for Foreign Trade of the USSR will continue a Central Account with the Reserve Bank of India and one or several accounts with one or more commercial banks in India authorised to deal in foreign exchange; b. the Central Account will be used for depositing the rupee balances and for replenishing the accounts with the commercial banks and for operating transactions relating to technical credit; c. the accounts with the commercial banks in India will be used for carrying out all operations of commercial and non-commercial nature. 3. a. The Central Account will be replenished by transfer of funds from the account(s) with commercial bank(s) mentioned in paragraph 2 and by receipts on account of technical credit; b. the account(s) with commercial bank(s) will be replenished by transfer of funds from other similar account(s) mentioned in paragraph 2 and from the Central Account/ . . .

6. Any balance in the Rupee Account of the Bank for Foreign Trade of the USSR or any debt of the Bank for Foreign Trade of the USSR in connection with the grant of technical credit will, upon expiry of this Agreement, be used during the ensuing 12 months for the purchase of Indian and Soviet goods as the case may be or shall be settled in such other ways as may be agreed upon between both Governments.'

Appendix 2 Coverage of imports from and exports to the USSR in Indian trade statistics

The main source of Indian trade statistics for this study has been the *Monthly Statistics of the Foreign Trade of India (MSFTI)* (published by the Directorate General of Commercial Intelligence and Statistics (DGCIS)), which gives the quantity and value of exports (vol. 1) and imports (vol. 2) by commodity/

country. The raw data initially had to be laboriously input into the computer at a highly disaggregated level, i.e. at 7-digit commodity classification level. Commodities are classified according to the Revised Indian Trade Classification (RITC), 1965; this classification was revised somewhat in April 1977, and is now known as RITC 2. The RITC is based on the Standard International Trade Classification (SITC).

It was found that the coverage of export data for Indo-Soviet trade in *MSFTI* was very high, i.e. 90 per cent or over. This was revealed by calculating the yearly aggregate of data input into the computer for the period 1970/1 to 1981/2. In fact, for most years the coverage was 95 per cent.

However, the coverage of imports from the USSR was extraordinarily poor, e.g. in 1976/7 it was as low as 50 per cent. Computing the yearly aggregate of data revealed that the coverage ranged between 50 and 91 per cent over the period 1970/1 to 1981/2. What is interesting is that in the early seventies (until 1973/4) the coverage is nearly 90 per cent. However, it drops dramatically after the oil price hike of 1973. For instance, the coverage is as follows: 74 per cent for 1974/5, 52 per cent for 1975/6, 50 per cent for 1976/7, 62 per cent for 1977/8, 60 per cent for 1978/9, 53 per cent for 1979/80 and 1980/1, and 51 per cent for 1981/2.

It may be of interest that while the source of crude petroleum imports is recorded in India's trade statistics since 1977/8 (though not between April 1971 and March 1977), details of petroleum product imports have not been published at any time through the seventies. India started importing petroleum crude from the USSR only in 1977/8; so while the crude oil import data is available, the sources of petroleum product imports are not published. We know from Soviet foreign trade statistics *Vneshnaia Torgovlya* (External Trade Statistics of the USSR), however, that the USSR has been exporting petroleum products through the seventies and eighties. The petroleum product imports from the USSR consist largely of middle distillates, i.e. kerosene and diesel. This fact is confirmed by DGCIS itself, which, curiously enough, published the source of petroleum product imports by India in 1977/8. In fact, in that year, all middle distillate imports happened to be from the USSR. We can reasonably infer from these two sets of facts, i.e. the fall in coverage of imports after the oil price hike of 1973 and the substantial imports of petroleum products from the USSR through the seventies, that if details regarding the petroleum product imports from the USSR had been furnished in the *MSFTI*, the coverage of total imports from the USSR would have been much higher. For some inexplicable reason, the DGCIS continues to keep the sources (though not the total value of imports from all sources) of petroleum product imports a secret.

Another anomaly about the coverage of imports from the USSR, which emerged during our analysis, was that while in every year after 1973/4 the coverage was less than 74 per cent, in 1977/8 it turned out to be 111 per cent, i.e. our total for imports from the USSR for 1977/8 (Rs4,918m) was higher by Rs500m than the total given by DGCIS in the same volume of *MSFTI* (Rs4,418m). Quite clearly, publishing the details of imports of petroleum products in 1977/8 was not the only mistake that DGCIS committed that year! It is rather interesting that, for 1977/8, if we deduct the value of petroleum product imports from the USSR (Rs2,163m) from our calculation of total imports from the USSR (Rs4,918m), the coverage of imports, by DGCIS statistics, would fall from 111 to 56 per cent, which is, as we have shown above, close to the level of coverage one finds in DGCIS statistics for imports from the USSR in the latter half of the seventies. In any case, in our reconstruction of India's balance of payments with the USSR, we have had to make an adjustment of Rs500m for incomplete coverage of Indian imports in official Indian trade statistics for 1977/8.

Appendix 3 Comparison of Indian and Soviet trade statistics

Comparing statistical records referring to the same flow of goods, but kept by two trading partners, is always a hazardous business. Problems may arise on account of differences of definitions, valuation (f.o.b. or c.i.f.), coverage (inclusive or exclusive of defence imports/exports), the exchange rates used for conversion to a common currency, and simple leads and lags.

Datar's calculation for defence-related payments based on Indian statistics (i.e. the excess of RBI's payments data over DGCIC's customs data) came to Rs750m for the period 1961/2 to 1965/6 (see main text). Datar also found that Soviet exports, given in Soviet foreign trade statistics *Vneshnaia Torgovlya*, exceeded Indian imports for the period, as recorded in DGCIS statistics, by approximately Rs1,000m (after taking into account unrecorded imports by India and payments to the USSR for technical assistance). After discussions with Indian foreign trade officials, Datar concluded that this payment of Rs1,000m must be related to defence imports.

However, we cannot be absolutely certain that Datar's and for that matter, Nayyar's (Nayyar 1977, pp. 112–13) methodology, i.e. of regarding the excess of Soviet exports to India over Indian imports from the USSR as consisting largely of Soviet defence exports, is wholly correct. This is because we cannot be certain that Soviet arms exports were actually included in the volume of exports to individual countries. A recent CIA estimate suggests, however, that a certain proportion of Soviet exports of arms is included in the individual country statistics of the USSR (Zoeter 1982, USJEC). The consensus, in any case, is that the bulk of Soviet arms deliveries is not concealed in individual country statistics, but rather in other residuals in Soviet trade data.

Our own calculations (see table VII.1) show that total exports by the USSR to India from 1970 to 1985, according to Soviet records, were slightly lower than Indian records of imports from the USSR. Therefore, unlike Datar, we cannot conclude that Soviet exports of arms to India were actually concealed in Soviet export statistics. While Soviet exports to India over 1970–85 come to Rs114,697m, Indian imports from the USSR (in Indian data) are somewhat higher at Rs116,489m; the difference can almost certainly be explained by errors and omissions, and leads and lags.

It is necessary to explain the methodology and sources used for arriving at

Table VII.1. *Indo-Soviet trade balances: Soviet statistics, 1970–1985* *(million rupees)*

	Soviet exports (c.i.f.)	Soviet imports (f.o.b.)	Balance
1970	1,123	2,026	−903
1971	1,068	2,136	−1,068
1972	1,338	2,798	−1,460
1973	2,151	3,214	−1,063
1974	3,117	3,641	−524
1975	3,710	4,545	−835
1976	3,562	4,349	−787
1977	4,682	6,500	−1,818
1978	4,802	4,875	−73
1979	5,683	5,018	665
1980	9,230	8,558	672
1981	10,932	12,460	−1,528
1982	11,285	14,532	−3,247
1983	14,012	10,529	3,483
1984	18,038	13,560	4,478
1985	19,964	17,305	2,659
Total	114,697	116,046	−1,349

Note: Vneshnaia Torgovlya gives the f.o.b. value of exports. To make these comparable with Indian statistics, 10 per cent has been added on to the f.o.b. value of Soviet exports.
Source: Vneshnaia Torgovlya, various issues.

the above figures. Indian import data is drawn, as usual, from official DGCIS figures. However, since Indian data is published for financial years (April–March) rather than calendar years, the Indian data has been recalculated to make it comparable to Soviet import data, which is only available for calendar years. This is why Indian imports for calendar years 1970–85 (Rs116,489m) are different from Indian imports for financial years 1970/1 to 1985/6 (Rs120,352m).

To make Soviet trade data comparable to Indian data, we had to carry out two exercises. First, since Soviet exports are recorded f.o.b., while Indian imports are recorded c.i.f., we have added 10 per cent to the value of Soviet exports to take account of insurance and freight. (Datar too had taken 10 per cent to be the value of insurance and freight, while comparing Soviet and Indian trade statistics for the period 1961/2 to 1965/6.) Secondly, we have converted the rouble values of Soviet exports as given in *Vneshnaia Torgovlya* to rupees using the official rupee–rouble exchange rate. This is the practice adopted by the CPEs in compiling their foreign trade statistics (see UN, *Yearbook of International Trade Statistics*, 1981, p. 10). Like the rouble–dollar exchange rate, the rouble–rupee exchange rate had also remained stable (at Rbls1=Rs8.33) until the collapse of the Bretton Woods system. After 1971, just as the rouble–dollar had fluctuated, so had the rouble–rupee rate. The rupee was depreciating against the convertible currencies, and the Soviet authorities accordingly adjusted the rupee–rouble rate between 1972 and 1978 (when finally an agreement was signed – see text for details). It is these official exchange rates which we have used in converting Soviet exports in roubles to rupees.

8   Bilateral trade

Indo-Soviet trade had by the early seventies acquired its own dynamic. Indian imports from the USSR up to the mid-sixties were largely supported by utilisation of Soviet developmental credits. Soviet aid utilised by India accounted for over four-fifths of Indian imports from the USSR between 1956/7 and 1960/1, and nearly two-thirds between 1961/2 and 1965/6. However, that share had fallen considerably by the early seventies (see table 8.1). Although the share of development credits repaid as a share of Indian exports to the USSR has not shown a consistently falling trend since the mid-fifties, for most of the period it was well below 20 per cent, falling to under 10 per cent in the eighties.[1] In this sense, one can justifiably argue that Indo-Soviet trade has acquired its own dynamic, and is not determined to any significant extent by India's utilisation and repayment of Soviet loans.

However, the question may still be raised: has bilateral trade with the USSR in the seventies led to trade creation for India or have India's exports merely been diverted from hard currency areas? This question is addressed in section 1. Section 2 considers the commodity composition of Indo-Soviet trade, comparing it to India's trade with the rest of the world, and Soviet trade with other LDCs. Section 3 discusses the stability of India's export earnings from the USSR, comparing it to the stability of India's export earnings from the rest of the world. This issue acquires its analytical significance from the fact that frequent fluctuations in export earnings are a major concern for most LDCs. While trade on a multilateral basis is subject to many factors beyond the control of most LDCs, bilateral trade agreements have often been recommended to moderate the fluctuations in export earnings. Finally, section 4 investigates India's import and export prices and compares the terms of trade with the USSR with those obtained from the rest of the world. An analysis of these four sets of issues enables one to assess the costs and benefits to India of bilateral trade with the USSR.

Table 8.1. *Share of credit repayment in exports to the USSR and credit utilisation in imports from the USSR (percentages)*

	Credit repaid as percentage of Indian exports	Credit utilised as percentage of Indian imports
1956/7–1960/1	11	82
1961/2–1965/6	18	64
1966/7–1969/70	27	32
1970/1	29	35
1971/2	15	16
1972/3	16	7
1973/4	17	5
1974/5	11	3
1975/6	11	9
1976/7	18	8
1977/8	19	5.5
1978/9	27	4.6
1979/80	7	5.8
1980/1	3	4.4
1981/2	1	2
1982/3	2.4	1.7
1983/4	5.7	1.3
1984/5	5.7	1.1
1985/6	6.7	2.0

Sources: Table 7.1 and Banerji 1977.

8.1 Trade diversion or creation

8.1.1 Diversion by India

During the early 1970s there was considerable concern among Indian economists that the substantial increase in exports to the USSR and east Europe during the sixties might be a spurious one. This would be the case if a part of the increase resulted from diversion of exports from hard currency markets to east Europe. It would also be the case if the USSR (or an east European country) re-exported goods imported from India under bilateral trade to hard currency markets at a discount. In the latter case, not only would India's hard currency earnings be reduced to the extent of east European re-exports of Indian goods, but it could adversely affect India's terms of trade by pushing the world prices of India's exports downwards.

This concern dates back to the sixties; the source of this concern over whether Indo-east European trade constituted trade diversion or creation was that trade and payments arrangements had only just been fully bilateralised in 1959/60. Since trade with the USSR and east Europe expanded very rapidly in the sixties (from a rather low base in the fifties) there was justifiable concern among Indian academics and policy-makers alike that the expansion of exports to bilateral trade partners, in particular, should not take place at the expense of India's traditional hard currency markets.

An examination of India's direction of trade in the sixties reveals that 43 per cent of the increase in India's exports in current prices between 1960 and 1970 went to east Europe. This is likely to be close to their share in real growth, considering that the US dollar unit value of exports changed only slightly. Martin Wolf, in a study for the World Bank (concerned about the bias against exports of India's trade regime), noted: 'Indeed, bilateral trade with eastern European countries and expanded exports of iron ore to Japan were the saving factors of the 1960s for export growth' (Wolf 1982, p. 39). The study, in fact, goes on to argue that during the fifties and sixties India did not exploit sufficiently the fast-growing markets of the DMEs. Thus, although the total imports of manufactures of DMEs from all market economies increased by 240 per cent between 1960 and 1970, and their imports of manufactures from LDCs went up by 260 per cent, India increased its exports to DMEs by only 22 per cent.

However, the consensus among economists who have examined Indo-east European trade in the sixties is that most of India's exports to east Europe were additional and not diverted from her traditional markets (Narain 1968; Datar 1972; Banerji 1977; Nayyar 1977).

In the face of overwhelming evidence that India's exports to the CMEA were of an additional character, it is rather curious that Wolf should suggest that 'the motivation for this trade (with east Europe) was the problem India faced in expanding its exports to countries conducting their trade on a multilateral basis (which, in turn, was largely the result of India's trade regime)' (Wolf 1982, p. 39). One may argue that over the sixties India could have increased her exports (especially of manufactures) to DMEs more than it did (32 per cent of the increase in India's total exports went to DMEs). But such diversion of manufactures was improbable since the share of manufactures in India's exports to east Europe over the sixties was lower than their share in India's exports to DMEs. Moreover, with the abandonment of autarkic policies by the USSR in the late fifties, it was inevitable that Indian exporters would move to take advantage of new markets opening up (particularly after Stalin's death, when political relations between the two countries were warming up). Whatever the criticism (often justifiable) of India's trade regime, even if India had fully exploited DME markets, the latter could still not have absorbed the entire 43 per cent (or even a substantial part) of the increase in India's exports between 1960 and 1970 which went to east Europe. The reason lies in the commodity composition of India's exports to east Europe over the sixties, which consisted overwhelmingly of traditional, primary and semi-processed products. While it is legitimate to argue that India's export policies resulted in poor exploitation of DME markets for labour-intensive manufactures in the sixties, India's traditional exports did face serious external demand constraints (see Nayyar 1976, p. 339). The strong empirical evidence apart, it should be patently obvious, given the low base of Indo-Soviet trade in the fifties, that India's exports to east Europe in the sixties would have been of an additional character.

In the seventies, the possibility that India's exports to east Europe, and in particular to the USSR, were diversionary is less likely than the possibility of diversion in the sixties. This is because the most dynamic market for India's exports in the seventies 1970/1–1980/1 were DMEs. As table 8.2 shows, over 46 per cent of the increase in India's exports went to the OECD countries; the DMEs thus displaced the CPEs as the fastest growing market for India's exports during this decade, even though their share in India's exports declined over the period from 50 per cent to about 47 per cent. By comparison, the east European contribution to the increase in India's exports over the same period was much less – 26.3 per cent (23.1 per cent for the USSR). East Europe's share in India's total exports tended to decline from 21.1 per cent in 1970/1 to 16.3 in 1975/6 and further down to 13.1 in 1979/80 before rising to 25.3 per cent in 1981/2.

The USSR's share in India's exports also tended to decline over the seventies, before picking up dramatically in the early eighties.[2] If we were to take only the period 1970/1 to 1979/80 into consideration, the USSR's contribution to the increase in India's exports would be under 9 per cent (east Europe as a whole 10.5 per cent). Even in the eighties, the OECD absorbed a larger share of the increment in India's exports than east Europe. As table 8.2 demonstrates, over the seventies the growth areas for India's exports lay in North America, Europe and the oil-exporting countries of the Middle East, rather than in east Europe. This tends to suggest that the risk of trade diversion to the USSR and east Europe over the seventies would be low, although it could be argued that DME and LDC markets might have grown faster still without Indian exports to the CPEs.

Table 8.2. Direction of India's trade: exports, 1970/1–1985/6 (in current prices)

	1970/1 Value Rsm	Share %	1975/6 Value Rsm	Share %	1979/80 Value Rsm	Share %	1980/1 Value Rsm	Share %	1981/2 Value Rsm	Share %	1982/3 Value Rsm	Share %	1983/4 Value Rsm	Share %	1984/5 Value Rsm	Share %	1985/6 Value Rsm	Share %
OECD	7,691	50.1	20,233	50.1	36,106	55.9	31,262	46.8	34,271	43.9	35,576	40.4	43,668	44.2	52,723	44.9	56,692	51.5
OPEC	985	6.4	6,161	15.2	7,014	10.9	7,446	11.1	9,403	12.1	8,201	9.3	8,815	8.9	9,439	8.0	8,528	7.7
East Europe of which	3,231	21.1	6,589	16.3	8,449	13.1	14,863	22.2	19,749	25.3	20,247	23.0	16,103	16.3	22,419	19.1	23,370	21.2
USSR	2,098	13.7	4,167	10.3	6,382	9.9	12,263	18.3	16,610	21.3	16,697	18.9	13,059	13.2	18,796	16.0	19,374	17.6
LDCs	3,047	19.8	7,081	17.5	6,126	10.2	12,857	19.2	12,325	15.8	10,684	12.1	14,702	14.9	14,408	12.3	16,147	14.7
Others	398	2.6	359	0.9	511	0.9	402	0.6	2,311	2.9	13,325	15.1	15,433	15.6	18,477	15.7	5,381	4.9
Total	15,352	100.0	40,423	100.0	58,206	100.0	66,831	100.0	78,059	100.0	88,033	100.0	98,721	100.0	117,466	100.0	110,119	100.0

Source: Ministry of Finance, Economic Survey, 1986–7.

The overall impression that diversion was minimal derived from examining the direction of India's exports at an aggregate level is reinforced by comparing the trend growth rates of exports to the USSR and the rest of the world (by volume) at a more disaggregated level. Thus, as table 8.4 shows, the exports of traditional goods to the rest of the world tended to either decline or stagnate over the seventies. Manufactures were the main source of growth of exports to the rest of the world. In fact, manufactures accounted for 95 per cent of the total growth of Indian exports between 1973/4 and 1978/9 (Wolf 1982, p. 43). On the other hand, the share of manufactures in India's exports to the USSR has shown no increase between 1970/1 and 1981/2 and, in fact, tended to decline between 1970/1 and 1978/9. At the same time, the share of traditional, primary products (including tea, coffee, cashews, spices and tobacco) in exports to the USSR tended to increase between 1970/1 and 1981/2 (particularly up to 1978/9), largely at the expense of raw/crude materials (groundnut, raw wool, raw jute and vegetable oils) (see table 8.10 below). Thus, while the exports of traditional commodities showed some buoyancy in the east European markets, the main thrust of Indian exports in the seventies came from manufactured exports to the rest of the world.

We have seen that although the USSR's share in India's total exports decreased from 13.7 per cent to 9.9 per cent in 1979/80, it recovered dramatically in the following three years to 18.3 in 1980/1, 21.3 in 1981/2 and 19 per cent in 1982/3. This sudden increase in exports to the USSR, coupled with an absolute decline in India's exports to the OECD countries (from Rs36,106m in 1979/80 to Rs31,262m and Rs34,271m in 1980/1 and 1981/2 respectively), can reasonably lead one to speculate that the growth in India's exports to the USSR in the early eighties may have been at the expense of exports to hard currency markets.[3] The Soviet Union accounted for 76 per cent of the increase in India's exports between 1979/80 and 1981/2. An examination of trend growth rates by commodity category (see table 8.4) suggests that such a diversion in the case of cotton and jute textiles, wool carpets/rugs and some items of clothing may have occurred. In the case of each of these items, the growth rate of exports to the world shows an absolute decline (over 1977/8 and 1981/2), while the growth rate of exports to the USSR shows substantial increases.

At the same time, it is precisely in these commodities (e.g. cotton textiles and garments, jute textiles, and tobacco) that quantitative restriction in the USA, the EEC and Japan may have affected India's exports to them (Wolf 1982, p. 74). If it can be shown that India's

Table 8.3. Direction of India's trade: imports, 1970/1–1985/6 (in current prices)

	1970/1		1975/6		1979/80		1980/1		1981/2		1982/3		1983/4		1984/5		1985/6	
	Value Rsm	Share %	Value Rsm	Share %	Value Rsm	Share %	Value Rsm	Share %	Value Rsm	Share %	Value Rsm	Share %	Value Rsm	Share %	Value Rsm	Share %	Value Rsm	Share %
OECD	10,422	63.8	32,257	61.2	43,907	48.1	57,395	45.7	63,780	46.9	68,123	47.7	81,837	51.7	83,393	48.7	105,510	53.4
OPEC	1,255	7.7	11,511	21.9	23,610	25.8	34,875	27.8	37,702	27.7	38,989	27.3	32,249	20.4	41,876	24.4	33,780	17.1
East Europe of which	2,200	13.5	5,659	10.7	11,024	12.1	12,963	10.3	15,069	1.11	17,115	11.9	19,647	12.4	21,522	12.6	21,584	10.9
USSR	1,061	6.5	3,098	5.9	8,243	9.0	10,137	8.1	11,369	8.3	14,132	9.9	16,456	10.4	17,881	10.4	16,728	8.5
		(48.2)		(54.7)		(74.7)		(78.2)		(75.4)								
LDCs	2,388	14.6	3,111	5.9	11,280	12.3	19,664	15.7	19,106	14.0	18,000	12.6	24,169	15.3	23,816	13.9	35,568	18.0
Others	76	0.5	115	0.2	1,525	1.7	706	0.5	419	0.3	699	0.5	412	0.3	733	0.4	1,025	0.5
Total	16,342	100.0	52,652	100.0	91,346	100.0	121,583	100.0	136,076	100.0	142,927	100.0	158,315	100.0	171,342	100.0	197,736	100.0

Note: Figures in brackets show share of the USSR in India's imports from east Europe.
Source: Ministry of Finance, Economic Survey, 1986–7.

exports of these commodities could not be increased to these major markets on account of protection by the DMEs, one can reasonably conclude that exports of these products to the USSR were of an additional character. In the case of textiles and textile products, exports which are the most important and the most tightly constrained, India fulfilled only 30 per cent of its quotas in 1978 and only 24 per cent in 1979 in the US market. In the case of clothing, although India filled over 90 per cent of its quotas in 1978 and 1979 to the USA, the reason for this fulfilment was that a few products, of which knit blouses were the most significant, exhausted their quotas. In most other products, quotas remained unfulfilled. This suggests that in certain items of clothing, men's and women's, and finished fabrics, diversion to the USSR may have taken place. However, the opportunity cost of diversion could not be high, since table 8.19 shows that the prices received from the USSR between 1977/8 and 1981/2 for cotton fabrics, dresses and garments for men, were higher than prices received from the rest of the world. Although the prices received may not be in hard currency, as long as imports from the USSR are of an essential nature (which they were, as we show later), the opportunity cost of diversion will not be high. As regards jute manufactures, India's exports to the USSR between 1977/8 and 1981/2 tended to grow while exports to the rest of the world were declining or stagnant. This must be explained by the higher elasticity of substitution with polypropylene in the DMEs as compared with the USSR. Wolf rightly argues that India's labour-intensive exports, especially garments, will increasingly face severe quantitative restrictions in the future; hence exports of these products to the USSR and east Europe are likely in the future to remain of an additional character, instead of being diversionary.

Although a part of the increase in exports to the USSR between 1979/80 and 1981/2 may have been diversionary, the sudden spurt during that period seems to have petered out, and there was absolute decline in exports to the USSR in 1983/4 (from about Rs17,000m in the previous two years to Rs13,000m). The USSR's contribution to the increase in India's total exports (in current prices) between 1970/1 and 1985/6 is approximately 18 per cent, which is roughly equivalent to the USSR's share in India's total exports in 1985/6. At the same time, exports to the rest of the world seemed to pick up again in recent years. Taken together, these facts seem to suggest that diversion from hard currency markets was almost non-existent in the seventies and marginal in the early eighties. Whatever small diversion did take place was, in any case, quite insignificant in scale compared with the

Table 8.4. *Growth rate of exports to the USSR and the rest of the world,*
1970/1–1981/2

	USSR		Rest of the world	
	Volume	Value	Volume	Value
Cashews		23.6		4.9
Coffee	27	69.1	9	36.1
Tea	6.6	23.0	−1.0	16.8
Pepper	11.9	22.8	−1.1	6.0
Other spices	9.0	23.0	12.5	14.2
Oilcakes	7.9	18.6	−3.6	9.0
Jute, raw	4.1	12.8	−0.7	2.4
Mica	2.9	15.9	6.9	3.3
Tobacco, unmanufactured	17.3	32.3	2.5	16.1
Lac	6.3	17.6	−4.3	9.6
Cotton piecegoods (1970/1–76/7)	11.4	31.3	4.1	28.5
Leather		16.2		16.0
Cotton fabrics, woven (1977/8–81/2)	257.7	332.5	−33.3	−14.5
Jute fabrics, woven (1977/8–81/2)	49.5	32.2	−4.7	−4.9
Manufactures of textile materials (1977/8–81/2)	−56.8	−27.8	155.9	51.9
Floor coverings: wool carpets (1977/8–81/2)	148.6	67.6	−40.9	−20.6
Mineral manufactures (1977/8–81/2)	45.0	74.1	27.8	9.3
Aluminium	16.5	36.3	−22.5	7.6
Clothing (1977/8–81/2): Dresses	143.9	168.2	97.1	124.2
Textile fabrics (men's shirts)	41.5	50.9	−41.5	−28.7
Knitted garments	45.5	45.5	76.6	65.4
Dresses, skirts	411.2	243.7	13.3	27.9
Cotton undergarments	95.1	87.1	13.1	39.9
Cotton fabrics		73.1		5.4
Textile fabrics (1970/1–76/7)	−6.4	13.1	125.0	154.1
Jute manufactures (1970/1–76/7)		25.1		5.6
Clothing (1970/1–76/7)		18.9		66.9
Footwear (1970/1–76/7)	−1.4	11.1	4.0	39.5
Art works, antiques		76.6		35.8
Imitation jewellery		36.0		9.0

Source: Calculations based on raw data in DGCIS, *Monthly Statistics of the Foreign Trade of India,* various issues.

diversion found in the earlier studies to have occurred in the sixties (which itself, as we have seen, was not large).

8.1.2 Diversion by the USSR

In addition to diversion by India, it is possible that some diversion of Indian exports may have been carried out by the USSR. This could have occurred in two ways: either by reconsignment in transit or by re-export after import.

Reconsignment in transit could occur when shipments from India meant for the USSR are unloaded in ports in hard currency areas and never actually reach Soviet shores. It is next to impossible to estimate this kind of switch trading on a commodity basis. If the USSR indulges in switch trading of this kind, India's exports to the USSR will not actually enter Soviet import statistics. Thus a comparison of Soviet and Indian trade statistics can prove useful here (just as such a comparison proved useful in calculating defence-related payments to the USSR). If India's exports to the USSR as recorded in Indian trade statistics are higher than Soviet imports from India as recorded in Soviet trade statistics, we can reasonably infer that Indian exports were being reconsigned in transit by the USSR with the intention of earning hard currency. Such a comparison is facilitated by the fact that Soviet imports and Indian exports are both recorded f.o.b. Since Indian trade data is recorded for calendar years (April–March), it had to be adjusted to make it comparable to Soviet data.

Tables 7.1 and VII.1 (see previous chapter) show that Indian exports over the period 1970–81 exceeded Soviet imports from India (Rs64,532m – Rs60,120m = Rs4,412m). The difference of Rs4,412m is 6.8 per cent of India's exports to the USSR. If we include 1982 and 1983, the difference rises even further to Rs12,411m (Soviet imports: Rs85,181m; Indian exports: Rs97,592m), which is 13.8 per cent of Indian exports to the USSR.

It may be interesting here to compare the experience in the seventies and eighties with that in the sixties. Datar, comparing Indian exports as reported in DGCIS statistics, and Soviet imports as reported in *Vneshnaia Torgovlya* (External Trade Statistics of the USSR), found that during 1960–5, the aggregates were quite comparable: Rs3,162m for Indian exports and Rs3,054m for Soviet imports. Nayyar, comparing Indian and Soviet statistics, as reported in the UN *Yearbook of International Trade Statistics*, also found that during 1960–72, Indian exports exceeded Soviet imports to the USSR by under 2 per cent of total Indian exports to the USSR over the period. Our calculations for the seventies would therefore seem to suggest that the phenomenon of reconsignment of Indian exports by the USSR in transit showed marked increase. In fact, such switch trading was not at all significant in the sixties, but was tending to acquire significant proportions in the seventies.

A more detailed examination of Indian and Soviet data for the period since 1970 reveals that this increase in switch trading by the USSR is concentrated in the late seventies and early eighties. Up to 1978, Soviet imports seem to be roughly equal and even somewhat in excess of the figures for Indian exports. All the switch trading, in fact, seems to have occurred from 1979 onwards, coinciding with a period of dramatic increase in Indian exports to the USSR. We have therefore presented some detailed evidence of large-scale switch trading by the USSR in certain commodities in Appendix 5.

We can now turn to a discussion of re-export of Indian goods imported by the USSR. Re-exports of India's non-traditional exports (e.g. machinery, footwear, chemicals, clothing, etc.) to hard currency areas are unlikely to have occurred, since Western markets are fairly brand conscious, and the need for product differentiation and the marketing costs would probably make switch trading in manufactured/non-traditional goods quite difficult.

As regards India's traditional exports, an Indian study for the period 1965–80 has concluded that the argument that the USSR made substantial hard currency earnings by re-exporting Indian goods to DMEs is not valid. The study is based on twelve traditional commodities exported by India to the USSR.[4] The USSR is a large producer of three commodities (tea, tobacco and cotton textiles) which are exported regularly but which are also imported from India. However, only a small proportion of these commodities is exported to hard currency areas, most exports going to east Europe. Besides, the unit values of exports in hard currency areas are far lower than the unit values of imports of the same commodities. Further, the share of exports in domestic production for these three commodities is 1 or 2 per cent. All this suggests that the USSR's hard currency earnings from re-exports of imports from India are minimal.

At the same time, the study rightly argues that the USSR could have been exporting domestically produced tea or tobacco which might be qualitatively inferior to the Indian product. Firm evidence is difficult to find in this regard. Imports may have increased the export potential of the USSR for these products. Imported tea or tobacco could also have been blended with the domestic product by the USSR before export to east Europe.

The overall conclusion on the question of trade creation/diversion must be that a fairly small proportion of India's exports to the USSR over the seventies and eighties was diverted from hard currency markets. India may have been responsible for a small amount of diversion from 1979 onwards. This is suggested by the phenomenal increase in India's exports to the USSR which occurred after 1979. However, considering that demand had slackened in DME markets after the second oil shock of 1979, most of the increase in exports to the USSR in the eighties is likely to have been of an additional nature. This is all the more likely since there are no special government incentives to private exporters to export to the USSR.

Diversion of Indian exports for which the USSR may be held responsible is more likely to have occurred in the form of reconsignment of Indian goods to Western ports, rather than re-exports of Indian goods. Comparison of Soviet and Indian statistics showed that such switch trade seemed to be concentrated in the late seventies and eighties. Dharam Narain has estimated the switch trade at 3.5 per cent of India's total exports to east Europe, and Indian officials put it at around 5 to 10 per cent up to the mid-sixties. Compared with these estimates, our estimates for re-exports by the USSR certainly seem to be comparable for the period 1970 to 1981, and higher for the period up to 1983. It is also noticeable that while in the sixties the phenomenon of switch trade was confined to the smaller east European countries, in the late seventies and eighties the major complaints have been against the USSR (see Appendix 5).

8.2 Commodity composition of trade

A comparison of the commodity structure of 1. Soviet-LDC trade and Soviet-Indian trade and 2. India's trade with the USSR and the rest of the world gives us very interesting insights into the present stage of development of both the Soviet as well as the Indian economy. We shall pursue each comparison in turn in this section.

We have suggested in chapter 3 that Soviet-Indian economic relations are rather different in character from Soviet-LDC economic relations in general. The commodity composition of Soviet imports from, and exports to, India is one aspect of this difference in character. According to UN data (table 3.8 above), the share of manufactures in Soviet (and east European) imports from LDCs, far from rising, has

Table 8.5. *Commodity composition of India's imports from the USSR, 1970/1–1984/5 (percentages)*

	70/1–72/3	73/4–75/6	76/7–78/9	79/80–81/2	82/3–84/5
Petroleum and petroleum products	5.7	20.5	49.8	76.8	74.8
Raw materials	5.4	3.1	4.1	0.5	0.3
Food	—	23.3	—	—	—
Manufactures	77.3	42.8	37.5	15.0	11.8
Others	11.6	10.3	8.6	7.8	13.1

Note: Average share of machinery and transport equipment as follows: 70/1–72/3: 46.3%; 73/4–75/6: 16.7%; 76/7–78/9: 21.9%; 79/80–81/2: 8.3%; 82/3–84/5: 6.6%.
Source: As table 8.4.

tended to decline from its peak between 15–20 per cent in the early 1970s to under 10 per cent in the late seventies; on the other hand, the share of manufactures in India's exports to the USSR rose steadily from around 17 per cent in 1960/1 to about 25 per cent in 1964/5 to over 50 per cent in the early seventies (at which level it has stabilised). These high shares of manufactures in India's exports to the USSR are not particularly surprising, considering that already in 1960 manufactures constituted as much as 45 per cent of India's exports to the world (World Bank 1983, p. 166).

8.2.1 Structure of Soviet exports to India

The commodity composition of Soviet exports to India is also quite different as compared to Soviet exports to most other LDCs. Machinery and transport equipment (SITC 7) constituted well over a fifth of all exports by the USSR to LDCs over the seventies. Its share in Soviet exports to India dropped from a high 46.3 per cent in the early seventies (1970/1 to 1972/3) to 16.7 per cent in the mid-seventies (1973/4 to 1975/6), recovering slightly to 21.9 per cent towards the end of the decade. In the early eighties (1979/80 to 1981/2) that share had dropped sharply to 8.3 per cent. Capital goods have been replaced by intermediate goods as the single most important category of civilian exports by the USSR to India. At the same time, the share of manufactures in Soviet exports to India has fallen consistently over the seventies: from 77.3 per cent in 1970/1 to 1972/3 to 15 per cent in 1979/80 to 1981/2.

Table 8.5 shows that the most dramatic changes have taken place in the structure of India's imports from the USSR. The share of petroleum and petroleum products, which averaged 5.7 per cent over 1970/1 to 1972/3 (and never rose above 8.5 per cent in the sixties), rose steeply to nearly half (over 1976/7 to 1978/9) and then to over three-quarters of Indian imports from the USSR by the early eighties. There are three sudden increases in the share of petroleum and petroleum products: 1. from 1973 to 1974, caused by the oil price increase; 2. from 1977 to 1978, the result of the introduction of petroleum crude oil to the import-mix; and 3. from 1979 to 1980, caused by the second oil price hike. Thus, the increase in the share of fuels has been the result of both volume and price increases.

In chapter 2 we quoted Marshall Goldman as saying that 'the Soviet Union is a one-crop economy', because petroleum accounted for a high proportion of Soviet hard currency earnings and overall export earnings. That proposition is even truer in the case of Soviet-Indian trade than it is in the case of the USSR's overall export structure. The high share of petroleum products appears even more striking if petro-chemicals like crude/manufactured fertilisers are also taken into account; their share in total Soviet exports to India over the seventies has normally been between 5 and 10 per cent.

This picture is confirmed by a detailed examination of India's imports from the USSR in table 8.8 (and table 8.6). The only commodity categories which have shown significant trend growth rates have been petroleum and petroleum products (63 per cent) and fertilisers (38.6 per cent). Almost all other commodities have either stagnated or declined in value (in current prices). Non-ferrous metals, paper and paperboard, and medicines, which together constituted 10 per cent of India's imports from the USSR in the early seventies, show growth rates of just 3.1, 2.0 and 2.7 per cent respectively. Iron and steel and non-metallic mineral manufactures show a trend decline (of 13.5 and 70.9 per cent per annum). Imports of machinery (mostly non-electrical) which stood at Rs542m in 1970/1, when it was the single most important category of import, had barely risen to Rs604m after twelve years, having fallen (in current prices) in the early seventies.[5] Even chemicals, imports of which were tending to rise in value until the mid-seventies, had by the early eighties declined to their earlier level. So overwhelming is the importance of fuels in the import-mix from the USSR, that no commodity categories (at 2-digit commodity classification) other than machinery and fertilisers have had a share of over 2 per cent since the late seventies.

Table 8.6. *India's imports from the USSR, 1970/1–1984/5 (million rupees)*

	RITC	70/1	71/2	72/3	73/4	74/5	75/6	76/7	77/8	78/9	79/80	80/1	81/2	82/3	83/4	84/5
Cereals	04	—	—	—	1037	1109	—	—	—	—	—	—	—	—	—	—
Textile fibres	26	neg.	—	74	43	22	neg.	70	80	neg.	neg.	—	neg.	neg.	neg.	neg.
Crude fertilisers and minerals	27	22	31	45	45	101	86	109	136	86	57	9	86	38	34	70
Petroleum, crude	33	—	—	—	—	—	—	—	2,978	1,286	2,835	3,630	4,616	6,108	7,617	7,925
Chemicals, organic and inorganic	51	17	21	25	34	95	88	22	63	29	24	18	21	6	6	2
Medicines	54	8	5	3	4	13	12	8	—	5	13	4	6	4	5	7
Fertilisers	56	42	22	54	35	425	145	200	289	216	134	637	252	77	92	518
Paper, paperboard and manufactures	64	52	56	55	78	156	102	151	156	134	112	188	13	284	331	329
Non-metallic mineral manufactures	66	32	39	12	10	5	6	10	5	7	3	1	neg.	neg.	40	40
Iron and steel	67	80	70	80	83	181	171	107	63	24	44	35	51	52	5	15
Non-ferrous metals	68	48	24	80	460	208	123	98	65	56	89	101	86	130	206	295
Machinery, electrical and non-electrical		542	382	358	304	545	718	708	555	550	579	718	604	796	1000	1388
Transport equipment		22	28	78	9	31	15	26	508	263	429	20	1	64	11	15
Instruments scientific, controlling	86	17	12	19	5	28	4	7	—	—	—	—	—	15	10	11

Source: As table 8.4.

Table 8.7. *India's exports to the USSR, 1970/1–1984/5 (million rupees)*

	70/1	71/2	72/3	73/4	74/5	75/6	76/7	77/8	78/9	79/80	80/1	81/2	82/3	83/4	84/5
Food															
Rice	—	—	—	—	68	—	—	—	—	—	—	1,217	2,337	1,414	442
Cashews	51	180	240	297	730	181	295	839	244	430	902	1,272	646	0.2	48
Fruit and vegetable juice	—	9	9	16	6	—	10	15	9	1	—	1,966	—	—	—
Fresh vegetables	—	—	neg.	neg.	neg.	6	34	16	neg.	15	62	81	—	—	—
Coffee	58	65	101	3	178	172	292	642	319	437	726	366	772	662	610
Tea	263	330	324	326	595	730	535	1,263	588	805	1,213	1,375	1,170	1,714	3,002
Pepper	36	72	58	98	101	152	162	193	139	139	241	202	145	109	341
Other spices	9	4	9	8	34	22	25	5	21	35	24	34	55	32	118
Oilcakes	44	34	102	95	112	24	neg.	38	—	2	295	414	238	5	101
Tobacco															
Tobacco, unmanufactured	55	153	294	186	172	289	240	300	246	293	504	690	1,003	812	626
Cigarettes	3	15	16	13	2	33	18	5	1	21	54	160	176	83	64
Crude materials															
Groundnut	23	18	22	112	60	101	45	—	—	27	92	181	357	114	294
Raw wool	32	19	15	33	93	14	36	—	—	—	neg.	neg.	—	—	—
Raw jute	41	24	38	1	4	11	10	11	8	15	37	51	—	—	—
Mica	54	49	57	52	71	71	81	69	80	98	72	172	126	88	99
Lac	2	3	4	11	49	26	11	5	12	14	8	3	4	18	6
Oils and fats															
Vegetable oils	45	55	73	122	108	101	82	94	neg.	15	—	—	8	518	152

Chemicals															
Pigments, paint	28	18	29	15	64	50	41	47	42	80	88	92	284	280	351
Opium, quinine	6	4	neg.	2	17	7	10	4	3	4	10	7	—	—	—
Medicaments	—	neg.	—	18	24	36	41	59	66	357	26	759	—	—	35
Essential oils	18	3	9	17	22	24	12	17	5	20	25	11	29	14	35
Cosmetics	6	8	13	3	3	3	4	11	8	35	148	577	478	34	260
Soap	—	neg.	—	neg.	—	1	1	—	—	3	134	287	149	25	neg.
Detergents	3	7	10	11	6	33	34	37	14	69	176	247	207	4	30
Manufactures															
Leather	189	130	257	428	324	394	384	479	368	334	899	397	576	600	881
Leather manufactures	neg.	neg.	neg.	1	neg.	neg.	neg.	3	3	46	96	182	315	451	637
Rubber manufactures	5	7	—	3	14	18	20	13	10	21	46	176	356	194	243
Cotton piecegoods, cotton manufactures	101	74	287	146	222	180	354	170	216	438	633	1,193	1,837	1,350	1,894
Jute manufactures	344	315	530	326	589	668	501	645	330	828	1,281	844	821	750	2,101
Floor coverings	13	24	14	17	18	25	25	29	23	60	88	285	256	15	17
Mineral manufactures	—	—	—	—	—	—	—	9	13	19	21	51	39	28	61
Precious stones	—	neg.	neg.	—	neg.	—	—	13	1	7	29	7	—	—	—
Iron and steel	173	77	94	79	17	1	167	265	300	68	27	11	neg.	—	203
Aluminium and alloys	6	11	16	7	2	2	8	19	24	28	14	34	150	23	60
Metal manufactures	47	10	18	14	16	14	17	53	23	45	40	67	120	95	124
Machinery and transport equipment	9	15	40	53	95	162	250	215	216	228	497	992	1,410	1,245	1,685
Miscellaneous manufactures															
Clothing	178	182	197	237	229	260	383	437	316	544	896	1,223	1,270	560	1,639
Footwear	46	34	48	38	44	44	58	36	20	12	5	6	19	24	10
Art works	neg.	6	11	12	9	8	10	16	—	52	96	178	91	25	55
Imitation jewellery	neg.	neg.	4	2	6	9	9	8	—	9	10	4	4	neg.	4

Source: As table 8.4.

However, to put this overwhelming importance of fuels in the import-mix in perspective, one must point out that their share in India's total imports has also risen considerably since the first oil price increase. But this relative (and absolute) increase is far from being as dramatic as the change in the commodity composition of India's imports from the USSR. The share of fuels in India's total imports rose from just over 10 per cent in 1970/1 to a maximum of 42 per cent in 1980/1 (following the second oil price rise); in most other years it has remained well under 40 per cent.

The share of machinery in India's imports from the USSR has declined partly because of the slow-down in the growth of public investment in general since the mid-sixties, and in capital goods and basic goods industries in particular, which account for about 50 per cent of the value added in industry. These are just the industries in which technology was being imported from the USSR till the early seventies. Moreover, even the industries set up with Soviet assistance over the fifties and sixties were now opting for Western technology (see chapter 6). As a result, there is no continuing demand for Soviet machinery from the public sector. Following the slow-down in the growth of public investment, the growth of private investment also decelerated, from an annual rate of 4.9 per cent during 1956/7 to 1965/6 to 3.9 per cent during 1967/8 to 1978/9. This also affected the demand for capital goods and basic goods adversely. However, the slow-down in private sector investment could not have affected demand for Soviet machinery very much, since Soviet links with India's private sector remained minimal until the late seventies. No formal technology transfer has taken place between Soviet FTOs and Indian private firms. It was only in 1977 that, in response to the decline in importance of machinery in Soviet exports to India, a cooperation agreement was signed between the Federation of Indian Chambers of Commerce (FICCI) and the USSR Chamber of Commerce (USSR CCI). The results of this cooperation agreement are yet to be seen.

There is no doubt that India's imports of machinery from the USSR over the fifties and sixties were crucial to the implementation of the import substitution strategy, particularly in certain key sectors. But how important have Soviet exports of petroleum and petroleum products over the seventies been for the Indian economy? After several Indian requests, the USSR agreed to supply crude oil in 1977 (soon after India, it has been suggested, had made some friendly noises towards China). Since then crude oil supplies have continued uninterrupted. From the Soviet point of view the supply of crude oil, the

Table 8.8. *Trend growth rate of value of India's imports from the USSR,
1970/1–1981/2 (2-digit level)*

Commodities	Code	%
Crude fertilisers and minerals	27	4.9
Petroleum and petroleum products	33	63.0
Crude petroleum (1977/8–81/2)	33	31.8
Medicines	54	2.7
Fertilisers	56	38.6
Paper, paperboard and manufactures	64	2.0
Non-metallic mineral manufactures	66	−70.9
Iron and steel	67	−13.5
Non-ferrous metals	68	3.1
Manufactures of metals	69	14.6

Source: As table 8.4.

opportunity cost of which should be measured in hard currency, is a
considerable gesture; it is even more significant at a time when exports
of energy to the east European allies are being cut back (see Coker
1984).

For India, however, the petroleum products are perhaps more important. Since Indian official publications do not reveal the source of
petroleum product imports, we have used Soviet statistics (see table
8.9) to estimate that nearly 61 per cent of India's total middle distillate
imports between 1970 and 1976 and just over 23 per cent of middle
distillate imports between 1977 and 1981 came from the USSR. (All of
India's middle distillate imports in 1977/8 came from the USSR.) Indian
consumption of petroleum products is, somewhat unusually, heavily
biased towards the consumption of middle distillates, especially diesel
and kerosene, as against light distillates and heavy ends. Kerosene is
largely used as domestic fuel and for lighting purposes, while road and
rail transport are major consumers of diesel. The sales and excise tax
structure seems to encourage this consumption pattern. The USSR has
been a major source of middle distillate imports for India.

The USSR has gradually become a very important source of petroleum crude. Between 1977/8 and 1982/3 the USSR's share in India's
total imports of crude never rose above 15.1 per cent but by 1984/5 had
risen to 23.1 per cent. The Middle Eastern countries (Iran, Iraq, Saudi
Arabia, the United Arab Emirates) accounted for over 80 per cent of

Table 8.9. *Soviet exports of oil and oil products to India, 1970–1985*

	Soviet exports: oil and oil products (Rblsm)	Conversion factor (Rs per Rbl)	Soviet exports: oil and oil products (Rsm)	Indian imports: oil only (Rsm)
1970	4.3	8.33	35.9	—
1971	9.8	8.33	81.9	—
1972	7.0	8.78	62.0	—
1973	10.8	8.78	94.8	—
1974	66.5	10.52	699.2	—
1975	93.6	11.55	1,080.9	—
1976	98.0	11.55	1,131.9	—
1977	191.0	11.55	2,196.9	814.5
1978	220.0	11.97	2,634.6	1,286.3
1979	403.2	9.84	3,967.2	2,835.0
1980	650.8	9.74	6,339.3	3,629.7
1981	830.5	9.34	7,756.9	4,616.0
1982	815.7	9.86	8,042.8	6,108.0
1983	972.3	10.02	9,742.4	7,617.0
1984	1,066.8	10.66	11,372.1	7,925.0
1985	867.1	11.54	10,006.3	—

Notes: 1. Soviet statistics do not distinguish between Soviet exports of oil and oil products. 2. Only oil products were exported to India between 1970 and 1976. 3. The source of India's imports of oil products is not disclosed in Indian statistics.
Sources: Vneshnaia Torgovlya, various issues; DGCIS, *Monthly Statistics of the Foreign Trade of India,* various issues.

India's imports of crude between 1977/8 and 1982/3. Acceptance of an Indian request for an increase in Soviet oil exports in response to the Iran-Iraq war in 1980 was very helpful; most of the increases since the war have come from Saudi Arabia and the USSR (as table 8.9 demonstrates). The domestic production of crude oil has indeed gone up to two-thirds of annual consumption, but for India, the advantage of being able to pay for Soviet crude in rupees has certainly helped her hard currency balance of payments to weather the oil price storms of the 1970s. Besides, but for Soviet exports of crude oil, the absorption of India's overall trade surplus with the USSR may have become a serious problem. Crude oil has constituted a substantial proportion of India's imports from the USSR every year between 1977 and 1981: 18.6, 27.3, 34.5, 35.9 and 40.6 per cent respectively. India's exports to the USSR would almost certainly have had to be curtailed in the eighties in the absence of Soviet oil exports; the constraints of bilateral balancing would have prevented the colossal increases in India's exports to the USSR which occurred in the eighties.

8.2.2 Structure of India's exports to the USSR

We mentioned in the previous section that manufactures were the most dynamic category among India's exports to the world as a whole over the seventies. Between 1970/1 and 1978/9, manufactured exports to the world grew at a rate of 11.2 per cent annually, while food and raw materials grew at a rate of only 4.4 per cent and 1.3 per cent per annum (Wolf 1982, p. 27). In the case of the USSR, however, it is the three categories of food, tobacco and crude materials (RITC 0, 1 and 2) – all three primary commodities – which have continued to grow rapidly over the seventies. But these commodities (excepting tobacco) have tended to either stagnate or decline in volume terms in the case of the rest of the world (see table 8.4). Taken together with the fact that the DMEs were the most dynamic markets for Indian exports in the seventies, one can reasonably hypothesise that most of the increases in manufactured exports went to these dynamic markets, while the increases in primary products were absorbed by the USSR.

Coffee exports, one of India's main non-traditional primary exports, have grown faster to the USSR than to the world as a whole (see table 8.4). Exports of tea, one of India's major traditional exports, have more than doubled in real terms between 1970/1 and 1981/2; on the other hand, exports to the rest of the world have tended to decline somewhat. Exports to the USSR of pepper, another product (like tea) in which India is an important contributor to world trade, doubled between 1970/1 and 1971/2, stabilised at that level over the seventies, and then rose again sharply in the eighties. On the other hand, pepper exports to the rest of the world rose (in volume terms) over the seventies, but by the early eighties had returned to the same level as in the early seventies. Exports of oilcakes to the USSR fell dramatically in the latter half of the seventies (though they simultaneously rose to the rest of the world) but rose again very sharply in the early eighties.[6] Exports of tobacco grew both to the USSR and to the rest of the world; but as table 8.4 shows, the growth rate of export volume was 17.3 per cent for the USSR, but only 2.5 per cent for the rest of the world. Exports to the USSR of cashews, in which again India is an important contributor to world trade, while fluctuating considerably, still grew; on the other hand, exports to the rest of the world, markedly declined after the mid-seventies.

For many major traditional commodities (tea, tobacco, spices, oil-cakes, and jute and cotton textiles) the pressure of domestic demand on slow-growing or even stagnant production was a possible reason for poor export performance in DME markets. It is possible that in-elastic supply meant that export growth to the USSR of these primary commodities may have been at the expense of increases to DME markets (although this question cannot be firmly resolved without investigating in detail demand conditions in DME markets as well as India's competitive position in these markets in respect of each com-modity). It is equally possible that low price and income elasticity of demand for these primary commodities in DME markets may mean that India could not increase its exports of these commodities to these markets without a sharp deterioration in its terms of trade. At the same time, it is certain that with India's deteriorating ratio of land to labour and with high income elasticities of demand for agricultural products, income growth is bound to result in falling export proceeds. However, yield increases (especially in raw cotton and jute) could still result in output increases, and appropriate agricultural policies many need to be devised for the purpose. Besides, income increases in India have not been rapid enough to justify a fall in exportable surpluses of agricul-tural commodities (Nayyar 1976, pp. 342–3; Wolf 1982, pp. 72–3).

In the light of the buoyancy of primary commodity exports to the USSR discussed above, it would be interesting to see how exports of manufactures to the USSR have fared in comparison with manufac-tured goods in India's exports to the world. This issue is of particular interest since earlier studies of India's exports to east Europe showed that over the sixties, the share of manufactures in exports to these markets was normally lower than their share in India's total exports (Alagh 1975, p. 1; Ambegaonkar 1974, p. 419; Chisti 1973, p. 33; Nayyar 1976, p. 25; Nayyar 1977, p. 117). Interest has also been focused on this issue since the targets for primary commodity exports to these markets were met consistently and often over-fulfilled; but exports of non-traditional items normally fell below targets specified in trade plans.[7] This conclusion assumes further significance if we recall our finding in an earlier chapter that manufactured goods had a smaller share in LDC exports to the East than they did in LDC exports to the world as a whole.

Table 8.10 shows the commodity composition of India's exports to the USSR. The share of manufactures in exports to the USSR has

Table 8.10. *Commodity composition of India's exports to the USSR,*
1970/1–1984/5 (percentages)

	70/1–72/3	73/4–75/6	76/7–78/9	79/80–81/2	82/3–84/5
Food and tobacco	38.1	41.2	46.3	41.8	34.6
Raw materials	9.2	10.4	4.0	5.6	4.3
Manufactures	52.7	48.4	49.6	52.6	61.0

Source: As table 8.4.

stabilised around 50 per cent, while the share of manufactures in India's overall exports is quite close to 60 per cent. So while the share of manufactures in India's exports to the USSR has risen over the seventies, it is still not quite as high as its share in India's overall exports. However, this difference is not so surprising, considering that the USSR is itself an industrialised country. Between a quarter and third of India's exports over the seventies went to LDCs (including OPEC countries), the commodity composition of which is naturally biased in favour of manufactures. Another striking fact about Table 8.10 is the high share of food in India's exports to the USSR; the share of food has risen while that of crude materials and oils and fats has fallen. Although the share of manufactures in exports to the USSR has remained relatively stable, machinery and transport equipment has risen from a negligible share in the early seventies to an average of 4.8 per cent over 1976/7 to 1978/9 and 4.6 per cent over 1979/80 to 1981/2; this, however, is still lower than the 7.3 per cent share over 1976–8 and 7.5 per cent share over 1979–80 in India's exports to the world. Over 1982/3 to 1984/5, however, the share of manufactures in Indian exports to the USSR has indeed shot up, and so has the share of machinery and transport equipment to around 9 per cent.

The commodity composition has undergone a sea-change over the two decades from 1960/1 to 1984/5. Commodities which together accounted for as much as 94 per cent of India's exports to the USSR in 1960/1, contributed only 42 per cent to them in 1984/5. Between 1970/1 and 1984/5, however, the commodity composition has not altered so substantially. The share of raw leather had fallen over the period while that of leather manufactures was rising. Non-traditional manufactures like machinery (RITC 7), medicines, cosmetics and toilet preparations and soaps and detergents (the latter in the early eighties), and traditional products like cotton manufactures, had recorded colossal

Table 8.11. *Traditional and non-traditional goods in India's exports to the world, 1950/1–1979/80 (percentages)*

	50/1	55/6	60/1	65/6	70/1	75/6	76/7	77/8	79/80
Traditional goods, of which:	70.6	68.9	64.4	60.0	42.6	28.9	26.9	31.6	39.0
Tea	13.4	17.9	18.7	14.3	9.7	5.9	5.7	10.3	5.6
Jute manufactures	18.9	19.4	20.5	22.7	12.4	6.2	3.9	4.5	5.2
Cotton textiles	19.7	9.3	8.7	6.9	4.9	4.0	5.2	4.1	6.3
Non-traditional goods, of which:	6.5	7.0	15.2	24.5	40.0	53.7	53.3	50.5	61.0
Iron ore	—	1.0	2.6	5.2	7.5	5.3	4.6	4.5	4.4
Silver	n.a.	n.a.	n.a.	n.a.	n.a.	4.3	3.3	1.5	8.0
Gems	n.a.	n.a.	—	1.8	2.7	3.7	5.6	10.1	—
Leather and manufactures	4.3	3.8	4.1	4.3	5.3	5.6	4.6	4.9	8.6
Iron and steel	0.3	n.a.	1.5	1.6	5.9	1.7	5.6	3.5	1.6
Engineering goods	0.1	n.a.	2.7	2.5	7.6	10.2	11.0	11.5	10.1
Chemicals	1.4	0.9	0.5	1.1	1.9	2.1	2.2	2.2	3.2
Clothing	—	—	0.1	0.8	2.0	5.0	6.5	6.1	7.5

Source: Balasubramanyam 1984.

increases in absolute and relative terms. Although the relative share of clothing (RITC 8) has not changed, it has also recorded substantial increases in absolute terms.

Since manufactures have traditionally constituted a high proportion of India's exports since the fifties, primarily on account of the predominance of cotton textiles and jute manufactures, it is now common practice, while discussing India's export structure, to use 'traditional' and 'non-traditional' goods as the conceptual categories. Just as traditional goods have included important manufactures among them, non-traditional goods have consisted not just of manufactures but have included primary commodities such as iron ore, marine products and coffee.

It is quite plain from a comparison of tables 8.11 and 8.12 that the share of non-traditional products in India's exports to the USSR has been well below their share in India's total exports throughout the seventies. It appears that in this respect the position has not changed from that prevailing in the sixties. Since exports of non-traditional items were repeatedly falling short of annual trade plan provisions, a determined effort was made in the latter half of the sixties to include a larger number of non-traditional items in the trade plan. Efforts to diversify exports by restricting the level of exports of the traditional items to east Europe by pegging exports to the then current level did not seem to yield results. Another fact that stands out about table 8.12 is that the share of non-traditional goods has certainly risen over the seventies. From an average annual share of about 30 per cent in the first half of the seventies, it rose to around 41 per cent over 1976/7 to 1978/9 and even higher over 1979/80 to 1981/2.

Especially interesting in this increase of non-traditional manufac-tured exports to the USSR in the eighties is the role of the two Special Export Zones (SEZs or Free Trade Zones) set up by India off the west coast.[8] Several Western multinationals decided to set up plants in these SEZs in order to penetrate the Soviet market. Ciba-Geigy, Hoechst, Helene Curtis and American Home Products are among the companies whose local subsidiaries set up factories in the Kandla SEZ to manu-facture mainly for export to the USSR. A combination of multinational technology and cheap Indian labour has given the Soviet Union access to similar quality drugs, toothpaste, soap, shampoo, cosmetics and so on without having to spend hard currency. In fact it is precisely these commodities (medicines, cosmetics and toilet preparations, and soaps and detergents) which climbed to being among the top ten exports to the USSR in 1981/2. In 1982/3, 15 per cent of all exports of the Santa Cruz SEZ and 85 per cent of the Kandla SEZ were being exported to the Soviet and east European markets (Kumar 1985). By 1983/4, however, exports to the USSR of soaps, detergents and cosmetics had plummeted.

A recent ILO study on Asian export processing zones concluded that the direct employment effect of industries set up in these zones is insignificant. Barring Singapore and Malaysia, the contribution of SEZs to employment in manufacturing has been negligible. Signifi-cantly, in the case of India, the proportion is 0.1 per cent of total employment in the manufacturing sector. Secondly, since the goods produced in the zones use relatively simple technologies, the back-ward and forward linkages of these industries have been minimal. Regarding the policy's impact on government revenues and the sub-sequent impact on increased employment, the governments of host countries had to spend sizeable funds to create infrastructural facilities in the SEZs. The tax holidays further reduce the advantage to govern-ment revenue. More significantly, as soon as tax holidays expire, the industrial processing units are reallocated to more favourable sites in other countries, especially in the context of competition among

Table 8.12. *Traditional and non-traditional goods in India's exports to the USSR, 1970/1–1981/2 (percentages)*

	70/1	71/2	72/3	73/4	74/5	75/6	76/7	77/8	78/9	79/80	80/1	81/2
Traditional goods	52.4	67.8	66.1	58.9	64.2	60.2	53.2	57.6	47.1	48.6	41.2	36.2
Tea	13.4	17.6	11.0	11.4	14.1	17.5	12.2	20.2	14.8	12.6	9.9	8.3
Spices	1.8	4.0	2.3	3.5	3.2	4.1	4.3	3.2	4.0	2.7	2.2	1.4
Tobacco, unmanufactured	2.8	8.1	10.0	6.5	4.1	6.9	5.5	4.8	6.2	4.6	4.1	4.2
Raw jute	2.1	1.3	1.3	neg.	neg.	neg.	neg.	neg.	neg.	neg.	0.3	0.3
Mica	2.8	2.6	1.9	1.8	1.7	1.7	1.8	1.1	2.0	1.5	0.6	1.0
Vegetable oils	2.3	2.9	2.5	4.3	2.6	2.4	1.9	1.5	neg.	neg.	—	—
Essential oils	0.9	0.2	0.3	0.6	0.5	0.6	0.3	0.3	0.2	0.3	0.2	neg.
Cotton piecegoods	5.1	3.9	9.8	5.1	5.3	4.3	8.1	2.7	5.4	6.8	5.2	7.2
Jute manufactures	17.4	16.6	18.0	11.4	14.0	16.0	11.4	10.4	8.3	13.0	10.5	5.0
Groundnuts	1.2	1.0	0.8	3.9	1.4	2.4	1.0	—	—	0.4	0.8	1.1
Cashews	2.6	9.6	8.2	10.4	17.3	4.3	6.7	13.4	6.2	6.7	7.4	7.7
Non-traditional goods	38.1	28.7	28.2	32.2	25.5	30.9	41.2	37.4	44.4	51.5	47.2	35.3
Coffee	3.0	3.5	3.4	neg.	4.2	4.1	6.6	10.3	8.0	6.8	5.9	2.2
Leather and manufactures	9.6	6.9	8.7	15.0	7.6	9.5	8.7	7.7	9.2	10.5	8.1	3.0
Chemicals	3.3	2.6	2.2	2.5	4.3	4.8	5.7	3.4	5.3	9.5	6.4	13.7
Floor coverings	0.7	0.5	0.5	neg.	0.4	0.6	—	0.5	0.6	1.0	0.7	1.5
Iron and steel	8.3	3.7	3.1	2.7	neg.	neg.	3.7	4.0	7.5	1.0	neg.	neg.
Aluminium and alloys	neg.	neg.	0.5	neg.	neg.	neg.	0.3	0.6	0.4	neg.	neg.	—
Metal manufactures	2.2	0.5	0.4	0.5	0.3	0.3	0.4	0.8	0.5	0.7	0.3	0.4
Machinery and transport equipment	0.4	0.7	1.4	1.9	2.3	4.0	5.7	3.4	5.3	3.6	4.1	6.1
Clothing	8.4	8.7	6.5	8.3	5.4	6.2	8.4	6.7	7.6	8.5	7.3	7.4
Footwear	2.2	1.6	1.5	1.3	1.0	1.0	1.3	neg.	neg.	neg.	neg.	neg.
Rubber manufactures	neg.	neg.	neg.	neg.	neg.	0.4	0.4	neg.	neg.	neg.	0.3	1.0
Rice	—	—	—	—	—	—	—	—	—	9.9	14.1	—

Source: As table 8.4.

developing countries. For example, in one of the leading SEZs of the Philippines, out of sixty-eight units twenty have already closed down. Similar evidence is appearing for the Indian SEZs, where after making a killing on the east European market, the firms are beginning to close. The average life span of firms in the Kandla SEZ is 3.19 years (Santa Cruz 4.09 years) (Kumar 1985).

Even in terms of foreign exchange earnings the sudden increase of non-traditional manufactures from the SEZs may be an uncertain gain. In 1982/3 the total exports of the Kandla SEZ were valued at Rs1,326.9m, while imports totalled Rs856.8m (surplus Rs470.1m).[9] If dividends, royalty payments and profit repatriation are taken into account, not to speak of transfer pricing, the net foreign exchange contribution of these zones may be negative.

In tables 8.13 and 8.14 we have analysed the significance of the USSR as a source of imports and as a market for exports. If the commodity specification of Soviet exports to India is defined as those commodity categories where the share of imports from the USSR is greater than the share of Indian imports from the USSR in India's total imports, the following three commodities can be identified: petroleum, petroleum products and paper (mainly newsprint). Except for certain years, even the share of crude and manufactured fertilisers and machinery and transport equipment in imports from the USSR is not as high as the USSR's share in India's total imports.

Table 8.14 shows that the USSR's share in India's exports of primary commodities far exceeds the USSR's share in India's total exports. However, its share in India's exports of machinery and transport equipment has been consistently below its share in India's total exports; though this is not the case for clothing, leather, jute manu-factures, footwear and certain chemicals. Thus in recent years, the USSR has been the biggest buyer of Indian cotton fabrics, garments, knitwear, detergents, cosmetics, medicines, handicraft products and carpets. More than 90 per cent of the output of India's knitwear industry goes to the USSR.

8.3 Stability of India's export earnings

Fluctuations in export earnings have been a matter of concern for most LDCs, especially those dependent on primary exports. At the very least, this instability in export earnings results in uncertainty in regard to import capacity and hence to general development prospects (MacBean 1966). Hence, most of the discussion in international

Table 8.13. *The USSR's share in total Indian imports by commodity category, 1970/1–1981/2 (percentages)*

	70/1	71/2	72/3	73/4	74/5	75/6	76/7	77/8	78/9	79/80	80/1	81/2
Wheat	—	—	—	31	16	—	—	—	—	—	—	—
Crude fertiliser and minerals	6	9	12	9	9	10	13	12	8	3	—	4
Chemical elements and compounds	3	3	3	3	5	5	2	3	1	1	—	—
Medicines	3	2	2	2	4	3	—	2	—	2	—	—
Fertilisers	7	3	6	2	10	3	10	11	6	4	10	5
Paper, paperboard and manufactures	21	16	18	27	27	18	24	19	13	7	10	neg.
Non-metallic mineral manufactures	10	10	2	1	—	—	—	—	—	—	—	—
Iron and steel	6	3	4	3	4	6	5	2	—	—	—	—
Non-ferrous metals	4	2	7	15	12	2	—	3	2	3	2	2
Manufactures of metal	2	11	5	4	13	5	5	7	3	—	2	1
Machinery, non-electrical	19	11	7	6	11	11	9	6	6	6	6	4
Machinery, electrical	9	8	10	6	7	4	6	3	3	2	3	2
Transport equipment	3	3	8	1	3	—	—	22	12	13	—	—

Source: As table 8.4.

Table 8.14. *The USSR's share in India's total exports by commodity category, 1970/1–1981/2 (percentages)*

	70/1	71/2	72/3	73/4	74/5	75/6	76/7	77/8	78/9	79/80	80/1	81/2
Rice	—	—	—	—	—	—	—	—	—	—	60	32
Cashews	10	29	34	38	61	18	27	54	27	33	62	66
Coffee	24	31	32	—	35	27	26	76	23	28	35	27
Tea	18	21	22	22	27	30	18	23	17	22	29	35
Pepper	22	43	40	31	29	41	40	36	28	34	54	63
Other spices	4	2	6	3	13	neg.	8	neg.	2	42	4	5
Oilcakes	8	9	13	6	12	3	neg.	3	—	neg.	24	35
Tobacco, unmanufactured	19	—	48	27	21	31	25	31	25	33	47	36
Cigarettes	—	4	96	94	78	98	78	43	11	59	77	90
Groundnuts	41	34	41	34	24	20	7	—	—	20	17	100
Raw jute	95	18	78	2	2	11	64	46	51	70	69	41
Mica	35	32	34	41	39	48	47	39	41	46	38	56
Lac	2	3	4	6	15	14	7	3	6	6	4	1
Vegetable and fruit juice	66	65	74	28	—	43	30	21	2	—	31	62
Castor oil	93	89	32	41	35	23	30	69	neg.	neg.	—	—
Chemical elements compounds	9	11	—	3	10	13	22	—	10	—	3	20
Dyeing, tanning, colouring materials	41	37	33	14	36	30	23	23	22	32	29	—
Medicines	7	5	2	15	18	22	22	20	12	42	10	65
Essential oils	37	22	31	27	19	42	27	28	13	38	69	81
Leather and leather goods	27	14	15	25	22	20	15	20	11	14	30	12
Textile fabrics (cotton, jute, synthetics)	14	10	19	9	14	16	13	12	9	14	20	24
Iron and steel	19	19	23	14	2	neg.	4	9	14	6	6	41
Metal manufactures	17	4	4	4	2	2	—	3	1	2	2	3
Machinery and transport equipment	1	2	5	5	5	6	8	6	5	5	10	16
Clothing	59	52	35	25	17	13	12	13	7	11	16	19
Footwear	40	29	37	29	21	20	20	15	8	4	1	2
Jute manufactures	18	12	22	15	20	28	26	27	26	40	34	—

Source: As table 8.4.

economics literature on instability in foreign trade is limited to an examination of exports stability. Export earnings stabilisation has been a major concern at various UNCTAD conferences and a major issue of the New International Economic Order called for by LDCs at these conferences. International commodity agreements have been seen as an instrument for commodity price and earnings stabilisation; bilateral trade and payments agreements have been seen as another such instrument.

Trade on a multilateral basis is subject to many factors beyond the control of the individual LDCs. But bilateral trade and payments agreements in which quantities and prices are agreed upon in advance are considered to mitigate the fluctuations in a country's export earnings. Hence, we have attempted to compare the degree of instability in India's exports to the USSR with that in India's exports to the rest of the world (see table 8.15). Although a part of India's trade with the rest of the world is conducted under clearing agreements (mainly with Czechoslovakia, East Germany, Poland, Rumania and a small number of LDCs), this constitutes less than 5 per cent of India's total exports to the rest of the world. Its effect on the instability index for the rest of the world will therefore be marginal.

The instability index we have constructed is the coefficient of variation, which expresses the standard deviation (of export earnings) as a percentage of the arithmetic mean (of export earnings) over the period 1970/1 to 1981/2.[10] These coefficients are especially suitable for comparing the instability of two time series where arithmetic means differ; this will naturally be the case for India's exports to the USSR and the rest of the world.

Table 8.15 gives the value of the instability indices by commodity categories for export earnings from the USSR and from the rest of the world. Comparison is aided by column 3 in the table which gives the same information, except that the instability index for the USSR is set to 100. From the table the following conclusions can be drawn.

In most cases, the export earnings from the USSR were more unstable. The value of India's exports to the rest of the world was less stable than India's exports to the USSR only in the case of a small number of commodities: groundnuts, raw jute, spices (other than pepper), castor oil and cashews (the difference in clothing is very small). Cashews is the only major commodity in this list; the rest of the commodities together do not account for more than 5 per cent of India's exports to the USSR. The five commodities (including cashews) in which India's export earnings from the USSR are more stable than

Table 8.15. *Instability index of India's export earnings from the USSR and the rest of the world (by commodity category), 1970/1–1981/2*

	USSR	Rest of the world	Rest of the world (USSR = 100)
Food and tobacco			
Cashews	80.0	100.3	125
Coffee	82.8	70.9	84
Tea	56.6	45.9	79
Pepper	45.8	40.6	89
Other spices	62.5	74.9	125
Oilcakes	115.6	56.0	47
Tobacco	62.8	41.6	64
Cigarettes	147.6	99.0	65
Crude materials			
Groundnuts	68.0	92.0	125
Raw jute	88.0	120.1	144
Mica	19.3	16.1	75
Lac	104.2	31.2	30
Linseed oil	141.4	112.5	80
Castor oil	57.4	77.8	136
Manufactures			
Chemicals	144.0	52.0	36
Detergents	131.3	116.5	81
Leather	49.7	48.2	97
Cotton piecegoods (1970/1–76/7)	51.6	43.2	64
Textile fabrics (cotton/jute manufactures, floor coverings)	61.5	29.8	49
Iron and steel	106.5	82.0	77
Machinery and transport equipment	114.0	58.6	51
Clothing	76.7	77.3	101
Footwear	54.0	52.8	98

Source: As table 8.4.

from the rest of the world constitute no more than 15 per cent of India's total exports to the USSR in any year (except 1974/5).

It must be pointed out at this stage that the stability of India's export earnings from bilateral trading is significant for two reasons: first, its impact on India's capacity to import from the USSR; second, its impact on the profits, employment and capacity utilisation in industries which are dependent to a large extent on exports to the USSR. It must be emphasised at the same time that the impact of stability/instability in India's exports to the USSR will not make any difference to stability of overall export earnings for the obvious reason that trade is conducted in different currencies, and the earnings generated in exports to the USSR cannot be used by India to make purchases elsewhere. In this sense, stability/instability of earnings from the USSR are not as significant as that in hard currency.

Nevertheless, as stated above, instability can affect India's import capacity as well as the exporting industries. Several industries or economic activities in many different states are crucially dependent on exports to the USSR; tea, jute, floor coverings and some engineering products in West Bengal; carpets, handicrafts, handlooms and leather in Uttar Pradesh; rice and agricultural products in Haryana; knitwear in the Punjab; textiles, drugs, chemicals and engineering products in Gujarat and Maharashtra; coffee in Karnataka; cashews, cardamoms and spices in Kerala; leather in Tamil Nadu; tobacco in Andhra Pradesh; and groundnut extractions (oilcakes) and fruit juices in Madhya Pradesh. The significance of stability in export earnings was particularly brought home to many Indian exporters in 1981 and 1982, when the USSR suddenly cancelled orders because it was unable to generate sufficient rupee funds when oil prices fell. The Soviet FTOs seem to have over-contracted in 1979 and 1980, when increased oil prices gave them larger than expected rupee funds, on the assumption that prices would hold in 1981 and 1982. However, when oil prices fell, their generation of funds proved less than expected. Once technical credits could not be extended beyond a point, the Soviets withdrew from certain contracts.

Instability in export earnings can be the result of either price variations or quantity variations. In table 8.16 we present an instability index of price and quantity for exports to the USSR and the rest of the world for sixteen commodities. These constitute well over 50 per cent of India's exports to the USSR in most years (the remaining categories had to be excluded since no quantity or price data is possible at 1- or 2-digit level classification). Table 8.16 shows that prices of India's exports to the USSR are more stable than export prices to the rest of the world in the case of ten of the sixteen commodities. On the other hand, the volume of India's exports to the USSR is more stable than export volumes to the rest of the world in only six cases –

Table 8.16. *Instability index of volume and price of India's exports to the USSR and the rest of the world (by commodity category), 1970/1–1981/2*

	Quantity			Price		
	USSR	Rest of the world	Rest of the world USSR = 100	USSR	Rest of the world	Rest of the world USSR = 100
Food and tobacco						
Coffee	43.6	27.2	63	58.1	58.7	103
Tea	27.2	10.3	44	39.3	46.3	119
Pepper	36.0	33.1	93	30.8	28.5	93
Other spices	42.4	41.6	98	45.0	50.0	111
Oilcakes	99.2	37.7	39	36.9	34.5	87
Tobacco, unmanufactured	41.9	24.4	58	27.8	29.7	107
Cigarettes	121.4	84.2	69	24.9	22.1	89
Crude materials						
Groundnuts	50.5	84.3	167	62.2	56.5	91
Raw jute	92.7	100.9	109	21.2	39.2	185
Mica	11.8	30.0	254	23.1	25.4	110
Lac	48.5	22.1	46	77.3	36.8	48
Oils and fats						
Linseed oil	129.8	126.4	97	38.0	31.3	82
Castor oil	43.3	77.1	178	34.4	35.3	103
Manufactures						
Detergents	109.7	125.1	114	36.0	66.4	185
Leather	40.3	53.5	133	64.7	48.9	76
Cotton piecegoods	52.4	25.3	48	27.4	31.7	116

Note: For other manufactures it is not possible to calculate instability indices for volume and price because units of measurement within broad 1- or 2-digit categories are not comparable.
Source: As table 8.4.

groundnuts, raw jute, mica, detergents, leather and castor oil, of which only leather is a major commodity. For most major commodities exported to the USSR – tea, coffee, tobacco, mica, cashews and cotton piecegoods – export prices to the USSR are more stable than prices obtained by India from the rest of the world. Table 8.16 therefore suggests that quantities are a more important factor explaining the greater instability of India's export earnings from the USSR compared with earnings from the rest of the world.

To test whether fluctuation in volume is actually more responsible than price variation for the instability in India's export earnings from the USSR, we carried out a Spearman's rank correlation test. We found that the volume of exports is more responsible for fluctuations in value of exports both to the USSR and to the rest of the world. However, the relationship is stronger in the case of the USSR. The coefficient of correlation between the value and volume of exports is 0.816 for the USSR, and 0.587 for the rest of the world. At the same time, the coefficient of correlation between value of exports and unit value (or price) was 0.29 for the USSR, but 0.411 for the rest of the world. Thus the relationship between the instability of India's export earnings from the USSR and fluctuations in unit values seems to be relatively weak.

It is rather interesting that two earlier studies covering the sixties and early seventies had come to conclusions similar to ours. Both Banerji (1977) and Sharma (1977) found that fluctuations in export earnings from east Europe (including the USSR) were greater than from the rest of the world.[11] They also found that instability of export volume, rather than price, was critical in explaining the instability of India's export earnings from east Europe.

It appears, therefore, that while the USSR offers relatively stable prices to India, the physical volume of goods lifted from India varies from year to year. This is not to suggest that prices are not important at all; in certain commodities (e.g. leather) they are. A regression run to test the price elasticity of Soviet imports from India revealed that only in the case of leather was the correlation coefficient between price and exports significantly different from zero. Besides, although the prices of India's exports to the USSR may be relatively stable compared with prices to the rest of the world, India's competitors in the Soviet market may offer lower prices in particular years. For example, a detailed study of the Soviet market in respect of twelve major commodity categories exported by India to the USSR showed that the USSR lifted a greater quantity of cotton textiles and jute from India or Pakistan depending upon which country offered the lower prices (Gidadhubli 1983, p. 158). Table 8.17 shows that in all commodities in which India has an absolute monopoly or near monopoly on the Soviet market – tea, black pepper, cashews, jute bags, jute packing materials – the instability index of total Soviet imports (in physical terms) is either the

Table 8.17. *Instability index of Soviet imports for selected commodities,*
1965–1979

	Total Soviet imports	Imports from India
Tea	35.4	36.1
Coffee	25.1	43.0
Raw tobacco	18.4	56.6
Raw wool	17.7	58.2
Jute	21.3	80.9
Cotton textiles	21.8	48.5
Black pepper	18.1	17.8
Cashews	33.4	33.4
Jute bags	23.8	21.3
Jute packing materials	20.8	18.6
Raw leather, small	156.7	57.1

Note: The index measures instability of *volume* of imports. The instability index
used is the coefficient of variation.
Source: Gidadhubli 1983.

same or very close to the instability index of imports from India. On the
other hand, for commodities in which India is an important supplier
but is faced with some competition – coffee, raw tobacco, raw wool,
jute and cotton textiles – the instability index of total Soviet imports
is lower than the index for imports from India. Since the USSR has
been importing these commodities from many different countries,
it is reasonable to infer that the USSR allocated a given expenditure between countries depending on the price offered by each
country.

   Fluctuations in the physical volume of India's exports to the USSR
(which we saw was the major cause of instability in India's export
earnings) may occur on account of two reasons: first, domestic factors
affecting the country's exportable surplus (e.g. profitability of domestic sales to exports, fluctuations in supply, etc.), and/or second,
changes in demand conditions in the USSR. It has been rightly suggested that the reasons will vary from commodity to commodity. Needless
to say, appropriate policy measures may have to be taken to minimise
irregularities in supply. While the domestic factors could be taken care
of through policy measures, the Indian government may find it difficult to influence Soviet FTOs, which make their purchases from private
exporters by entering the market directly.

8.4 Terms of trade

Before we present the evidence on the terms of trade India obtained from the USSR and the rest of the world, the limitations of the available data should be pointed out. Among the usual limitations, the first is the non-availability of actual price data. Hence, unit value data has to be used instead. For primary products, which tend to be homogeneous, unit values should be perfectly adequate. But for manufactured products unit values for broad groups of commodities can only serve as poor proxies for actual price data, primarily for two reasons. First, differences in unit values of exports to/imports from different countries may be caused by a divergence in composition of products included in a commodity category, no matter how disaggregated the trade data. Second, differences in unit values may result from quality differences in products.

In addition, there are some special problems which relate to Indian data. Indian traders are known to have indulged in the practice of under-invoicing exports and over-invoicing imports in trading with convertible currency areas. In situations of exchange control the exporter gains direct access to foreign exchange overseas through such practices and the importer gains a larger claim to import-entitlement licences. It is possible, therefore, that the unit values of exports to the rest of the world are understated whereas the unit values of imports from these multilateral trade partners are overstated. These caveats must be kept in mind while interpreting the evidence below.

We have found it necessary to break up our period, 1970/1 to 1981/2, into two parts – 1970/1 to 1976/7 and 1977/8 to 1981/2 – for two reasons. First, the Indian trade classification became much more detailed particularly for manufactured goods. Many commodity categories at 4-digit level (and even at 3- and 2-digit level) ceased to be comparable after April 1977 with the commodity codes used earlier. Second, the number of commodities being traded between the two countries had also increased considerably by the mid-seventies as exports in particular diversified. Therefore, it was felt necessary that the base year be changed from 1970/1 to 1977/8.

Earlier studies which have attempted to construct India's net barter terms of trade index for east Europe and the rest of the world have found that the terms of trade India obtained from the former were certainly no worse than those from the latter. Our own analysis for the seventies and early eighties is conducted at two levels – aggregative and disaggregative. Our aggregative analysis is in terms of the move-

Table 8.18. *India's terms of trade with the USSR and the rest of the world, 1970/1–1981/2*

	USSR			Rest of the world		
	X unit value index	M unit value index	Terms of trade	X unit value index	M unit value index	Terms of trade
1970/1	100	100	100	100	100	100
1971/2	100.9	93.1	108.4	103.7	92.0	112.7
1972/3	101.0	101.7	99.3	109.4	86.3	126.8
1973/4	126.1	109.8	114.8	127.2	105.2	120.9
1974/5	162.1	218.2	74.3	134.6	182.9	73.6
1975/6	157.2	227.6	69.0	132.8	202.8	65.5
1976/7	200.1	167.8	119.3	174.1	189.6	91.8
1977/8	100	100	100	100	100	100
1978/9	92.5	91.2 (82.9)	101.4	90.6	101.5 (102.8)	89.3
1979/80	93.6	141.3 (105.3)	66.2	64.1	128.4 (110.3)	49.9
1980/1	92.1	195.0 (125.8)	47.2	92.5	190.4 (152.2)	48.6
1981/2	108.4	256.4 (139.7)	42.3	88.8	154.1 (96.1)	57.6

Notes: 1. Figures in brackets give the import unit value index after excluding crude. 2. Import unit value index excludes petroleum products, since the source(s) of Indian petroleum product imports are not revealed in published data.
Source: As table 8.4.

Table 8.19. Ratio of unit values of exports to the USSR and the rest of the world, 1970/1–1981/2 (Rest of the world = 100)

	70/1	71/2	72/3	73/4	74/5	75/6	76/7	77/8	78/9	79/80	80/1	81/2
Cashews	80	92	94	150	103	98	88	44	84	94	99	99
Coffee		100	75	91	100	85	83	87	90	87	116	108
Tea	113	109	109	118	131	119	113	99	95	99	102	106
Pepper	103	116	101	108	100	109	104	110	169	131	131	106
Spices	69	87	188	127	121	143	120		148	190		139
Oilcakes	103	104	120	91	103	104		118		97	95	92
Tobacco	106		148	110	117	116	126	102	115	89	103	109
Groundnut	107	103	126	104	109	105	109			94	130	110
Wool, greasy	102	97	76	68	88	92	91					
Wool, degreased	91	106	85	113	108		101					
Raw jute	99	101	145	112	139	149	121	131	92	217	191	182
Lac	71	89	74	113	173	13	97	79		88	66	103
Mica	672	218		369	213		291	707	741	320	1,228	1,193
Castor oil	118	112	121	107	101	106	117	117		99		
Pigments, paint	188	177	150	152	217	190		141	132	148	138	148
Essential oils	42	13	42	42	29	45	41	43	53	33	25	36
Detergents	141	124	136	77	99	195	107	129	41	76	74	87
Leather	61	50	—	57	63	55	78	60	68	89	145	71
Rubber tyres	176	120	—	206	174	235	93					
Cotton piecegoods	143	159	129	115	117	135	133					
Floor coverings	103	13	43	86	33	36.	98					
Jute bags/sacks	108	133	153	137	140	113	105					
Jute fabrics	88	84	87	94	99	91	95	93	104	164		95
Aluminium	108	107	99	87	88	89	90	90	79	80	89	72

Cotton fabric (bleached)								114	115	135	119	121
Cotton fabric (bleached)								111	141	104	231	121
Sacks and Bags (jute/cotton)								114	902	136	417	678
Wool carpets								51	47	11	72	53
Mica manufactures								136	128	78	1,010	330
Textile fabric	113	100	101	121	152	132	127					
Dresses								111	154	108	91	130
Shirts (men/boys)								121	117	106	104	119
Knitted garments								159	182	133	200	162
Skirts, dresses (women/girls)								464	99	92	45	162
Footwear	405	354	383	670	268	217	222	269	222	186	261	111

Source: As table 8.4.

ments of terms of trade. However, considering the problems discussed above connected with such aggregative analysis, we have also carried out a more detailed disaggregative analysis (based on Tables 8.19 and 8.20) to find out whether India's export and import prices have remained comparable with those obtained from the rest of the world over the seventies and early eighties.

Table 8.18 shows that the unit values of India's exports to the USSR were usually slightly higher than those to the rest of the world obtained during the two periods, 1970/1 to 1976/7 and 1977/8 to 1981/2. Although the export prices were gradually rising in both sets of markets, there were two sharp rises in India's import unit value index – 1974 and 1979 – both on account of oil price increases. The result has been that India's terms of trade have suffered sharply over the seventies and early eighties. The effect is particularly noticeable in India's terms of trade with the USSR. This is hardly surprising given that oil constitutes a high proportion of India's imports from the USSR.

Table 8.18, however, cannot capture the precise effect of the oil price increases on India's terms of trade because the import unit value index does not take into account petroleum product imports. As we have pointed out earlier, Indian trade statistics do not reveal the sources of imports of petroleum products. Considering that petroleum products (as distinct from crude petroleum) are such a large proportion of India's imports from the USSR, the import unit value index in table 8.18 is somewhat less reliable than its export unit value index. Nevertheless, it does demonstrate how dramatic has been the impact of oil price rises on Indo-Soviet terms of trade. The sudden increase in the volume of India's exports to the USSR in the early eighties can almost certainly be explained by the sharp increase in Soviet purchasing power resulting from these oil price increases in 1979. However, an examination of table 8.18 does not enable one to conclude whether India's overall terms of trade with the USSR are worse (or better) than her terms of trade with the rest of the world.

Perhaps an examination at a more disaggregated level may suggest whether India obtained more favourable prices from the USSR than from her multilateral trade partners.

In table 8.19 we compare the unit values of India's exports to the USSR and the rest of the world. The commodities listed in table 8.19 constitute at least two-thirds of India's exports to the USSR. To facilitate comparison, unit values are expressed in terms of index numbers using the rest of the world as base. The number of commodities in which the USSR pays somewhat better prices than those commodities

Table 8.20. *Ratio of unit values of imports from the USSR and the rest of the world, 1970/1–1981/2 (Rest of the world = 100)*

	70/1	71/2	72/3	73/4	74/5	75/6	76/7	77/8	78/9	79/80	80/1	81/2
Sulphur	—	108	—	108	140	102	98	—	—	137	—	99
Asbestos, crude	84	71	67	77	75	57	53	55	—	68	63	63
Fertiliser, nitrogenous	81	99	79	75	80	95	133	96	106	85	81	82
Fertiliser, other	—	80	90	66	78	79	—	110	—	—	89	96
Newsprint	102	106	101	118	126	95	95	91	94	92	95	82
Refractory	7	40	59	63	73	71	—	—	65	67	34	39
Iron and steel bar rods	68	289	195	157	220	305	262	130	210	327	535	531
Iron and steel heavy plates, vessels	99	105	99	79	98	159	104	—	—	—	—	—
Iron and steel medium plates and sheets	97	118	140	168	88	96	318	—	—	—	—	—
Iron and steel, thin (below 3mm. thickness)	72	78	109	182	104	72	228	—	—	—	—	—
Iron and steel wire (except wire rod)	—	85	256	82	197	252	—	81	75	135	90	—
Tubes and pipes of cast iron	95	64	105	—	82	76	50	100	—	—	382	136
Tubes and pipes (except cast iron)	83	144	124	100	65	84	91	110	114	129	117	206
Tubes and pipes (except cast iron, welded, clinched)	197	357	291	486	112	115	38	178	—	—	—	133
Tubes and pipes fittings	50	—	29	115	66	78	67	39	37	60	68	179
Copper and alloys worked	210	112	60	66	89	69	54	266	107	—	120	—
Nickel and alloys worked	121	103	80	99	107	92	100	—	110	66	106	—
Aluminium and alloys worked	96	50	160	51	108	—	—	117	180	61	75	91
Zinc and alloys worked	100	102	123	190	195	83	99	96	110	124	102	—

Source: As table 8.4.

in which it pays slightly less is higher. However, in regard to manufactured exports, the price differences may very well exist on account of differences in quality.

The unit values of crude imports from the USSR and the rest of the world are comparable, given that world oil market prices are simply converted from their dollar prices to rupees. In table 8.20, on the unit values of India's other imports, the sample is much smaller than in table 8.19.[12] As was discussed in the case of India's oil imports, the prices India pays for her imports from the USSR appear to be comparable to those from the rest of the world. And again, as in the case of India's exports, the picture appears to be mixed: in certain commodities (e.g. fertiliser) India has paid less to the USSR, while in others (e.g. certain kinds of iron and steel products) prices paid appear to be higher.

It was noted in earlier studies that over the sixties the gap between the prices of India's bilateral and multilateral trade partners had narrowed. Our analysis for the seventies and early eighties does not seem to contradict that conclusion. We have found no evidence to suggest that India's terms of trade with the USSR were any more unfavourable than those obtained in her trade with the rest of the world. By and large, her terms of trade have worsened during the seventies and early eighties on account of rising petroleum prices.[13]

8.5 Summary

The arguments in this chapter can be summarised as follows:
1. An examination of India's exports to the USSR and the rest of the world, both at an aggregate as well as a disaggregated level, suggested that India did not divert its exports from hard currency markets to the USSR during the seventies and early eighties. The extent of switch trading by the USSR of imports from India was quite limited during the seventies. However, it may have increased in the late seventies and early eighties. We present further evidence on switch trading in the eighties in Appendix 5.
2. We found that the commodity composition of Soviet-LDC trade during the seventies is rather different from that of Indo-Soviet trade over the same period. Manufactures constitute a very high proportion of Soviet imports from India; their share stabilised around 50 per cent of LDC exports to the USSR over the same period. The share of oil and oil products in Soviet exports to India has risen sharply during the seventies, and stood at nearly 80 per cent in the early eighties. But the

average share of SITC 3 (mineral fuels, lubricants and related materials) in Soviet exports to LDCs over the seventies never rose above
17 per cent, although that share was much higher in the case of certain
countries, many of which are political allies of the USSR.[14]

The demand for India's exports of primary commodities has
remained buoyant in the USSR, unlike in the markets of the rest of the
world. In fact, the share of manufactures in exports to the USSR has
tended to lag behind the share of manufactures in India's total exports.
However, that may simply be because the USSR is itself an industrialised country. The more disturbing fact, perhaps, about the commodity composition of India's exports to the USSR is that
non-traditional goods account for a much smaller share of Indian
exports to the USSR than they do in India's total exports. The factors
underlying this phenomenon may be twofold. First, India, like other
LDCs, has been viewed by the USSR (and other east European economies) as a source of traditional primary commodities; through the
fifties and sixties, in spite of Indian efforts at diversification of exports
to east Europe, primary commodities still accounted for an overwhelming share in her exports to these countries. That underlying
trend appears to have continued, in spite of the increasing importance
of non-traditional manufactures in India's exports to east Europe since
the early seventies. Secondly, the USSR has presumably seen east
Europe, rather than semi-industrialised economies like India, as the
source of imported manufactured goods. The fact about the inter-
sectoral nature of Soviet-east European trade (i.e. energy for machinery) is too well known to need repetition here.
3. We found that as in the sixties, India's export earnings from the
USSR had fluctuated more than her earnings from the rest of the world.
Instability in rupee earnings from exports to the USSR should make no
difference to India's hard currency export earnings. Moreover, considering the comparatively small share of the USSR (and east Europe)
in India's total exports, instability in earnings from exports to the
former is unlikely to make such a difference to overall export earnings
either. However, the limited impact of export earnings instability
could be felt on India's capacity to import from the USSR; but given
that India had faced problems in identifying goods to import from the
USSR, both in the sixties and the seventies, the significance of this
factor in practice could not have been great. It is true, though, that the
impact of instability in export earnings from the USSR may have been
great on factor earnings, employment and capacity utilisation in industries exporting a large proportion of their output to the USSR.

4. Analysis at both an aggregated as well as a disaggregated level revealed that the unit value index of India's exports to the USSR rose over the seventies; however, the dramatic oil price increases of 1973 and 1979 have more than offset the improvements in export prices. Considering that oil constitutes such a high proportion of Soviet exports to India, it has enormously increased Soviet purchasing power over Indian goods. There was, in fact, a sudden increase in Soviet imports from India (including rice) after the 1979 oil price increase in particular. Our calculation of the unit value index of India's imports from the USSR with, and without, petroleum showed a wide variation; the unit value index of imports including petroleum was higher than when petroleum was excluded. However, overall India's terms of trade were not any more unfavourable than her terms of trade with the rest of the world.

Appendix 4 Technical credits

The problem of unequal generation of funds in the bilateral account during a plan period is tackled through the instrument of temporary swing credits called 'technical credits'. This is the most important management instrument in the bilateral trading system and exists in all clearing systems. The unit of account being the rupee, the credit is advanced in rupees. There is no need for such an advance to be given to the Indian side. Technical credits find mention in the trade and payments agreements.

There are occasions when India's imports from a given east European country are comparatively slow and the rupees available in the central account are not sufficient to pay for its imports from India, e.g. when purchases of seasonal commodities like tea, coffee, pepper, cashews, etc., have to be made in bulk by an east European trade partner. To help tide over the situation, the Indian government has agreed to make temporary advances or 'technical credits' to the foreign banks concerned. These loans are repaid as soon as funds are generated in the central account (through payment for goods purchased by India or by repayments of economic credits). There is a ceiling up to which loans can be advanced. In the case of the USSR, however, there is no such ceiling. Usually the ceiling is calculated at about 15 per cent of the three-year moving average of total exports. The ceilings are fixed usually at the time the trade and payments agreements are concluded. Occasionally ad hoc requests for increasing the ceiling temporarily are received by India and the ceilings are increased for short periods. A small proportion of the technical credit is interest-free and when the foreign governments draw more, interest is charged at prevailing three-month Indian Treasury Bill rate. The account is kept by the Reserve Bank of India on behalf of the Indian government.

The technical credits are treated by the Indian government as export promotion measures, as they help the CMEA countries to make their purchases from India at times when they do not have sufficient funds in their central account. The technical credits drawn over a year are by and large repaid in the same year. It is assumed that at the end of a year the technical credit account would show a 'nil' balance in a bilaterally balanced system, though in fact, this is not the case. The balancing of payments takes place over a long period and therefore a 'nil' balance rarely arises. This account actually becomes the indicator of the balance of payments at the end of the year. However, this account is kept confidential by both governments, although on the Indian side it is budgeted and voted on by Parliament.

Once the technical credit account is drawn to its limit, the smaller east European countries have to go slow and virtually stop their purchases till the account is replenished by generation of funds through their exports. But there is no ceiling on technical credit which can be drawn by the USSR. It can be argued that giving short-term low interest credit for promotion of exports in a planned regime is not necessarily a bad thing, given that exports to a DME carry the additional burden of promotion, intermediary and other charges which are absent in this trade. However, since the technical credits are an important tool of management on the Indian side it should not be so lax as to permit over-exploitation. A graded rate of interest has been suggested as an alternative to act as a break after a certain stage. At times 'swap' arrangements in free foreign exchange have also been tried but only in the case of countries where technical credits had a limit. But where there are no limits the bilateral partner can use this instrument to promote (and in fact force) its exports on the partner by overdrawing.

Appendix 5 Switch trade

In section 1 of chapter 8 we argued that in the late seventies and early eighties there had been growing evidence of switch trading by the USSR; in this appendix we present further evidence of this phenomenon. Switch trade refers to the practice by the east European countries of re-exporting goods imported from India (either by reconsigning Indian goods in transit or actual re-exporting after import into the USSR) in order to earn hard currency. In this appendix we present evidence of such switch trading in Indian oilcakes. The evidence presented here corresponds with information in table 8.7. This shows that there was hardly any export of oilcakes to the USSR in the latter half of the seventies, but it seemed to rise dramatically in the eighties, while at the same time, oilcake exports to the rest of the world fell.

In summary, the mechanism of the switch trade is as follows. The USSR sells large sums of Indian rupees, running into millions of rupees annually, to west European importers of goods from India. In the process, the USSR secures convertible currency to finance its imports from the West; and the west European importers of goods get their imports cheaper since the Soviet Union sells them Indian rupees at a 10 to 12 per cent discount. In the process India is deprived of convertible currency on the goods bought by west European buyers.

As regards oilcakes, the EEC countries have been traditionally the main buyers of oilcakes from India. In 1979 these countries accounted for over 80 per cent of all Indian exports of oilcakes. Four large importers, one based in London and the other three in Hamburg, used to account for 90 per cent of all imports of oilcakes from India into the EEC. However, all this changed dramatically at the beginning of 1980. In 1981, on paper, these four west European importers did not purchase a single tonne of Indian oilcakes. In their place, two new 'importers' emerged: Messrs Generalexport and Messrs Sojuchimport, Moscow. The direction of India's exports of oilcakes changed completely suddenly, with the USSR ostensibly emerging as a principal buyer and the erstwhile west European buyers disappearing altogether from the scene. In other words, Indian exports of oilcakes suddenly ceased to earn any foreign exchange.

In reality, the oilcakes were still going to the same west European nations as before. The Indian agents of the same four west European bulk buyers of Indian oilcakes continued to be as active in the Indian oilcakes market as ever. In 1980 when on paper their foreign principals did not import a single tonne of Indian oilcakes, these Indian agents are believed to have bought over substantial quantities of oilcakes. These purchases were not made on behalf of the two Soviet firms which had formally opened the letters of credit in respect of export of these commodities. The letters of credit explicitly enjoin the Indian sellers not to enter into any correspondence with the two Soviet firms but to appropriate the shipments directly to the specified Indian agents and to send one set of shipping documents to the latter for further action. This is quite understandable since apparently Messrs Generalexport and Sojuchimport merely sell Indian rupees to the west European importers of Indian oilcakes and so are not concerned with the actual shipments of the goods. The shipping arrangements leave no doubt as to the real destination of the goods. The destination ports are mentioned as Rotterdam/Hamburg in transit to Leningrad/Odessa. The shipping vessels continue to be chartered in rotation by the four west European buyers and the goods are discharged at various ports as per their instructions.

It is unlikely that the concerned Indian authorities were unaware of this elaborate operation. What makes this unlikely is that the export of groundnut extractions (i.e. oilcakes) are canalised through the Indian State Trading Corporation (STC) and copies of all export contracts and related letters of credit are submitted to and registered by the sellers with the STC.[15]

9 Conclusions

The Soviet planning experience deeply influenced India's planners in the fifties, both in regard to their commitment to planning and to the particular strategy of planning. Although an assessment of the precise extent of Soviet influence on the strategy adopted in India's Second Plan (i.e. 'heavy-industry first') would be of interest to a student of the history of economic thought, it is outside the scope of this study. The available evidence suggests that Mahalanobis was fairly impressed with Soviet thinking on industrialisation.

Soviet and east European economic/technical assistance and Indo-east European trade played an important role in implementing the chosen planning strategy. The Mahalanobis strategy neglected the role of foreign trade, and from 1950 to 1969 India's total exports did not expand much. However, over the same period, Indo-east European trade expanded very rapidly due to bilateral trade and payments agreements. Bilateralism created secure markets for India's traditional exports, producing the purchasing power for India to import plant and machinery to implement the chosen import-substitution strategy in certain sectors.

In the seventies and eighties the macro-economic role of Indo-Soviet trade and Soviet aid in India's economy has been changing. Given the near absence of fresh aid authorisations by the USSR in the seventies and the changing structure of trade, the continuing macro-economic significance of the Indo-Soviet economic relationship consists increasingly in alleviating the balance of payments difficulties of the economy. Oil/oil products and arms have an overwhelming share in Soviet exports to India, both of which India also buys from hard currency markets. The special advantage for India of purchasing these commodities from the USSR lies in being able to pay for them in inconvertible rupees.

Our examination of Soviet economic interests in LDCs showed that the available data is consistent with the hypothesis that in the seventies the pursuit of economic advantage has become a major objective of Soviet economic relations with LDCs, as distinct from the period from 1954 to 1964 when economic relations were used largely as a political weapon.

It was also found that Soviet economic interests in India were rather different from Soviet economic interests in LDCs in general. Structural problems with the Soviet economy have compelled the Soviet leadership to increase technology and grain imports from hard currency areas since the late sixties. The result in the seventies has been a large Soviet debt to Western banks and governments. Soviet hard currency trade surpluses with LDCs, resulting largely from arms exports, have been playing a key role in relieving Soviet trade deficits with the West.[1] At the same time, a growing scarcity of raw materials in the USSR over the last decade or so has resulted in an increasing LDC role in meeting primary commodity (raw materials and tropical foodstuffs) demand in the USSR.

However, India plays no role in relieving the USSR's hard currency trade deficits with the DMEs, since Soviet arms exports to India are not paid for in hard currency; civilian trade is also conducted in inconvertible rupees. The fact that the USSR has been prepared to sell oil/oil products to India, which could have been exported elsewhere in exchange for hard currency, suggests that it is for strategic-political reasons that India is important to the USSR rather than for economic ones. In fact, Soviet oil/oil product exports to India might be very much to the USSR's economic and political disadvantage, in terms of its political relationship with east Europe. Given that oil is central to the USSR's economic relationship with east Europe, Soviet oil exports to India may even have an opportunity cost in political terms, especially considering that the USSR intends to raise prices and cut quantities of oil exports to east Europe. However, India is not the only LDC to which the USSR exports energy; Afghanistan, Bangladesh, Cuba, Ethiopia, Liberia, Morocco, Yemen and Nepal were the other LDCs importing Soviet oil in 1980 and 1981, though with most of them trade was paid for in hard currency.

Although economic relations with India play no hard currency role, Soviet imports of Indian consumer goods, both agricultural and, increasingly, manufactured goods, have tended to increase sharply in the eighties, particularly after oil price increases improved Soviet terms of trade with India. Raw materials form a negligible proportion of Indian exports to the USSR; but in the Third World India is among the few politically stable countries with a sufficiently large and diversified manufacturing sector for the USSR to consider it a reliable source of consumer goods in the long run. In the eighties the USSR has probably been saving hard currency by importing certain manufactured goods from India rather than from the West. In the Third World, it is unlikely that the newly industralised countries could fulfil this role given that Soviet relations with these countries are improving very slowly.

Soviet aid was an engine of growth of Indo-Soviet trade in the fifties and sixties, and it will resume that role in the eighties and nineties. Soviet aid utilised by India was 82.4 per cent of India's imports from the USSR between 1956/7 and 1960/1 and 66.1 per cent between 1961/2 and 1965/6. That share has fallen dramatically since the late sixties. It is, however, rising again because of the authorisation of several new credits since 1977. In fact, an increase in Soviet exports of machinery and equipment to India, an important policy objective of the USSR, depends crucially on the utilisation of these loans. At the same time, credits utilised by India during the fifties and sixties served to expand Indian exports in the seventies; these credits had been mostly repaid by 1980/1. Whether the share of credits repaid in Indian exports rises in the eighties and nineties will itself depend on the rate of utilisation of recent Soviet aid.

We found that Soviet aid and technology transfer involved the following benefits for India. The burden of servicing Soviet loans through bilateral exports was lower than that of loans to be repaid in hard currency. Soviet offers of aid enabled the Indian government in many cases to break the monopoly of transnational companies in India and strengthened the government's bargaining position vis-à-vis the transnationals; the combined result was considerable foreign exchange savings for India. The planned nature of the Soviet and Indian econ-omies enabled the USSR to commit project aid for the duration of a whole five-year plan period, and extend project aid for investments of an interlocking character. Thus, Soviet assistance has led to the creation of several vertically integrated industrial complexes. These enterprises were created as part of an overall strategy of import-substituting industrialisation with the aim of giving the Indian econ-omy an independent technological capability in basic and capital goods industries.[2]

Since the Soviets are committed to handing over charge of the project soon after erection is complete, project aid generally included the training of Indian personnel. Training programmes were not special or peculiar to Soviet technology transfer. However, in certain sectors (e.g. steel), training of Indian personnel in the USSR took place on a particularly large scale. As regards use of local inputs, we found strong evidence of progressive indigenisation of equipment in steel and oil refining, the two sectors which have been recipients of Soviet technology on more than one occasion and over a period of time. The significance of indigenisation lies in the resulting backward and forward linkages and externalities in terms of skill formation. Although the USSR has not been as willing to share design and engineering work as to use local inputs, Indian consultants were usually associated in the execution of Soviet-aided projects. While the Soviets' preferred mechanism of technology transfer was the 'near-turnkey' arrangement, and the original Soviet contracts only required the transfer of know-how rather than know-why, later on the Soviets did assist in the setting in motion of a local design capability in certain industries. In other industries (e.g. coal mining and heavy engineering) the weakness of the design capability of Soviet-aided enterprises is undeniable. However, that fact alone was not responsible for their extremely poor performance; domestic factors were equally important. As regards the permissibility of horizontal technology transfer, although the contracts do not categorically state that the recipients of technology have the unhindered right to transfer the know-how to any other party in India, recent agreements in the eighties (involving the modernisation of Soviet-built steel plants) specifically provide that all improvements effected in the older steel plants can also be utilised in other steel plants. In any case, in practice, the ambiguity about the permissibility of horizontal technology transfer under the terms of the original contract document has not been an effective constraint. We found that Soviet equipment was observed to be less sophisticated, but more hardy than similar Western equipment. The hardiness of Soviet equipment and, in addition, the excellence of the Soviet maintenance system constitute two good arguments for LDCs to buy from the USSR in the early stages of their industrialisation. Finally, on the basis of the limited comparison we attempted (for the steel and oil-refining industries), we found that India's experience as a recipient of Soviet technology compared favourably with its experience as a recipient of Western technology. In particular, we found that the Soviets were more willing transferrers of technology (e.g. steel) and prepared to share design and engineering work (e.g. oil refining).

One can now summarise the costs or problems associated with Soviet technology transfer which whittled away many of its advantages noted above. The sheer variety of the financial and technological performance of Soviet-aided enterprises suggests that domestic factors may have been more important in explaining the 'success' or 'failure' of an enterprise than external ones. Having said this, we can note the costs of Soviet technology transfer. Several Soviet-aided enterprises were set up to manufacture products with specifications for which there was no demand in India. In addition, they were equipped to manufacture an overly specialised product-range; as a result they were unable to meet a very large part of the overall demand for the products of that industry. A market survey prior to project execution would have demonstrated the need for adapting product design/specifications to Indian conditions and also for producing a broader product-mix. These problems of Soviet-aided enterprises in India appear to derive from the interaction of two inefficient bureaucracies in the process of setting up new industries in a market economy. Soviet-aided enterprises in India exhibited a tendency towards excess built-in capacity. In a centrally planned economy, which is primarily supply-constrained, the government's control over investment ensures that a demand constraint for producer goods will not arise. In a developing market economy creation of capacity must match projections of demand; otherwise, under-utilisation of capacity is inevitable. However, it is debatable to what extent the Soviets can ultimately be held responsible in this regard. Even Mahalanobis assumed, rather unrealistically, that the government could completely control the consumption–savings balance and saw no difficulties in transforming savings into desired forms of investment. The problems of certain Soviet-aided enterprises were the result of rigidity on the part of the Soviets: existing plant sizes were simply transferred to India without any adjustments being made to the capacity of the plant. However, foreign firms from DMEs have also done little, according to the existing literature, to adapt and restructure technologies under technical collaboration agreements. A peculiar feature of Soviet technology transfer was running a parallel management in enterprises, analogous to the tradition in plants in the USSR, with party and technical experts working in tandem. However, from the Indian point of view, the resulting proliferation of Soviet specialists meant two kinds of additional costs: the extra payment necessitated on the technical assistance account, and the dependence on Soviet specialists generated as a consequence. A further problem of collaborating with the Soviets was that the sale of technology had been a one-off sale; no improvements or updated models were transferred later. The reason why modifications or new models were not passed on is probably that, unlike capitalist enterprises, enterprises in these administratively planned economies have no direct interest in foreign trade, and hence no marketing strategy. However, this may change if the reforms proposed by Gorbachev are actually implemented by the time the next Five-Year Plan commences. Finally, we found strong evidence in support of the hypothesis that turnkey contracts, i.e. packaged transfer, involve a high price for the recipient. The capital and foreign exchange cost of the first generation steel plants and oil refineries, executed on a turnkey or near-turnkey basis, was high relative to later plants/refineries, irrespective of whether the collaborator was a Soviet or a Western firm.

The analysis of technology transfer revealed the growing technological capability of Indian industry. This capability was evident in the increasing proportion of equipment for Soviet-aided enterprises being supplied indigenously, the growing share of Indian design and engineering work in these enterprises, the reverse transfer of technology being undertaken by these enterprises to the USSR (e.g. BHEL, IDPL), and the technology exports to other LDCs undertaken by some of these enterprises (e.g. BHEL, MECON).

However, some of the present weaknesses of the Indian economy may possibly derive from the same policies that have resulted in such an impressive technological performance by Indian industry. India's industrial and trade strategy, characterised by both protection of production and protection of 'learning', may have given rise to numerous high-cost and inefficient industries which would probably have never come into existence in a less protected environment. Nowhere have the high costs of India's import-substituting industrialisation been more in evidence than in the cases of certain Soviet-aided enterprises (e.g. HEC, MAMC), some of their losses being so large as to exhaust their paid-up capital and even consume their loans.

However, it must be admitted that these financial losses might not have occurred had capacity utilisation in these capital goods industries, i.e. demand for these goods, been higher. Low demand for these industries can be traced back to the financial resource constraints of the Indian state, and the resulting deceleration in the growth of public investment since the mid-sixties.

We also obtained some insights into the functioning of the Soviet economy. Soviet attempts at introducing new institutional forms in Indo-Soviet economic relations are evidence not only of a greater commercial approach, but also an attempt to give a new dynamism to Soviet exports of machinery to India. Thus the repeated Soviet proposals in inter-governmental meetings to set up joint plants with

Indian firms in third countries, and joint production of manufactures in India on a compensation basis, are all primarily motivated by the desire to increase Soviet machinery exports. New Soviet aid in the eighties appears to have the same objectives. However, the wide and relatively sophisticated industrial base India has acquired (in certain sectors, paradoxically, with Soviet assistance), does make the prospect of a major increase in Soviet machinery exports to India in the near future a somewhat remote possibility.

In part III we examined, first, the payments aspects, and secondly, the real side of Indo-Soviet trade. Our major analytical concern in regard to the payments aspect of Indo-Soviet trade has been: why does bilateralism still prevail in Indo-Soviet trade in the nineties, although the USSR has been multilateralising trading arrangements with most LDCs?

For India, the possibility of paying for defence equipment without the expenditure of scarce foreign exchange has been the main factor precluding multilateralisation of Indo-Soviet trade. In addition, India's adverse experience after multilateralising trade with certain smaller CPEs (Yugoslavia, Hungary, Bulgaria) will also dissuade India's decision-makers to consider an early abandonment of bilateralism.

The USSR, too, will not be keen to multilateralise Indo-Soviet trade, given that India has consistently been able to generate trade surpluses with her during the seventies and eighties, primarily in order to repay developmental and military credits. In fact, during personal interviews within India's Commerce Ministry it was learnt that, in certain years in the 1980s, India had generated trade surpluses with the USSR over and above the amount required for repayment of developmental *and* defence credits. Considering that utilisation of developmental credits is not especially large, though it rose in the eighties, future trade surpluses will largely be used to repay defence credits. The USSR will be averse to multilateralisation because of the fear that it may possibly result in hard currency trade deficits with its largest LDC trade partner. This underlines even further the Soviet need to increase machinery exports to India.

In our study of Indo-Soviet trade we found that the most dynamic markets for India's exports in the seventies were the developed market economies. Unlike in the sixties, we found that the USSR and east Europe contributed a very small part of the increase in India's total exports in the seventies. Thus, at an aggregate level, an examination of the direction of India's exports does not suggest that India diverted exports from hard currency markets. However, it could be argued that DME markets might have grown faster still without India's exports to the USSR. But an examination of the composition of India's exports to different markets at a disaggregated level revealed that while the exports of traditional primary commodities showed buoyancy in the CPE markets, the main increase in Indian exports in the seventies came from manufactured exports to the rest of the world. In other words, the risk of diversion was limited. Throughout the seventies there were relatively few complaints of switch trading of Indian goods by the USSR. Hence, the overall conclusion must be that, as in the sixties, an overwhelming proportion of exports to the USSR over the seventies and early eighties constituted trade creation, not diversion.

We found that as in the sixties, India's export earnings from the USSR fluctuated more than her earnings from the rest of the world. This instability in export earnings from the USSR will not make any difference to the stability of India's total export earnings since the earnings generated in exports to the USSR cannot be used to make purchases in hard currency markets. Nevertheless, its impact is felt on India's capacity to import from the USSR and on factor earnings, employment and capacity utilisation in industries dependent on exports to the USSR.

We also found that India's terms of trade with the world deteriorated sharply in the seventies as a result of two oil price increases. However, we found no evidence to suggest that India's terms of trade with the USSR were any more unfavourable than those obtained in her trade with the rest of the world.

Finally, we noted that major structural changes have occurred in the commodity composition of Indo-Soviet trade. Intermediate goods have replaced capital goods as the single most important category of Soviet civilian exports to India over the seventies and eighties. India's exports have diversified, with a larger share for manufactures and non-traditional goods in the seventies/eighties than in the sixties. This raises the question: has there been a permanent loss of complementarity between the two economies or is this the beginning of a new stage in the international division of labour between an industrialised CPE and a semi-industrialised LDC? In 1970 a Moscow Institute study for UNCTAD expressed fears about how 'the mutually advantageous nature of economic relations' between the CPEs and the LDCs can be preserved after the latter eliminate their backwardness. The study suggested that over the next ten to twenty years the exchange of goods will be mainly of an inter-sectoral nature (i.e. manufactures for primary commodities), but after that mainly of an intra-sectoral nature (i.e. within the manufacturing sector).

The predominance of agricultural commodities in India's exports to the USSR through the sixties, and also the continued buoyancy of traditional and primary exports through the seventies, fits in with the inter-sectoral nature of exchanges mentioned in the Moscow Institute's study. Increasingly in the eighties, however, non-traditional manufactured exports to the USSR have grown, and are likely to continue to grow. There is now some evidence of production cooperation or joint ventures in manufactures on a compensation basis between the two governments and the Chambers of Commerce of both countries. The inter-sectoral nature of complementarity between the two economies may now be changing. The big question mark, however, remains about the Soviet ability to expand exports of manufactures, in particular machinery, to India's private sector. Unless these exports rise, a new stage in the international division of labour hoped for by the Soviets may not develop. According to one estimate, 70 per cent of India's imports from the USSR (and 30 per cent of her exports to the USSR) are made by the public sector.[3] This must change if Soviet exports of machinery to India are to increase. Formal contacts between the two Chambers of Commerce were established in 1977; the 'information gap' about Soviet products, particularly machinery, in India's private sector should have been filled by now. Annual exhibitions and trade fairs have helped to provide such information. However, the expectation that over the current trade agreement (1986–90) the share of industrial products (such as chemicals, iron and steel, plant and machinery) in Soviet exports to India will rise to 47.5 per cent from the 16.7 per cent share in the trade agreement valid over 1981–5 seems highly unlikely on the basis of present trends.

We have not attempted to draw any general conclusions (or 'lessons') for other LDCs on the basis of our analysis of economic relations between India and the USSR. This is because quite apart from the truism that relationships between different states are always sui generis, we have demonstrated the Soviet-Indian economic and political relationship to be a special case. India is the USSR's biggest LDC trade partner and the largest recipient of Soviet development aid. India's level of technological development makes possible certain kinds of collaborative arrangements with the Soviet Union not possible in most poor developing countries. India not only buys Soviet arms but manufactures them in India under licence; in fact, it is probably the only non-socialist country which manufactures major Soviet defence equipment under licence. Unlike other LDCs it also exports quite a few manufactures to the USSR. The Soviet Union takes one-fifth of India's exports, while the share of all CMEA countries in LDC exports is about 5 per cent. The closeness of ties between India and the USSR may have had its origin in, and be sustained by, the relationships between the USSR, the USA, China and Pakistan. But they are also built on mutual economic interest, and a compatibility of strategic-political interests. However, their interests are not necessarily identical: there are not only conflicts of interests between India and the USSR, but India has also simultaneously tried to maintain good relations with the West.

Notes

1 The Indian development strategy and the USSR

1 Nehru and even Mahalanobis, the architect of the Second Plan, are known to have been influenced by such Fabian Socialists as Beatrice and Sidney Webb.

2 With the major exception of the army and naval factories, most Japanese state enterprises were disposed off to private entrepreneurs during the 1880s.

3 Cited in Clarkson (1979), p. 266.

4 In fact, after Nehru's death in 1964 the influence of the Planning Commission on strategy and policy declined.

5 Feldman's model was published in the USSR in 1928. For an English translation, see G. A. Feldman (1964).

6 At the same time, the Indian Statistical Institute had the benefit of visits from Jan Tinbergen, Ragnar Frisch, Charles Bettelheim and Joan Robinson.

7 The advantages of such assistance have been pointed out by economists like Patel (1970) and Reddaway (1962).

8 Naturally, since the utilisation of aid was slower than its authorisation, actual withdrawals peaked during the Third Plan.

9 Soviet aid constituted 11.4 per cent (14.2 per cent if the other east European countries are included) of total non-food aid authorised to India up to 1968/9 (i.e. the end of the Annual Plans). For further details see chapter 4.

10 Soviet aid strengthened not only India's bargaining position, but that of all LDCs. See Valkenier (1983), p. 11.

11 Chaudhuri (1977), p. 15; Datar (1972), p. 256.

12 See Sebastian (1975), Datar (1972), Chisti (1973), Nayyar (1977) and Banerji (1977), among others.

13 On the advantages and disadvantages of bilateral (as distinct from multilateral) aid, see T. Balogh (1967).

14 Japan's share in India's exports increased from 5.3 per cent in 1960/1 to 13.3 per cent in 1970/1; at the same time, the UK's share declined from 26.1 per cent to 11.1 per cent; that of the USA declined only slightly from 15.5 per cent to 13.5 per cent.

2 Indo-Soviet economic relations: geo-political and ideological factors

1 In the aftermath of the war, Indo-American relations reached such a low point that the USA, which had been extending economic assistance to India

since 1951, did not do so from 1972 to 1977. (It was resumed in August 1978 and since then it has been made available each year.)
2 Cited by Charles B. McLane (1973), p. 55.
3 The Soviet view of the character of the Congress Party has evolved from the early 1950s to a much more positive view in the 1970s. See Robert H. Donaldson (1974), pp. 61–266.
4 Even the Indian emergency (1975–7) received the unstinted support of the Soviet regime and its commentators. See *USSR and the Third World*, 5 (1975), pp. 196 and 288; and *New Times*, no. 29 (July 1975), pp. 11–13 and no. 10 (March 1977), pp. 13–15.

3 Soviet economic interests in non-socialist LDCs

1 Non-Marxists like Valkenier (1983, ch. 1) have argued that up to 1964, economic relations with LDCs were used by the USSR as a 'political weapon'; since then the pursuit of 'economic advantage' has become an important motivation for the USSR. Valkenier does not test this hypothesis by any detailed examination of Soviet-LDC trade and payments data; instead she argues her case on the basis of an extended analysis of the Soviet literature (i.e. academic and political debates) on the subject. However, in our examination of Soviet trade and payments arrangements with LDCs, we will be keeping Valkenier's hypothesis in mind.
2 'Foreign economic relations became an integral part of expanded social reproduction . . . increasing the effectiveness of social production, accelerating scientific and technological progress, and improving the well-being of the working people' (Iakovleva 1980).
3 Cited in D. M. Nuti (1979), p. 251.
4 Philip Hanson (1979) concluded: 'In civilian technology catching up, let alone overtaking, still seems a remote prospect' (p. 810).
5 On the increasing need for east Europe to turn to the Middle East for oil, see Christopher Coker (1984).
6 The macro-economic stimulus to the DMEs of exports to the CPEs is not great, since the share of exports to the East in total Western exports was only 5 per cent (6 per cent for western Europe). However, the impact for investment goods industries may be significant.
7 The increase in grain and technology imports in the sixties can easily be demonstrated statistically. See P. Hanson (1982) and USJEC (1982).
8 For interesting discussions of Soviet arms sales to LDCs, see Moshe Efrat (1983) and (1985), and Saadet Deger (1984).
9 '. . . comparing Soviet policy up to the early 1970s with what followed we have to conclude that the balance shifted to give more weight to economic considerations and less importance to political strategic ones' (Ofer 1976, p. 237).
10 The corresponding figures for LDC trade deficits with east European countries as a whole were: $269m (1965), $748m (1970) and $1,597m (1975).
11 The data for commitments and disbursements of Soviet and east European aid have been drawn from the CIA. While data for commitments is rela-

tively easy to come by in UN publications, there is no other recent series for Soviet disbursements. In any case the civilian aid disbursements were negligible outside the CMEA after 1980. The aggregates for commitments are roughly comparable between the CIA series and the UNECE series. The UN *Economic Survey of Europe* (UNECE Secretariat 1980) states that 'eastern credit disbursement reached the record level of $1.4bn in 1973, but has gradually declined to some $900m in recent years'.

12 In fact, in estimating the value of Soviet weaponry exports, Western scholars have generally relied on official Soviet foreign trade statistics. They have focused their attention on the 'unspecified residual' in Soviet exports to LDCs as a group and the aggregated amount of the reported exports to all individual non-communist developing countries.

13 This is precisely the reason why we have not used a deflator for surpluses, which are all expressed in current prices. If we were certain that the surplus was on the civilian account, then a deflator to take account of the fluctuations in international prices over the seventies and eighties could have been used. However, if the surplus includes Soviet arms exports, such a deflator would be meaningless.

14 Petroleum is such an important source of export revenue that 'in many ways, the USSR is a one-crop economy' (Goldman 1979, p. 188).

15 Moscow Institute (1969), p. 76. Valkenier (1974) writes that around 1961 the Presidium of the Academy of Sciences set up a research group in the Institute of the Economy of the World Socialist System to devise indices of the effectiveness of economic relations with the LDCs.

16 In 1976 Indo-Soviet trade accounted for 9.9 per cent of Soviet-LDC trade; Iraq was the USSR's largest LDC trade partner at 10.9 per cent. However, in the eighties, India has been the USSR's largest trade partner.

17 On switch trading by the USSR of imports from India, see chapter 8.

18 Gidadhubli (1982), p. 2057. India's share in total Soviet foreign trade turnover declined during this period. The share declined from 2.34 per cent in 1965 to 1.36 per cent in 1979 but recovered to 1.8 per cent in 1980.

4 Aid flows

1 Total non-food aid consists of loans plus grants. As far as loans were concerned, Soviet loans were 12.5 per cent (15.5 per cent including other CMEA countries) of total loans authorised by all donors.

2 Calculated from Ministry of Finance, *External Assistance*, 1980/1.

3 Calculated from Ministry of Finance, *External Assistance*, 1980/1.

5 The collaboration agreements

1 Chaudhuri (1977), pp. 156–62.

2 The discussion which follows is based on three sets of contracts – for a refinery (Koyali), a steel plant (Bokaro) and an aluminium smelter/fabrication unit (Korba). The refinery contracts were between Tiazhpromexport, Moscow, and Oil and Natural Gas Commission, Dehradun, and were

signed in 1961. The Bokaro contracts were again between Tiazhpromexport and Bokaro Steel Plant, and were signed primarily in 1965/6. The contracts for the aluminium project were between Bharat Aluminium Corporation (BALCO), and first with Tiazhpromexport (for the DPR) and later with Tsvetmetpromexport for the execution of the project itself; the contracts were signed between late 1968 and the end of 1971. Thus there is both a sectoral spread and a spread in terms of the time period over which these contracts were signed. Considering the overall similarity between these three sets of contracts, they constitute a fairly representative sample of Indo-Soviet firm level agreements. It was found impossible to gain access to contracts signed in the 1970s. They are likely to be still operative, hence they were obviously not made available to the author. In addition to Indo-Soviet contracts, for purposes of comparison we used contracts of certain Soviet-aided firms with Western corporations. The evaluation of these contracts in the text, it should be added, is based on a series of UN publications: UNIDO (1979 and 1973); UNECE (1970); UNCTAD (1978), TT/AS/5; and UNCTAD Secretariat (1971/2), TD/B/AC.11/9.

3 But now licence agreements, which are the normal mechanism for technology transfer between enterprises in industrialised countries, are assuming increasing significance in many LDCs, including India, where the technological base is already fairly diversified.

4 Of course, Indo-Soviet contracts did permit the purchase of residual machinery and materials from third parties.

5 For Soviet links with MECON and HEC, see chapter 6.

6 Thus Article 17 of the Bokaro agreement states: 'In case of any disagreement between the Indian and Soviet organisations on any matters arising from or connected with the implementation of the present Agreement, the representatives of the Government of India and the Government of the USSR shall consult with each other and endeavour to reach mutual settlement' (Ministry of External Affairs 1965, p. 62).

7 For instance, quoting a price, Article 8 of BALCO's contract for the preparation of the DPR states: 'The above price quoted is based on the Rouble gold content equal to 0.987412 gram of fine gold. Should the gold parity of the Rouble be changed, the price stipulated in the present Contract shall be recalculated in proportion corresponding to the change in the parity as on the date of the change.'

8 Thus the refinery contract states: 'The total weight of the equipment and materials delivered under the present Contract amounts to 15350 metric tons net' (Art. 2). The next para. says: 'The price of the equipment and materials to be delivered by the Supplier as per para. 2 of the present Contract including packaging amounts to 12500000 roubles, cif Bombay' (Art. 3).

9 Liquidated damages are specified in financial compensation and are always defined in relation to physical units as time, capacity or yield. Thus an engineering firm undertaking to supply engineering drawings by a certain date would warrant that should it not meet the schedule, due to the fault of the firm, it would pay the purchaser liquidated damages of $X per day for the period exceeding the guaranteed date of performance.

10 These plants were the heavy-machine building plant, coal-mining machinery plant, the three drugs and pharmaceuticals plants and the precision instruments plant. See CPU, *Management and Administration of Public Undertakings*, 1965, paras. 120–1.
11 This volume was seen quite by chance with one of the representatives of the consultants. The consultants handed over only twenty-four volumes while the twenty-fifth volume containing the time schedule was given only to their own representatives. See CPU, *BHEL*, 1967, para. 43.
12 A noteworthy sub-clause in the provisions on training in the most recent contract in hand (the BALCO contract) which did not exist in earlier contracts was that the buyer could suggest changes in the training programme drawn up by the seller.

6 Transfer of technology

1 Although today BHEL consists of a manufacturing division (plus ten service divisions), in the mid-sixties it started out as three divisions: one at Hardwar, producing steam (110–200mW sets) and hydro turbines and generators; another at Hyderabad, producing only steam turbines and generators (in different sizes up to 100mW); and the third at Tiruchirapalli, producing boilers. The Hardwar plant was set up with Soviet assistance, the Hyderabad and Trichy plants with Czech assistance.
2 The Bhopal unit, the first major heavy electricals plant in India, was set up with British financial assistance and in technical collaboration with Associated Electrical Industries, UK, and went into production during the Second Plan.
3 On account of the increased coal-raising targets, it was decided jointly by Indian and Soviet experts to raise the plant capacity to 45,000 tonnes. A report of the Parliamentary Estimates Committee later (in 1963/4) noted that the Soviet team had not considered it advisable to raise the rated capacity beyond 30,000 tonnes due to difficulty in producing a wide range of items and the long time required in mastering the techniques. The report added that the Soviet experts had subsequently agreed to the expansion of the project to 45,000 tonnes capacity and that the increase was mainly in the number of items planned.
4 These sizes are (in mW): 25, 26.6, 28.5, 30, 32, 50, 60, 62.5, 63.5, 75, 100, 120, 140, 150, 200 and 210.
5 For example, BHEL had more or less completely indigenised the 210mW turbine generator set based on Soviet design; in fact, its import content was as low as 12 per cent. But when it began manufacturing the 200mW set based on the Siemens design, the import content rose dramatically, as certain components could not be manufactured without augmenting production facilities. The manufacture of 500mW sets in fact has begun from 'completely knocked down' kits (Haribhushan 1985).
6 On India's technology exports, see a number of books and papers by Sanjaya Lall (1981), (1982a), (1982b) and (1984).
7 Statement of a SAIL executive in a personal interview.

8 This training, according to firm level contracts, was free of charge. However, the board and lodging expenses had to be borne by the Government of India from the Soviet credits.

9 A senior executive explained that the Indians circumvented the problem in Rourkela by resorting to photocopying the drawings for spares and also the operation manual.

10 As a former Chairman of Bokaro explained in a personal interview: 'If you want their [German or British] personnel, you must ask for them. But for Bhilai or Bokaro, the Russians will tell you so many experts are required, though perhaps not in so many words.'

11 While the basic design work for Vizag is being done by Dasturco, as the Prime Indian Consultant, design documentation for 15 per cent of the equipment to be imported from the USSR as well as for the 70 per cent to be manufactured in India will come from the USSR.

12 Government of India, Press Information Bureau press release, 15 August 1966, cited in Vedavalli (1976), p. 49.

13 Further, because the private oil companies refused to handle Russian products, the government established the Indian Oil Corporation (IOC) to import and distribute oil products from the USSR; this broke the foreign monopoly in marketing and strengthened the government's hand in its dealings with international firms.

14 EIL was set up at the same time that the Central Design Organisation of IOC was wound up. The establishment of EIL was, to a certain extent, made possible by the association of the Central Design Organisation with the design and construction of Barauni and Koyali expansion schemes.

15 For instance, for certain secondary processing facilities like the Fuel Catalytic Cracker (FCC) the technology is still patented and can only be obtained on licence (involving payment of royalty).

16 For projects in one of the world's most profitable industries, pharmaceuticals, this was quite a remarkable statement. As a matter of fact, except for a few years in the mid-seventies, IDPL has never made profits. On the contrary, IDPL is one of the ten largest loss-makers among public sector firms.

17 The Indian government had planned to build the antibiotics plant in two stages. Later on in the course of discussions the Soviets persuaded the Indian team that the capital cost per unit of output would be lower if bigger capacities were provided.

18 Information gathered from senior research scientists within and outside IDPL.

19 Even the surgical instruments plant of IDPL has diversified into the high profit area of formulations in an attempt to pull itself out of the red.

20 A partial explanation for IDPL's low share in the domestic formulations market may be that IDPL's formulations capacity was rather limited through the seventies. To overcome the problem a series of joint sector (joint state and central government) enterprises are being set up, with IDPL as a shareholder.

21 Thus a Technical School was set up at Cambay, Gujarat, for the ONGC; a

Technical Institute was set up at Bhilai; training courses were also developed at different sites, including one at Ranchi for HEC.

22 While 100 per cent of the consultancy services for Bhilai's 1mt stage were provided by the Soviet firm, the Soviet share had fallen to 45 per cent at the 2.5mt stage, and 10 per cent at the 4mt stage. Indian consultants have also been increasingly associated with Bokaro's work.

23 See Valkenier's discussion of economic relations with LDCs under Khrushchev, in Valkenier (1983), pp. 3–10.

24 The failures or successes of some enterprises can often be explained by the government. In our study we do not attempt to tackle the vast, and crucial, subject of the government's pricing policies for public sector products, since our interest in the financial, as opposed to the technological, performance of enterprises is peripheral.

25 However, Balasubramanyam (1973) has argued that the extent and quality of knowledge transferred under technology licensing agreements may be low relative to that under private foreign investment.

26 As many as 172 such firms have existed as far back as 1967, with East Germany, Czechoslovakia, Poland and Hungary, in that order, accounting for 117 such agreements between 1964 and 1967. Unlike the east European countries, the USSR has so far shied away from setting up equity firms engaging in production in LDCs.

7 Bilateral payments

1 See a series of country studies commissioned by the OECD Development Centre in the mid-seventies: R. Banerji (1977) on India, F. M. El Rafai (1978) on Egypt, K. Imboden (1978) on Ghana, I. Outters-Jaeger (1978) on Sri Lanka, and M. S. Rana (1978) on Nepal, and a synthesis report by I. Outters-Jaeger (1979). In addition, there exists a wealth of literature on the subject published by UNCTAD's Trade with Socialist Countries Division.

2 For a discussion of this crucial assumption and its implications for India's development strategy, see J. Bhagwati and S. Chakravarty (1969), and A. K. Sen and K. N. Raj (1961).

3 See Dharam Narain (1968), Datar (1972), Chisti (1973), Nayyar (1977), Sebastian (1975) and N. Ambegaonkar (1974). Later other studies appeared: R. Banerji (1977), and a Conference number of the *Indian Economic Journal* (1976). The last study brings the story up to 1975/6; the remaining studies cover the data available up to the mid- to late sixties or the early seventies.

4 Ten years became the normal repayment period in future defence credits until 1980, when it was increased to seventeen years. Information obtained during personal interview with a former Defence Ministry official.

5 *Economic and Political Weekly* (2 December 1978) reported that the compromise formula had been worked out about two years before it was actually signed in November 1978. The signing of the agreement became delayed because of the change of government in New Delhi in March 1977.

8 Bilateral trade

1 However, if repayment of defence credits were included, the share of credits repaid in India's exports to the USSR from the mid-sixties onwards would be likely to double.

2 A major reason for this dramatic increase in exports to the USSR in the early eighties is the introduction of a completely new commodity – rice. Twenty per cent of the increase of India's exports to the USSR between 1979/80 and 1980/1 and 54 per cent of the increase between 1980/1 and 1981/2 (all figures in current prices) can be explained by rice.

3 A similar fear is expressed in a report by a bureaucrat (with considerable experience of Indo-Soviet trade in the sixties and seventies). However, the extent of diversion in this period seems to have been limited (see Suresh Kumar 1985, p. 26). Besides, exports to OECD markets shot up again in 1983/4 as these economies recovered from an international recession.

4 R. G. Gidadhubli (1983). The twelve commodities are: tea, coffee, tobacco, black pepper, cashews, shellac, several raw materials and cotton textiles.

5 If machinery imports have stagnated in current prices, they must have declined in real terms, considering the inflation in international prices of machinery after the two oil price shocks of the seventies.

6 For a discussion of switch trading in oilcakes by the USSR in the late seventies, see Appendix 5.

7 Apparently, this was particularly so in the case of the east European economies, though not so much for the USSR. See Indian Institute of Foreign Trade (1977), p. 137.

8 One SEZ, at Kandla (near Ahmedabad), was set up in 1964, and the other, meant exclusively for electronics industries, at Santa Cruz (near Bombay), was set up in the seventies.

9 Net exports from Santa Cruz were much lower, Rs69m (exports Rs296m, imports Rs227m). (Rank Xerox has invested at Santa Cruz in a plant with an Indian partner, Modi, to export photocopiers to the USSR.)

10 Two other measures of export instability, the MacBean and Coppock indices, exist, which eliminate short-term cyclical deviations, thereby avoiding biased estimation due to explosive short-term fluctuations, but they require time series data for longer periods.

11 Both Sharma (1977) and Banerji (1977) covered roughly the same period. Other studies, by Datar (1972), Nayyar (1977), Chisti (1973) and Ambegaonkar (1974), had not examined the question of the instability of India's export earnings from east Europe.

12 Import prices for petroleum products imports cannot be included in table 8.20 because information on them is not available. As regards manufactures, not much purpose is served by making unit value comparisons for products which may differ vastly in quality.

13 In 1980 and 1981, the share of SITC 3 in total Soviet exports to the following countries was: Afghanistan, 30.5 and 21.2 per cent; Bangladesh, 35.3 and 17.3 per cent; Cuba, 27.0 and 31.1 per cent; Ethiopia, 69.4 and 81.8 per cent; Liberia, 92.4 and 35.5 per cent; Morocco, 81.8 and 87.1 per cent; Nepal, 86.7 and 91.8 per cent; Yemen, 18.2 and 17.6 per cent; and Yugoslavia, 61.5 and 65.1 per cent.

14 The Indian journalist on whose report (published in mid-1981 in *The Times of India*) this appendix is based, suggested during a personal interview that the sum of Indian rupees sold by the USSR to the west European importers

may amount to as much as Rs2,000m in 1980, i.e. around 20 per cent of Indian exports that year. For 1981, these buyers were likely to take Rs4,000m from Generalexport/Sojuchimport and enlarge the commodity lists to include other agricultural products like black pepper, cashews, rice, coffee, spices, tobacco, etc.

9 Conclusions

1 The precise extent to which Soviet trade surpluses with LDCs financed Soviet trade deficits with the West is impossible to determine because of the existence of varying estimates for 1. Soviet arms sales to LDCs, 2. the proportion of arms sales in hard currency, and 3. the share of hard currency arms transfers for cash, as against credits.
2 The strategy itself has been the subject of criticism from many quarters, both Indian and foreign (e.g. Little, Scitovsky and Scott 1970, Bhagwati and Desai 1970, and Bhagwati and Srinivasan 1975). But as we explained in the Introduction, a comprehensive evaluation of the strategy is outside the scope of this study. The discussion of the costs and benefits of Soviet technology transfer, therefore, is conducted within the terms of the goals of this strategy.
3 India's state trading enterprises are responsible for importing raw materials, such as oil, fertilisers, newsprint, etc., which account for the bulk of India's imports from the USSR.

Bibliography

1. Books and articles

Ahluwalia, Isher. 1982. 'Industrial Performance in India: 1959–60 to 1978–79. An Analysis of Deceleration in Growth since the Mid-Sixties.' Mimeo, Indian Council for Research on International Economic Relations, New Delhi.

Alagh, Yoginder K. 1975. *Intra-Industrial Specialisation and its Impact on Trade and Economic Cooperation between India and the Socialist Countries of Eastern Europe*. UNCTAD/TSC/25.

Amann, R. and J. M. Cooper. 1982. *Industrial Innovation in the Soviet Union*. London and New Haven, Conn.: Yale University Press.

(eds.). 1986. *Technical Progress and Soviet Economic Development*. Oxford and New York: Basil Blackwell.

Amann, R., J. M. Cooper and R. W. Davies (eds.). 1977. *The Technological Level of Soviet Industry*. London and New Haven, Conn.: Yale University Press.

Ambegaonkar, N. 1974. 'India's Trade with East European Countries – Trends and Problems', *Reserve Bank of India Bulletin*, March.

Balasubramanyam, V. N. 1973. *International Transfer of Technology to India*. New York: Praeger.

1984. *The Economy of India*. London: Weidenfeld & Nicolson.

Balogh, T. 1967. 'Multilateral versus Bilateral Aid', *Oxford Economic Papers*, vol. 19, no. 3.

Banerji, Ranadev. 1977. *The Development Impact of Barter in Developing Countries – the Case of India*. OECD, Paris.

Bardhan, Pranab. 1984. *The Political Economy of Development in India*. Oxford: Basil Blackwell.

Basak, Aroon. 1981. 'Comments', in Saunders (ed.) 1981.

Berliner, Joseph S. 1976. *The Innovation Decision in Soviet Industry*. Cambridge, Mass.: MIT Press.

1979. 'Prospects of Technological Progress', in USJEC 1979.

Bhagwati, J. N. and S. Chakravarty. 1969. 'Contributions to Indian Economic Analysis: A Survey', *American Economic Review Supplement*, part 2, September.

and P. Desai. 1970. *India, Planning for Industrialisation*. Oxford: Oxford University Press.

and T. N. Srinivasan. 1976. *Foreign Trade Regimes and Economic Development: India*. Delhi: Macmillan.

226

Bogomolov, O. 1981. 'The CMEA Countries and the New International Economic Order', in Saunders (ed.) 1981.

Cassen, Robert. 1985. *Soviet Interests in the Third World*. London: Sage.

Chakravarty, S. 1957. 'On a Model of Planned Growth', *Arthaniti*, November. and J. N. Bhagwati. 1969. 'Contributions to Indian Economic Analysis: A Survey', *American Economic Review Supplement*, part 2, September.

Chandra, Nirmal. 1977. 'USSR and Third World: Unequal Distribution of Gains', *Economic and Political Weekly*, Annual no., vol. 12, nos. 6, 7 and 8, February.

Chaudhuri, Pramit. 1977. 'East European Aid to India', in Nayyar (ed.) 1977.

Chisti, Sumitra. 1973. *India's Trade with East Europe*. Indian Institute of Foreign Trade, New Delhi.

CIA. 1978. *Communist Aid Activities in Non-Communist LDCs*. Washington, D.C.

Cilingiroglu, A. 1969. *Manufacture of Heavy Electrical Equipment in Developing Countries*. World Bank Staff Occasional Papers, no. 9. Baltimore, Md: Johns Hopkins University Press.

Clarkson, Stephen. 1979. *The Soviet Theory of Development. India and the Third World in Marxist-Leninist Scholarship*. London: Macmillan.

Coker, Christopher. 1984. 'The Forgotten Dimension of Soviet Policy: Eastern Europe and the Middle East'. Mimeo, Royal Institute of International Affairs, London.

Comecon Foreign Trade, various years. Institute of Comparative Economic Studies, Vienna.

Cooper, Charles. 1971. *The Channels and Mechanisms for the Transfer of Technology from Developed to Developing Countries*. UNCTAD (TD/B/AC.11/5), Geneva.

Cutler, R. 1983. 'Group D Countries in North–South Negotiations', *International Organisation*, Winter.

Dasgupta, Biplab. 1971. *The Oil Industry in India: Some Economic Aspects*. London: Cass.

1977. 'Soviet Oil and the Third World', in Nayyar (ed.) 1977.

Dastur, M. N. 1980. *Case Studies in the Transfer of Technology: Purchase of Capital Goods and Technology in the Iron and Steel Industry – the Case of Bokaro*. UNCTAD, Geneva.

Datar, Asha. 1972. *India's Economic Relations with the USSR and Eastern Europe, 1953–69*. Cambridge: Cambridge University Press.

Deger, Saadet. 1984. 'The Economic Rationale of Soviet Arms Trade in the Third World'. Mimeo, Royal Institute of International Affairs, London.

Desai, Padma. 1972. *The Bokaro Steel Plant. A Study of Soviet Economic Assistance*. Rotterdam: North Holland.

Dobozi, I. and A. Inotai. 1981. 'Prospects of Economic Cooperation between CMEA Countries and Developing Countries', in Saunders (ed.) 1981.

Donaldson, Robert H. 1974. *Soviet Policy Towards India*. Cambridge, Mass.: Harvard University Press.

Economist Intelligence Unit, various years. *India*, quarterly economic reviews.

Efrat, Moshe. 1983. 'The Economics of Soviet Arms Transfers to the Third World – a Case Study: Egypt', *Soviet Studies*.

1985. 'The Economics of Soviet Arms Transfer to the Third World'. Mimeo.

Ellman, Michael. 1979. *Socialist Planning*. Cambridge: Cambridge University Press.

El Rafai, F. M. 1978. *The Development Impact of Barter in Developing Countries – the Case of Egypt*. OECD, Paris.

Ericson, Paul and Ronald Miller. 1979. 'Soviet Foreign Economic Behaviour: A Balance of Payments Perspective', in USJEC, vol. 2, 1979.

Feldman, G. A. 1984. 'On the Theory of Growth Rates of National Income', in N. Spulber (ed.), *Foundations of Soviet Strategy for Economic Growth*. Bloomington: Indiana University Press, 1984.

Gidadhubli, R. G. 1982. 'India in the Soviet Union's Import Trade', *Economic and Political Weekly*, 18 December.

    1983. *Indo-Soviet Trade. A Study of Select Items of Export from India in the Soviet Market*. New Delhi: Somaiya Publications.

Goldich, Judith G. 1979. 'The USSR Grain and Oilseed Trade in the 1970s', in USJEC 1979.

Goldman, Marshall. 1967. *Soviet Foreign Aid*. New York: Praeger.

    1979. 'The Changing Role of Raw Material Exports and Soviet Foreign Trade', in USJEC 1979.

Gutman, Patrick. 1981. 'New Forms of Tripartite Industrial Cooperation and Third Countries', in Saunders (ed.) 1981.

Hanson, Philip. 1982. 'Foreign Economic Relations', in Kaser and Brown (eds.) 1982.

Haribhushan. 1985. *Indo-Comecon Economic Relations. Role of Aid and Technology Transfer*. Indian Council for Research on International Economic Relations, Working Paper no. 31, New Delhi.

Henderson, P. D. 1975. *India's Energy Sector*. New Delhi: Oxford University Press.

Hersh, Seymour. 1983. *The Price of Power: Kissinger in the White House*. New York: Faber.

Horn, Robert C. 1983. *Soviet-Indian Relations*. New York: Praeger.

Iakovleva, E. 1980. 'Production Cooperation', *Soviet Review*, Fall.

Imboden, K. 1978. *The Development Impact of Barter in Developing Countries – the Case of Ghana*. OECD, Paris.

Joshi, B. 1977. 'Economics of Transfer of Technology in the Public Sector: A Study of IDPL'. Unpublished Ph.D. thesis, Lucknow University (India).

Kaser, Michael and Archie Brown (eds.). 1982. *Soviet Policy in the 1980s*. London: Macmillan.

Kumar, Suresh. 1985. *Indo-Comecon Trade and Economic Relations: Problems and Prospects*. Indian Council for Research on International Economic Relations, Working Paper no. 30, New Delhi.

Lall, Sanjaya. 1981. 'Exports of Manufactures by Newly-Industrialising Countries: A Survey of Recent Trends', in *Developing Countries in the International Economy*. London: Macmillan, 1981.

    1982a. 'The Emergence of Third World Multinationals: Indian Joint Ventures Overseas', *World Development*, February.

    1982b. *Developing Countries as Exporters of Technology*. London: Macmillan.

    1984. 'India', *World Development* (Special issue: 'Exports of Technology by Newly-Industrialising Countries', May–June).

Laszlo, E. and J. Kurtzman (eds.). 1980. *Eastern Europe and the New International Economic Order*. New York: Pergamon.

Lawson, Colin W. 1980. 'Socialist Relations with the Third World: A Case Study of the New International Economic Order', *Economics of Planning*, vol. 16, no. 3.

———— 1983. 'Revealing Preferences: The East in North–South Negotiations'. Mimeo, Royal Institute of International Affairs, London.

Little, I., T. Scitovsky and M. Scott. 1970. *Industry and Trade in Some Developing Countries: A Comparative Study*. London: Oxford University Press.

MacBean, A. I. 1966. *Export Instability and Economic Development*. London: Allen & Unwin.

McLane, Charles B. 1973. *Soviet-Asian Relations*. London, Central Asian Research Centre.

McMillan, Carl H. 1981. 'Comments', in Saunders (ed.) 1981.

Maex, Rudy. 1979. 'Soviet Investment in the Industrialised Western Economies and in the Developing Economies of the Third World', in USJEC 1979.

———— 1984. *Employment and Multinationals in Asian Export Processing Zones*. ILO, Geneva.

Mahalanobis, P. C. 1953. 'Some Observations on the Process of Growth of National Income', *Sankhya*, September.

Moscow Institute of Economics of the World Socialist System. 1969. *Innovations in the Practice of Trade and Economic Cooperation between the Socialist Countries of Eastern Europe and the Developing Countries*. UNCTAD (TD/B/238), Geneva.

Nagy, A. 1981. 'Comments', in Saunders (ed.) 1981.

Narain, Dharam. 1968. *Aid through Trade: Case Study of India*. UNCTAD (TD/BC/C.3/57), Geneva.

Nayyar, Deepak. 1976. *India's Exports and Export Policies in the Sixties*. Cambridge: Cambridge University Press.

———— (ed.). 1977. *Economic Relations between Socialist Countries and the Third World*. London: Macmillan.

———— 1981. 'Comments', in Saunders (ed.) 1981.

Nuti, D. M. 1979. 'The Contradictions of Socialist Economies. A Marxist Interpretation', *The Socialist Register*, London.

OECD. 1973. *Flow of Resources to Developing Countries*. Paris.

Ofer, Gur. 1976. 'Soviet Military Aid to the Middle East – an Economic Balance-Sheet', in USJEC 1976.

Outters-Jaeger, I. 1978. *The Development Impact of Barter in Developing Countries – the Case of Sri Lanka*. OECD, Paris.

———— 1979. *The Development Impact of Barter in Developing Countries. A Synthesis Report*. OECD, Paris.

Panchamukhi, V. R. 1978. *Trade Policies of India. A Quantitative Analysis*. New Delhi: Concept Publishers.

Paszynski, M. 1981. 'The Economic Interest of the CMEA Countries in Relations with Developing Countries', in Saunders (ed.) 1981.

Patel, I. G. 1970. 'Foreign Capital and Domestic Planning', in J. H. Adler (ed.), *Capital Movements and Economic Development*. London: Macmillan, 1970.

Rana, M. S. 1978. *The Development Impact of Barter in Developing Countries – the Case of Nepal*. OECD, Paris.

Reddaway, W. B. 1962. *The Development of the Indian Economy*. London: Allen & Unwin.

Remnek, Richard B. 1975. *Soviet Policy towards India. The Role of Soviet Scholars in the Formulation of Soviet Foreign Policy*. Oxford and International Publishing House.

Saunders, Christopher T. 1981. *East–West–South: Economic Interactions between Three Worlds*. London: Macmillan.

Sebastian, S. 1975. *Soviet Economic Aid to India*. New Delhi: N.V. Publications.

Sen, A. K., and K. N. Raj. 1961. 'Alternative Patterns of Growth under Conditions of Stagnant Export Earnings', *Oxford Economic Papers*, February.

Sengupta, Bhabhani. 1976. *Soviet-Asian Relations in the 1970s and Beyond. An Interperceptional Study*. New York: Praeger.

Sharma, O. P. 1977. 'India's Exports to the East European Countries', in *Emerging Opportunities for India's Trade and Economic Cooperation with East Europe*. Indian Institute of Foreign Trade, New Delhi, 1977.

Singh, Manmohan. 1964. *India's Export Trends and Prospects for Self-Sustained Growth*. Oxford: Clarendon Press.

SIPRI Yearbook, various years.

Smith, Alan. 1984. 'Soviet Trade Relations with the Third World'. Mimeo, Royal Institute of International Affairs, London.

Smith, G. A. E. 1981. 'The Industrial Problems of Soviet Agriculture', *Critique*, no. 14.

Smyth, Douglas C. 1977. 'The Global Economy and the Third World: Coalition or Cleavage?', *World Politics*, vol. 29, no. 4, July.

Sridhar, D. R. 1981. 'The Role of In-House R&D in Indigenisation of the Drug Industry'. Mimeo, Seminar on The Drug Industry and the Indian People, New Delhi.

Subramaniam, K. K. 1972. *Foreign Private Investment in India*. New Delhi: People's Publishing House.

Subramanyam, K. 1981. 'Soviet Help for Self-Reliance in Defence', in S. D. Sharma, (ed.), *Studies in Indo-Soviet Cooperation*. New Delhi: Lancer International, 1981.

Tanzer, Michael. 1969. *The Political Economy of International Oil and the Under-developed Countries*. London: Beacon Press.

USJEC. 1976. *The Soviet Economy in a New Perspective*. Washington, D.C.

   1979. *Soviet Economy in a Time of Change*. Washington, D.C.

   1982. *The Soviet Economy in the 1980s: Problems and Prospects*. Washington, D.C.

Valkenier, Elizabeth K. 1970. 'New Trends in Soviet Economic Relations with the Third World', *World Politics*, vol. 22, no. 3, April.

   1974. 'Soviet Economic Relations with the Developing Nations', in Roger B. Kanet (ed.), *The Soviet Union and the Developing Nations*, Baltimore, Md: Johns Hopkins University Press, 1974.

   1979. 'The USSR, the Third World, and the Global Economy', *Problems of Communism*, July–August.

1983. *The Soviet Union and the Third World. An Economic Bind.* New York: Praeger.

Vassiliev, V. 1969. *Policy in the Soviet Bloc on Aid to Developing Countries.* OECD, Paris.

Vedavalli, R. 1976. *Private Foreign Investment and Economic Development. A Case Study of the Petroleum Industry.* Cambridge: Cambridge University Press.

Wharton Econometric Forecasting Association. 1984. 'Soviet Foreign Trade Performance in 1983', *Current Analysis*, vol. 3, nos. 22–3.

Wilzynski, J. 1972. *Socialist Economic Development and Reforms.* London: Macmillan.

Wolf, Martin. 1982. *India's Exports.* Oxford: Clarendon Press.

World Bank. 1983. *World Development Report.* Washington, D.C.

Zoeter, P. G. 1982. 'USSR: Hard Currency Trade and Payments', in USJEC, vol. 2, 1982.

2. Publications of international organisations

International Monetary Fund. *Balance of Payment Statistics*, various issues.

United Nations. *Monthly Bulletin of Statistics*, various issues.

Yearbook of International Trade Statistics, various issues.

UNCTAD. *Case Study in the Transfer of Technology: The Pharmaceutical Industry in India.* TD/B/C.6/20, 1977.

Payments Arrangements in India's Trade with the Socialist Countries of Eastern Europe. TD/B/AC.22/4, 1977.

Handbook on the Acquisition of Technology by Developing Countries. TT/AS/5, 1978.

The Experience of Socialist Countries of Eastern Europe in the Transfer of Technology to Developing Countries. TD/B/C.6/25, 1978.

Case Studies in the Transfer of Technology: Policies for Transfer and Development of Technology in Pre-War Japan (1868–1937). TD/B/C.6/26, 1978.

National Engineering and Design Organisations: Their Role in Strengthening the Technological Capacity of Developing Countries. TD/B/C.6/35, 1978.

Experience of the USSR in Building Up Technological Capacity. TD/B/C.6/52, 1980.

The Implementation of Transfer of Technology Regulations: A Preliminary Analysis of the Experience of Latin America, the Philippines and India. TD/B/C.6/55, 1980.

Technology Policies and Planning for the Pharmaceutical Sector in the Developing Countries. TD/B/C.6/56, 1980.

The Capital Goods Sector in Developing Countries: Technology Issues for Further Research. TD/B/C.6/60, 1980.

Energy Supplies for Developing Countries: Issues in Transfer and Development of Technology. TD/B/C.6/61, 1980.

Major Technology Issues in the Energy Sector of Developing Countries. TT/AS/5, 1980.

The Soviet Union in a Changing Global Economic Setting: the Prospects for Trade-Oriented Growth. ST/TSC/4, 1986.

Declaration of the Soviet Delegation at UNCTAD VII, 13 July 1987. TD/341, 1987.

Handbook of International Trade Statistics, various issues.

UNCTAD Secretariat. *Guidelines for the Study of the Transfer of Technology to Developing Countries.* TD/B/AC.11/9, 1971/2.

Review of the Present State of Payments between Less Developed Countries and the Socialist Countries of Eastern Europe. TD/B/AC.22/2, 1977.

Activities of the International Investment Bank. TD/B/AC.23/4, 1977.

Multilateral System of Payments in Transferable Roubles of the Members of the CMEA. TD/B/AC.23/5, 1977.

The Cooperation Mechanism among Countries having Different Economic and Social Systems. TD/243/Supp.3, 1979.

The Cooperation in Planning between Socialist Countries of Eastern Europe and Developing Countries: The Experience of the USSR. TD/243/Supp.4, 1979.

Tripartite Industrial Cooperation and Cooperation in Third World Countries. TD/243/Supp.5, 1979.

Draft International Code of Conduct on the Transfer of Technology. TD/CODE/TOT/25, 1980.

UNECE. *Economic Survey of Europe,* various years.

Guide for Use in Drawing up Contracts Relating to the International Transfer of Technology in the Engineering Industry. Trade/222/Rev.1, 1970.

UNECE Secretariat. *Economic Bulletin of Europe,* various issues.

UNIDO. *The Development of Engineering Design Capabilities in Developing Countries.* ID/67, 1972.

Guidelines for the Acquisition of Foreign Technology in Developing Countries, with Special Reference to Technology License Agreements. ID/98, New York, 1973.

Guidelines for Evaluation of Transfer of Technology Agreements. ID/233, New York, 1979.

3. Indian official publications

3.1 REPORTS OF THE PARLIAMENTARY COMMITTEE ON PUBLIC UNDERTAKINGS (CPU)

Bharat Aluminium Corporation. Seventh Lok Sabha, 71st Report, 1983/4.

Bharat Heavy Electricals Ltd. Third Lok Sabha, 39th Report, 1967.

Fifth Lok Sabha, 71st Report, 1971/2.

Seventh Lok Sabha, 44th Report, 1982/3.

Bhilai Steel Plant. Third Lok Sabha, 30th Report, 1966.

Bokaro Steel Ltd. Fourth Lok Sabha, 68th Report, 1969/70.

Durgapur Steel Plant. Third Lok Sabha, 29th Report, 1966.

Financial Management in Public Undertakings. Fourth Lok Sabha, 15th Report, 1967/8.

Foreign Collaborations in Public Undertakings. Fifth Lok Sabha, 89th Report, 1975/6.

Heavy Electricals Ltd. Fifth Lok Sabha, 19th Report, 1971/2.

Heavy Engineering Corporation. Fourth Lok Sabha, 14th Report, 1967/8.

Hindustan Aeronautics Ltd. Fourth Lok Sabha, 8th Report, 1967/8.

Hindustan Antibiotics Ltd. Fifth Lok Sabha, 1975/6.

Hindustan Steel Ltd. Fifth Lok Sabha, 1st Report, 1971/2.
Indian Drugs and Pharmaceuticals Ltd. Third Lok Sabha, 22nd Report, 1966.
  Fourth Lok Sabha, 44th Report, 1968/9.
  Fifth Lok Sabha, 56th Report, 1973/4.
Indian Oil Corporation (Refineries Division). Third Lok Sabha, 36th Report, 1967.
  Fifth Lok Sabha, 52nd Report, 1973/4.
Management and Administration of Public Undertakings. Third Lok Sabha, 13th
  Report, 1965.
Mining and Allied Machinery Corporation. Fourth Lok Sabha, 66th Report,
  1969/70.
National Coal Development Corporation. Fourth Lok Sabha, 10th Report, 1967/8.
  Fifth Lok Sabha, 75th Report, 1975/6.
Oil and Natural Gas Commission. Third Lok Sabha, 5th Report, 1965.
  Fifth Lok Sabha, 16th Report, 1971/2.
Production Management in Public Undertakings. Fourth Lok Sabha, 67th Report,
  1969/70.
*Public Undertakings – Delays in Commencement of Production, Under-utilisation of
  Capacity and Related Matters.* Sixth Lok Sabha, 1978/9.
Rourkela Steel Plant. Third Lok Sabha, 11th Report, 1965.
State Farms Corporation. Fifth Lok Sabha, 54th Report, 1973/4.
Steel Authority of India. Fifth Lok Sabha, 77th Report, 1975/6.

3.2 OTHER INDIAN OFFICIAL PUBLICATIONS (INCLUDING
   STATISTICAL SOURCES)

Bureau of Public Enterprises. *Lok Udyog* (monthly), New Delhi.
  Public Enterprises Survey, various issues.
Department of Science and Technology. *Research and Development in Industry,
  1978–79*, New Delhi, 1979.
Directorate General of Commercial Intelligence and Statistics. *Monthly Stat-
  istics of the Foreign Trade of India*, Calcutta.
Indian Institute of Foreign Trade. *Emerging Opportunities for India's Trade and
  Economic Cooperation with East Europe*, New Delhi, 1977.
Ministry of Chemicals and Fertilisers. *Report of Expert Committee on Surgical
  Instruments*, New Delhi, 1978.
Ministry of External Affairs. *Foreign Affairs Record* (monthly), New Delhi.
Ministry of Finance, Bureau of Public Enterprises. *Public Enterprises Survey.
  Annual Report on the Working of Industrial and Commercial Undertakings of the
  Central Government*, New Delhi.
  Department of Economic Affairs. *External Assistance*, New Delhi, 1980/1.
  Economic Survey, various issues.
  Explanatory Memorandum on the Budget of the Central Government (annual),
  New Delhi.
Ministry of Industry. *Guidelines for Industries*, New Delhi, 1979.
Ministry of Petroleum and Chemicals. *Report of the Committee on Drugs and
  Pharmaceutical Industry* (Hathi Committee Report), New Delhi, 1975.

234   Bibliography

Ministry of Steel. *Report of the Committee on Cost of Production of Steel*, New Delhi, 1966.
Report of the Planning Group on Design and Construction of Steel Plants, New Delhi, 1973.
White Paper on Steel Industry, New Delhi, 1976.
Reserve Bank of India. *Bulletin* (monthly), Bombay.
Report on Currency and Finance (annual), Bombay.

3.3 REPORTS OF THE FEDERATION OF INDIAN CHAMBERS OF COMMERCE AND INDUSTRY (FICCI)

First Working Meeting of FICCI and USSR Chamber of Commerce (USSR CCI), New Delhi, 1979.
Second Working Meeting of FICCI and USSR CCI, New Delhi, 1980.
Third Working Meeting of FICCI and USSR CCI, New Delhi, 1982.
Fourth Working Meeting of FICCI and USSR CCI, New Delhi, 1983.
FICCI Machine Tools Delegation to USSR, New Delhi, 1984.

3.4 ANNUAL REPORTS OF PUBLIC SECTOR UNDERTAKINGS

Bharat Aluminium Corporation. *Annual Reports*, 1965/6–1981/2.
Bharat Heavy Electricals Ltd. *Annual Reports*, 1964/5–1981/2.
Heavy Engineering Corporation. *Annual Reports*, 1959–1981/2.
Hindustan Steel Ltd (later Steel Authority of India). *Annual Reports*, 1955/6–1981/2.
Indian Drugs and Pharmaceuticals Ltd. *Annual Reports*, 1961/2–1981/2.
Indian Oil Corporation. *Annual Reports*, 1964/5–1981/2.
Instrumentation Ltd. *Annual Reports*, 1964/5–1981/2.
Mining and Allied Machinery Corporation. *Annual Reports*, 1965/6–1981/2.
Oil and Natural Gas Commission. *Annual Reports*, 1959/60–1981/2.

3.5 PLANNING COMMISSION

The Second Five-Year Plan, New Delhi, 1956.
The Third Five-Year Plan, New Delhi, 1961.
Draft Fourth Five Year Plan, New Delhi, 1966.
The Fifth Five-Year Plan, New Delhi, 1976.
The Sixth Five-Year Plan, New Delhi, 1981.

4. Soviet books, periodicals and translation journals

Eastern European Economies. New York: International Arts and Science Publishers.
Economic and Political Weekly. Bombay.
Foreign Trade (monthly). Moscow.
Indian Economic Journal. Conference number, 1976. Bombay.
International Affairs (monthly). Moscow.
Ministry of Foreign Trade. *Vneshnaia Torgovlya* (annual). Moscow.

New Times (monthly). Moscow.

Problems of Economics (monthly). New York: International Arts and Science Publishers.

Shirokov, G. K. *Industrialisation of India*. New Delhi: People's Publishing House, 1980.

Soviet and East European Foreign Trade (monthly). New York: International Arts and Science Publishers.

Soviet Review (monthly). New York: International Arts and Science Publishers.

Stanis, V. F., G. B. Khromushin and V. P. Mozolin. *The Role of the State in Socio-Economic Reforms in Developing Countries*. Moscow: Progress Publishers, 1976.

A Study of Soviet Foreign Policy. Moscow: Progress Publishers, 1975.

USSR and Third World (monthly). London.

V. I. Lenin on Peaceful Co-existence. Moscow: Progress Publishers, 1963.

Index

The following series titles are now out of print:

Soviet and East European Studies

For EU product safety concerns, contact us at Calle de José Abascal, 56–1°, 28003 Madrid, Spain or eugpsr@cambridge.org.

www.ingramcontent.com/pod-product-compliance
Ingram Content Group UK Ltd.
Pitfield, Milton Keynes, MK11 3LW, UK
UKHW042316180425
457623UK00005B/28